Keeper of Public Records

Deputy Keeper of Public Records in Ireland : seventh report with appendix

Keeper of Public Records

Deputy Keeper of Public Records in Ireland : seventh report with appendix

ISBN/EAN: 9783741105258

Manufactured in Europe, USA, Canada, Australia, Japa

Cover: Foto ©ninafisch / pixelio.de

Manufactured and distributed by brebook publishing software (www.brebook.com)

Keeper of Public Records

Deputy Keeper of Public Records in Ireland : seventh report with appendix

THE SEVENTH REPORT

OF THE

DEPUTY KEEPER

OF THE

PUBLIC RECORDS IN IRELAND.

[19TH MARCH, 1875.]

Presented to both Houses of Parliament by Command of Her Majesty.

DUBLIN:
PRINTED BY ALEXANDER THOM, 87 & 88, ABBEY-STREET,
FOR HER MAJESTY'S STATIONERY OFFICE.

1875.

[C.—1175.] *Price 7d.*

CONTENTS.

		Page
REPORT,	. . . .	5

APPENDIX.

1. Present places of custody of the Common Law Judgment Rolls, . 15
2. Extract from Report of Henry Berry, Esq., on the removal of the Records of the High Court of Admiralty, ... 15
3. Extract from Report of James H. Davies, Esq., on the removal of Records of the Revenue and Equity Exchequer, . . . 17
4. Note of removal of residue of Records of Law Exchequer, . . 18
5. Copy Order of the Lords Commissioners of the Great Seal dated 4th July, 1874, ... 19
6. Extract from Report of Henry Cox, Esq., on the removal of Records of the Court of Chancery from offices of J. J. Murphy, Esq., formerly Master in Chancery, ... 20
7. Report of Sir J. Bernard Burke, Ulster, Keeper of State Papers, . 21
8. Extract from Minutes of Trustees for the encouragement of the Linen Manufacturers in Ireland, ... 23
9. Particulars of Increment received from Court of Chancery in 1874, 25
10. Calendar of "Fiants" of Hen. VIII., with Index, and preliminary remarks, by J. J. D. La Touche, Esq., the Assistant Deputy Keeper, ... 27

☞ The marginal references to former Reports are by sections and by appendix numbers.

THE SEVENTH REPORT

OF THE

DEPUTY KEEPER OF THE PUBLIC RECORDS IN IRELAND.

TO HIS GRACE, JAMES, DUKE OF ABERCORN, K.G.,[1]

LORD LIEUTENANT-GENERAL AND GENERAL GOVERNOR OF IRELAND.

MAY IT PLEASE YOUR GRACE,

1. The removal of the bulk of the Records which, at the time of the passing of the Public Records (Ireland) Act, 1867, were of the age of twenty years and upwards from the making, has now been substantially completed. The only noticeable portions still left outstanding are the Judgment Rolls of the Courts of Common Law, that part of the Prerogative Collection comprising the Wills proved since the year 1820, and a portion of the State Paper Collection (*post*, 5), in process of preparation for transfer. *Removal of original bulk of records substantially completed.*

2. As regards the Common Law Judgment Rolls, I beg leave to refer to my former reports, and in particular to the letter of the Right Honorable the Master of the Rolls, dated 14th May, 1870, calling the attention of Her Majesty's Judges of the Courts of Common Law to the circumstances under which the removal to this office of the Judgment Rolls had been temporarily suspended, and to the expediency of framing rules for their treatment after removal. As they are Records of much public importance, I beg leave to refer to a note of their present places of custody, which will be found in the Appendix. *Outstanding Common Law Judgment Rolls. [III. App. 4; V. 3.] App. I.*

3. A sufficiently long experience tends to show that no sensible inconvenience to the administration of the Court of Probate need be apprehended from the removal of the residue of the Wills to 1846, inclusive, so that the Warrant already issued for that purpose will probably be carried into complete execution during the current year. *Outstanding Wills.*

4. The collections, by the removal of which to this office, during the past year, the primary work remaining to be done in execution of section 4 of the Act, has thus been completed, are the following:

a. Records of the High Court of Admiralty.—A portion of these, which had been deposited in the Chancery Recognizance Office, formerly occupied by the Marshal of the Admiralty Court, had been already removed to this office. The residue was deposited in presses in the present Court of Admiralty, and in the offices of the Queen's Proctor. Owing to the former practice of *Court of Admiralty. [I. 63.]*

transacting the administrative business of this Court at the private residences of the officials, the Records now remaining are of trifling bulk and little importance, as compared with the extent and antiquity of the jurisdiction. The removal was affected under the direction of Mr. Berry, to whose report I beg leave to refer.

App. II.

b. Records of the Court of Revenue Exchequer, and Equity Exchequer.—The Records of the Revenue Exchequer, completing the series to the year 1848, from the respective dates up to which they had already been removed to this office, from the Custom House and Bencher's Buildings, had remained deposited in a vault beneath the Offices of the Receiver Master in Chancery. In the same vault were deposited a miscellaneous collection of Replications, Rejoinders, and other documents from the Filacer's Office of the late Court of Equity Exchequer. The laborious duty of transferring the contents of this vault was committed to Mr. James H. Davies, and performed by him between the 11th and 21st May last.

Court of Exchequer, Revenue and Equity sides.

Appendix III.

c. Residue of Law Exchequer Documents from Chamber of the Lord Chief Baron.—Removed on 21st December, 1874, under the direction of Mr. Berry.

Court of Exchequer, Law side.

Appendix IV.

d. Records of Chancery from the offices of J. J. Murphy, Esq., formerly Master in Chancery.—Under the operation of the Chancery (Ireland) Act, 1867, and of several Orders of the Lord Chancellor and of the Lords Commissioners of the Great Seal, the Records relating to the several causes depending in Chancery at the date of the first Order had been concentrated in the offices of Master Brooke, Master Murphy, and the Receiver Master; and those pertaining to the jurisdiction of Master Brooke having been disposed of, by transfer to this office, and to that of Master Murphy, so that, for the purposes of section 4 of the Act, the latter office had come to be the ultimate repository of all the outstanding Cause Papers of the Court of Chancery, an order was made by the Lords Commissioners of the Great Seal, dated 4th July, 1874, whereby Masters Brooke and Murphy were released from their duties as such Masters, from and after the 8th of August next ensuing; and it was thereby directed that all the business then transacted in the offices of the said two Masters, which consisted in the passing of the accounts of Receivers, Guardians, and Committees of the estates of lunatics, and in the management of the estates wherewith they are entrusted, should, from and after the 8th of August then next, be transferred to the office of the Receiver Master, and that all other business then appertaining to the said two offices should, from and after the said date, be transferred to the Chambers of the Lords Commissioners. Warrants having been already issued for the removal of the Records, comprised in the 4th section of the Act, from the offices of the respective Masters, directions were given to proceed with Master Murphy's collections on the 20th of August. This duty, involving much detail of arrangement, separation, and redeposit, was confided to Mr. Henry Cox, by whom it was satisfactorily completed on the 20th October. The collection removed comprises the Cause Papers, and ancillary documents, chiefly of a date prior to 1850, in 2,960 causes, leaving

Court of Chancery. Records from offices of Master Murphy.

Order of 10th May, 1870.
[V. App. 6.]

Order of 4th July, 1874.
App. V.

Appendix VI.

the documents of a later date in 3,480 causes, in their former repositories. It not being possible to determine beforehand which of these latter causes should be deemed current business, to be left under the immediate control of the Receiver Master and Chief Clerk respectively, it has been considered that the intention of the Act would be best carried into effect, consistently with the convenience of the Court, by leaving the last-mentioned portions of the collection, newly labelled and indexed, under Mr. Cox's direction, in the custody of the Chief Clerk of the Court. *Residue of Cause Papers (Chancery) left unremoved.*

c. Ecclesiastical Collections of the Diocese of Clonfert and Kilmacduagh.—The 4th section of the Act, vesting in the Master of the Rolls the Records of any Court which shall have ceased to exist, rendered it my duty on some former occasions to remove to this office various collections of diocesan and other ecclesiastical documents, preserved at the private residences of the Custodians. The last collection of this nature of the existence of which I have been made aware, was at Aughrim, in the County of Galway, under the charge of the Reverend John F. T. Crampton, A.M., Registrar of the United Diocese of Clonfert and Kilmacduagh. These comprised, together with testamentary, matrimonial, and diocesan matter, some documents relating to Church property for which I held myself accountable to the Church Temporalities Commissioners. The collection was removed to this office on the 17th of September. *Ecclesiastical collections, Aughrim Rectory.*

5. The Keeper of the State Papers in his annual Report, which will be found in the Appendix, has given a detail of the operations now in progress, and nearly completed, at the Record Tower, for placing the residue of the State Papers in the same complete form of arrangement and accessibility as the portions already transmitted. Although these preparations did not admit of further removal of the State Paper series in the past year, the Keeper has sent to this office a collection of other Records, some of which are of no inferior interest to any hitherto transmitted. I refer particularly to the series of 139 folio volumes, containing the proceedings of the Trustees for the Encouragement of the Linen Manufactures in Ireland from the year 1711 to 1828. Considering the great past and present extent of the linen trade in this country, these Records of the first systematic steps, taken by public authority, for its regulation and development, possess a high interest for the historian and economist. It has been thought well to present in the Appendix an abstract of the first day's proceedings of the Board reciting the deed by which the original trustees for the respective provinces were appointed. *Record Tower, Dublin Castle. App. VII.*

App. VIII.

6. In conformity with the practice adopted in my former Reports of giving the number of pieces constituting each consignment, I annex a like return for the past year, which may be regarded as having witnessed the completion of the primary object of the Act.

Former Repository.	Classes of Documents.		Number of Pieces.
COURT OF ADMIRALTY,	Rule Books,	vols.	27
	Note and Rough Books,	"	11
	Log Books,	"	8
	Cause Papers,	bundles,	23
	Miscellaneous,	vols.	8
OFFICE OF THE QUEEN'S PROCTOR (COURT OF ADMIRALTY), 61, UPPER SACKVILLE-STREET	Rule Books,	vols.	3
	Rough Books, &c.,	"	16
VAULTS UNDER RECEIVER MASTER'S OFFICE.	*(Revenue Exchequer.)*		
	Sheriff's Accounts,	bundles,	16
	Green Wax Process,	"	11
	Nils,	"	10
	Miscellaneous,	"	7
	(Equity Exchequer).		
	Names of Commissioners,	bundles,	23
	Replications and Rejoinders,	"	31
	Orders,	"	17
	Appointments of Attorneys,	"	11
	Writs of Dedimus,	"	16
	" Attachment,	"	36
	Miscellaneous,	"	30
	"	vols.	6
LORD CHIEF BARON'S CHAMBER (COURT OF EXCHEQUER).	Issues and Verdicts, Venues and Jury Panels,	} bundles,	25
MASTER MURPHY'S COURT AND OFFICES (CHANCERY).	Interrogatories and Depositions,	bundles,	118
	Deeds and Leases,	"	62
	Cause Papers,	"	2,960
	Receivers' Accounts,	"	9
	Miscellaneous,	"	27
	Exhibits,	vols.	97
	Master's Note Books,	"	25
	Summons Books,	"	24
	Miscellaneous,	"	32
DIOCESAN REGISTRY OF CLONFERT AND KILMACDUAGH, AUGHRIM RECTORY.	Registries,	vols.	2
	Court Papers,	bundles,	1
	Cause Papers,	"	6
	Marriage Bonds,	"	1
	Subscription Rolls,	rolls,	6
	Miscellaneous,	bundles,	11
	"	vols.	4

Former Repository.	Classes of Documents.		Number of Pieces.
RECORD TOWER, DUBLIN CASTLE.	Proceedings of Trustees Linen Manufacture (Ireland),	vols.	139
	Returns of Schools (under 28 Hen. VIII.),	portfolios,	79
	Form of Answers (in taking an account of the Population of Ireland, 1813–14),	vols.	33
	Total,		3,971

Making, with the consignments of former years, viz:—

1868,	.	.	30,908		1871,	.	.	12,570
1869,	.	.	33,363		1872,	.	.	10,820
1870,	.	.	15,277		1873,	.	.	2,801

a total of 109,710 pieces, ranging in bulk from a sack to a volume, to which, if an estimated addition be made for all outstanding residues, the total of the original bulk will amount to about 115,000 pieces, the distribution, arrangement, and deposit of which will hereafter constitute the chief intern work of this office.

7. The primary work with which the office is charged having been thus substantially accomplished, it may be convenient to advert to the future duties which will be imposed on me and my successors by the 14th section of the Act. Under this latter enactment, the Records of all Courts or Public Offices in Ireland, after the passing of the Act (12th August, 1867) are placed under the care and charge of the Right Hon. the Master of the Rolls, for ultimate transmission to this office, as they shall respectively become twenty years old from the making; and this enactment is not limited as in the English Record Act, to particular courts or offices specified by name, but is general in its operation. It will depend on the means of supervision and correspondence placed at the disposal of this office, how far it may be enabled to carry the intention of the Act in this respect into operation. A beginning has been made in the case of the District Registries of the Court of Probate, in which, with the approval of the Right Honorable the Judge, the old method of putting up Wills and other Testamentary Instruments in bundles has been discontinued, and the system of separate envelopes of a uniform size for future transmission to this office has been adopted. Uniformity, in size and method, of Record-keeping, in all public offices, would be one of the most effective means towards economy of space, and facility of reference in the future central deposits contemplated by the Act; and as far as the facilities at the disposal of this office

Future operations under sec. 14 of Act.

1 & 2 Vic., c. 94. s. 8.

for the conduct of a necessarily extended correspondence will admit, no endeavour will be wanting to effect those important objects.

Accruing Increment, Chancery. App. IX.   8. The increment, over and above the original bulk, hitherto accruing under the last mentioned section of the Act has been chiefly derived from the Court of Chancery. In the Appendix will be found the detail of the several Records transferred from thence to this custody from time to time during the past year.

9. The diminished amount of extern duty has been attended with a corresponding increase in the intern work of arrangement and deposit. The accompanying diagram indicates in red the several changes effected in the Treasury during the year, the general nature and object of which has been to concentrate in the newly-fitted bays, in perfectly fire-proof fittings, and finally complete arrangement, the several collections which were deposited, in the first instance, in bulk, as received, on the wooden shelving of the original fittings.

Diagram of state of bays.

Intern operations.   10. The new fittings have been erected *pari passu* with the preparation for the ultimate intern deposits, and have been extended during the year through bays 1 S, 1 T, 1 U. The Cause Paper collections of the Offices in Chancery have been brought from their first place of deposit in the basement, and are now being incorporated with the fresh accretions, consequent on the abolition of the Masters' Offices, in preparation for ultimate deposit in self-indexing series. This process of interpolation must go on until the last of the outstanding documents shall have come in, when the entire collection will be capable of final deposit. The other collections of Deeds Boxes, &c., which were originally placed in the basement, owing to the large demand on the accommodation in the Upper Treasury for the reception of the first bulky consignments, have also been removed, so as to make room for the completion of the basement fittings in a uniform arrangement of presses.

Arrangement of Cause Papers, Chancery.

11. The other intern work of the year has consisted in the usual operations of Deposit, Indexing, Calendaring, and supplying the requirements of the public in inspections and compared copies of Records. The principal deposit has been in continuation of the Equity Exchequer Pleadings series, brought down to the year 1744, comprising 13,770 additional books or fasciculi.

Deposit. Eq. Exchequer Pleadings.

12. In the deposit of the Chancery Pleadings, space was left, in the respective series of Bills and Answers, for the introduction of the unindexed portion of the collection, anterior to 1624, kept formerly on files and known as "Ancient Pleadings." These, having been cleansed and flattened, have now been subjected to regular arrangement by date and series, which has proceeded through twelve bundles, but will necessarily be a tedious business, as the documents range back to the reign of Henry VIII, and are difficult to read from age and injury.

Ancient Pleadings in Chancery.

Indexing and calendaring.   13. In Indexing and Calendaring, a large addition has been made to those necessaries of the Search-Room.

Chancery decrees, 1852-4.   a. An Index of Chancery Decrees for 1852-4 (Vols. 89 to 92 inclusive), has been added to the General Decree Index.

OF THE PUBLIC RECORDS IN IRELAND. 11

b. The Index to Chancery Recognizances, 1847-1863, from the Record and Writ Office, has been copied, and the copy lodged in the Search-Room. *Chancery Recognizances, 1847-63.*

c. Mr. Cox has prepared a Calendar, by dates, titles of causes, and names of lands affected, with Index, of the Writs and Commissions for Perambulation, Returns thereto, and Maps; also of the Writs for the examination of Married Women and Returns thereto, transferred from the Record and Writ Office of the Court of Chancery at the time of the original removal of its Records. *Writs, &c., of perambulation. Examination of married women.*

d. Mr. Barry has prepared an Index to the MS. Calendar of the Memoranda Rolls of James I. and Charles I., transferred in 1870 from the Offices of the Master of the Court of Exchequer. *Mem. Rolls, James I.*

e. The Calendar of Disentailing Deeds has been advanced from Deed 2,872, enrolled 23rd June, 1854, to Deed 3,174, enrolled 11th July, 1856. *Disentailing Deed Roll.*

f. A Calendar and Index have been prepared by Mr. Mills, under the direction of Mr. LeTouche, the Assistant Deputy Keeper, to the Fiants of Henry VIII. A MS. Calendar and Index Nominum was already in existence, but as it indicates the nature of each Fiant only as Grant, Lease, Pardon, &c., it has been found too general to be of any substantial service. These Records, named "Fiants," from the initial words of one class of the instruments so known—"Fiant literæ patentes,"—are of great value as constituting the primary authority for grants under the great seal. Such grants, subsequent to 1665, had to be enrolled in Chancery as a condition to their validity, and the enrolments so made, where the Rolls have been preserved, dispense with the evidence of the Fiants; but, for Grants before that date, there was no certainty that any transcript would be found on the Roll, and in point of fact, great numbers of Letters Patent of early date remain unenrolled. To these Grants the Fiants afford the primary and, in most cases, the only clue accessible to the public, and sometimes, where the original letters are lost, to those representing the grantees. The importance of framing a well-indexed calendar of their contents has long been acknowledged, and it is hoped that this work, now completed for the reign of Henry VIII., will be found so far to supply all that is necessary. Considering the value of the work, it has been thought well to embody it in the Appendix to this Report; and it is proposed to continue it in like Appendices to future Reports, until the whole period shall be covered up to the point where the information already published by the Irish Record Commissioners will make such aid unnecessary. *"Fiants" of Henry VIII. Appendix X.*

g. An Index has been made to the Dublin Consistorial Grant Book, 1746-9, in which the volume was previously defective. *Dublin Grant Book, 1746-49.*

h. New Indexes have been made to the following Collections of Wills:— *Testamentary collections.*

Diocese or District.	Entries.
Clogher,	6,121
Armagh,	9,000
Raphoe,	1,546
Drogheda,	994
Newry and Mourne,	558

Also, Self-Indexing Envelopes for

	Envelopes.
Derry, ...	5,337
Connor, ...	8,407
Down, ...	7,520

Besides other indexing work arising out of the receipt of portions of collections supplemental to those originally transmitted.

14. Twenty volumes of the Testamentary series have been rebound. Two thousand three hundred and twenty-five membranes of Plea Rolls up to Roll 177 have been cleansed and flattened. I defer the further repair, by transparent tissue, till after the completion of endeavours to restore the faded ink, in which many experiments have been made without definite result. One hundred and seven Pleadings of the Equity Exchequer, and one hundred and forty-seven other Records of various kinds have been repaired.

15. From the Table of Fees annexed, it will be seen that the supply of certified copies to the public continues to increase. The amount for 1874 is £622 11s. 6d. as against £545 8s. 6d. for 1873.

FEES RECEIVED in the YEAR to 31st DECEMBER, 1874.

Date.	Inspections.	Traces.	Folios at 1s.	Folios at 6d.	£ s. d.	£ s. d.
1874. January,	117	–	–	–	5 17 0	
	–	4	–	–	1 2 6	
	–	–	509	–	25 8 0	
	–	–	–	1,813	45 6 6	
						77 14 0
February,	80	–	–	–	4 0 0	
	–	5	–	–	1 10 0	
	–	–	215	–	10 15 0	
	–	–	–	889	22 4 6	
	–	–	90 follios at 2d. (see post).		0 15 0	
						39 4 6
March, .	102	–	–	–	5 2 0	
	–	4	–	–	1 10 0	
	–	–	482	–	24 2 0	
	–	–	–	1,437	35 18 6	
						66 12 6
April, .	91	–	–	–	4 0 0	
	–	2	–	–	1 5 0	
	–	–	146	–	7 6 0	
	–	–	–	1,366	34 3 0	
	–		2 attendances.		4 4 0	
						51 9 0
May,	109	–	–	–	5 9 0	
	–	2	–	–	1 2 6	
	–	–	226	–	11 6 0	
	–	–	–	1,856	83 18 0	
						51 15 6
June,	109	–	–	–	5 9 0	
	–	2	–	–	4 0 0	
	–	–	212	–	10 12 0	
	–	–	–	1,710	42 15 0	
						62 16 0
July, .	84	–	–	–	4 4 0	
	–	3	–	–	8 0 0	
	–	–	352	–	17 12 0	
	–	–	–	1,599	39 19 6	
	–		4 attendances.		8 8 0	
						78 3 6

Fees received in the Year to 31st December, 1874—*continued*.

Date	Inspections	Traces	Folios at 1s.	Folios at 6d.	—	—
1874. August,	79	-	-	-	£ s. d. 3 19 0	£ s. d.
	-	4	-	-	3 15 0	
	-	-	50	-	2 10 0	
	-	-	-	719	17 19 6	28 3 6
September,	69	-	-	-	8 9 0	
	-	1	-	-	0 5 0	
	-	-	216	-	10 16 0	
	-	-	-	403	10 1 6	24 11 6
October,	102	-	-	-	5 2 0	
	-	3	-	-	1 12 6	
	-	-	153	-	7 13 0	
	-	-	-	975	24 7 6	38 15 0
November,	104	-.	-	-	5 4 0	
	-	1	-	-	0 15 0	
	-	-	433	-	21 13 0	
	-	-	-	1,880	34 10 0	62 2 0
December,	86	-	-	-	4 6 0	
	-	-	115	-	5 15 0	
	-	-	-	1,808	32 11 6	
		90 folios at 4d. (*see ante*).			1 10 0	
		1 attendance.			2 2 0	46 4 6
	1,182	31	3,108	15,040	—	£622 11 6

16. The literary inquiries during the year embraced Wills, Inquisitions (Chancery and Exchequer), Decrees of Court of Claims, Patent and Memoranda Rolls, Certificates of Adventurers and Soldiers, Documents connected with the River and Customs of Dublin, Hearth Money Rolls, Marriage Licences, Informations (Queen's Bench), Documents relating to Sir John Davys, Chancery Decrees, Bills (Chancery and Exchequer), Documents relating to Military Establishments, Royal Visitations, Munster Compositions, Desmond Survey, and Parliamentary Returns.

Literary Inquiries.

17. I have to acknowledge with thanks the receipt during the past year of seven volumes of Record Publications sent as donations to this office by direction of the Right Honorable the Master of the Rolls in England.

All which is humbly submitted to your Grace.

Dated at the Public Record Office
of Ireland, Four Courts, Dublin,
this 19th of March, 1875.

SAMUEL FERGUSON,
Deputy Keeper of the Public Records in Ireland.

I humbly certify to your Grace that this Report is made by the Deputy Keeper of the Public Records in Ireland, under my direction, pursuant to the Statute.

EDWARD SULLIVAN,
Master of the Rolls.

the University of

APPENDIX.

APPENDIX I.

NOTE of PRESENT PLACES of CUSTODY of the COMMON LAW JUDGMENT ROLLS.

REMAINING IN FORMER REPOSITORIES.

		No. of Rolls.	
QUEEN'S BENCH.—Debt Rolls, 1661–1850,			745
COMMON PLEAS.—Debt Rolls, 1760–1850,		157	
„ Case Rolls, 1836–1850,		61	
			218
EXCHEQUER.—Debt Rolls, 1660–1849,		767	
„ Case Rolls, 1772–1849,		537	
			1304
			2267

REMOVED TO PUBLIC RECORD OFFICE.

QUEEN'S BENCH.—Case Rolls, 1770–1850,		336	
„ Memorial Rolls, 1736–1850,		115	
			451
COMMON PLEAS.—Judgment and Case, 1596–1835,		453	
„ Recovery Rolls, 1821–1834,		25	
„ Memorial Rolls, 1786–1850,		37	
			515
EXCHEQUER.—Memorial Rolls, 1736–1850,			116
Total Transferred,			1082
Total remaining Untransferred,			2267
			3349

APPENDIX II.

EXTRACT from REPORT of HENRY F. BERRY, esq., on the removal of the RECORDS of the COURT of ADMIRALTY.

The Records of the High Court of Admiralty, now in this department, were transferred from three repositories, viz.:—a small room formerly used as Marshal's office, and which, at the time its contents were entered in our Transfer Books, belonged to the Chancery Recognizance Office; the Chamber which forms the present Court, and the offices of J. F. Hamerton, esq., the Queen's Proctor, at 61 Upper Sackville-street.

In former years, there was no fixed room for use as a Court, nor had the officials any offices for the transaction of business, with the exception of the small room above named, which, for a short time, was used by the Marshal. The officials discharged their duties at their own private residences, and so, in one instance, a quantity of documents had accumulated at the house of the late Dr. Anster, Registrar of the Court, which, after his death, were removed and placed in presses in the present Court.

The fact of business having been transacted at private houses, and the Records having been kept in them, will account for their want of regularity in series. In the preparation for Transfer, it was found impossible to arrange them satisfactorily, but very soon I hope to be able to arrange and index the Cause Papers, so as to make them, so far as they exist, readily consultable.

It was not till the year 1867, on the creation of the new jurisdiction of the Court of Admiralty, that the present commodious Court and offices were finally provided for the accommodation of the Judge and his staff.

In my Report on the Records belonging to the Chancery Recognizance Office, dated 11th December, 1868, at page 63 of the appendix to your First Report, there is a note to the effect that in an inner room were four presses, filled with documents belonging to the Court of Admiralty, which had been tied up, labelled, and entered in our Transfer Book, but which were not removed when the Transfer of the Chancery Recognizances, &c., took place. These Documents were brought over and deposited in this office on the 27th April, 1869, but no Report was made on them, as it was deemed advisable that all the Records of the Court of Admiralty should be dealt with together. They consisted chiefly of Affidavits, Warrants, Orders (circa 1800-35); several bundles of Cause Papers for about the same period, the titles and dates of the causes being entered in the Transfer Book; Protocols 1805-14; 1825 and 1830-2; 27 vols. Draft Rule Books, 1798-1852; some Log Books; a Book of Sale; two Appearance Books, and a Seal Book.

On 3rd August, 1874, in obedience to your instructions, I attended at the Court to prepare the contents of five presses in it for Transfer, which was effected on the following day. At the request of Judge Townsend, a Warrant to include all Documents connected with the old Court, up to its abolition in 1867 was issued, so that the following were transferred:—

Rule Books, (27 vols.), August, 1747 to 25th November, 1867.

Note and Rough Books (11 vols.), 8th Feb., 1856, to 23rd Mar. 1864.

Sales' Account Book, 1807 to 1823.

Marshal's Entry Book of Vessels seized, from 26th March,1862.

Judges' Crown Books (Admiralty Commission), (5 vols.), Antrim, Clare, and Cork Assizes, 1858-9.

Eight Log Books, 1857-1867; lodged during the progress of Causes.

Twenty-three parcels of *Cause Papers*, the titles of the principal Cause being given in the Transfer Book. Among these are some parcels of Letters Remissory.

J. F. Hamerton, esq., the Queen's Proctor, having intimated that he had found some Records of the Court in his offices, at 61 Upper Sackville-street, they were examined and were transferred on 17th October, 1874. They consisted of Three *Rule Books*, May 1797 to September 1800; 11th October 1855 to 20th May, 1858; and 1st February, 1862, to 7th October, 1863, which fill up gaps in the series brought from the Court.

Rough Court Books (15 vols.), 3rd November, 1856, to 29th October, 1860; and 1st February, 1862, to 7th October, 1863.

A Marshal's Book 1866.

All the above Records have been deposited in Bay 1 Q of the Record Treasury.

APPENDIX III

EXTRACT from the REPORT of JAMES H. DAVIES, Esq., on the removal of the RECORDS of the REVENUE AND EQUITY EXCHEQUER deposited in a VAULT beneath the OFFICES of MASTER FITZGIBBON.

The vault having undergone a thorough dusting and cleansing, I commenced proceedings, under your directions, on the 11th May. Owing to the crowded state of the vault, it was deemed advisable to carry on the actual transfer concurrently with the preparations. This was accordingly done, and on the 21st May, after some interruptions, I had the honour to report the deposit of the last load in the Record Treasury.

The Records of the Revenue Exchequer dealt with by me form a continuation of those previously removed to this office, and complete the series up to the year 1848; and as the Assistant Deputy Keeper, in his Report on the collection, has given full particulars of the nature and value of the different classes of documents, it would be useless for me to go over the same ground. I shall therefore ask leave to refer inquirers to that Report (see 2nd Report of Deputy Keeper, p. 61, Appendix 9).

The Equity Exchequer Records deposited in this vault were of slight value, and without arrangement, with the exception of four bundles of Replications and Rejoinders put up by the late Mr. Ferguson. The centre of the vault was taken up by a large wooden stand, supporting files of Replications, Rejoinders, Orders, Names of Commissioners, and other Documents from the Filacer's office. This stand was removed to the vaults of the Record Treasury, each file being properly docketed and easy of access if required. I append a Schedule of the Records transferred, which must still undergo further listing and arrangement.

REVENUE EXCHEQUER.

Book of Coroners' Returns. 1839.
  Do. *Extracts from Estreats.* 1838.
Certificates of Sheriffs' Tots paid, 1 bundle. 1835–1848.
Estreat Office Papers and Returns, 1 bundle.
Green Wax Process, 11 bundles. 1835–1848.
Nils, 10 bundles, unarranged.
Papers and Returns relating to Collection of Fines by Constabulary under 1 & 2 Vic., cap. 99, 2 bundles.
Sheriffs' Accounts, 15 bundles. 1835–1848. No bundle for 1839.
Besides these there were Miscellaneous Letters and Papers relating to *Petty Sessions' Clerks*, and various *Office Books*.

EQUITY EXCHEQUER.

Account Books (Official). 1806–1828.
Answers not filed, 4 bundles.
Appearances, 1 file. 1806–1808.
Appointments of Attorneys, 11 files. 1795–1814.
Attested Copies of Pleadings, &c., 8 bundles.
Chief Remembrancers' Certificates, 2 files. 1775–1782.
  Do. 1 file. 1816–1824.
Haberes, 1 bundle. Geo. III.
Letters and Papers of Filacer's Office, 2 files.

Names of Commissioners, 1 file. 1738–1739.
  Do.   2 files. 1757–1759.
  Do. 19 files. 1781–1822.
  Do.   1 file. 1837–1841.
Notices, 1 file. 1814–1816.
Orders, 17 files. 1794–1848.
Rejoinders, } arranged by Mr. Ferguson, { 2 bundles. 1682–1831.
Replications,   do. 1683–1831.
 Do. *and Orders*, 1 bundle. 1848–1850.
 Do. *and Rejoinders*, 26 files. 1778–1847, with occasional intervals.
Rough Bill Books, 1785–8, 1812–30, and 1832–8.
Subpœnas to Answer; Writs of Sequestration; Subpœnas to Hear Judgment; Writs of Distringas—1 bundle. Geo. II., III., and IV.
Writs, 1 file. 1821–1831.
 Do. *of Capias*, 2 bundles. Geo. III.
 Do. *Dedimus*, 16 bundles. Chas. II.—Geo. IV.
 Do. *Non Est*, 1 bundle. Geo. III.
 Do. *Replevin, Capias, and Levari*—1 bundle. Geo. III.
 Do. *Scire Facias*, 2 bundles. 1790–1812.
 Do. *Subpœnas*, 2 bundles. Geo. III.?

APPENDIX IV.

EXTRACT from REPORT of HENRY F. BERRY, Esq., on removal of RECORDS of LAW EXCHEQUER from the CHAMBER of the LORD CHIEF BARON.

The Lord Chief Baron having intimated that three presses in his Lordship's Chamber contained Records, these on examination were found to be Records of the Court of Exchequer, and I was instructed to prepare them for removal.

Twenty-five parcels were labelled, entered, and their transfer accomplished on 21st November, 1874; the Records were in no kind of order, and were very miscellaneous in their character. They seem to have belonged principally to the Rules Department of the Court, and consisted chiefly of the following:—

   Issues and Verdicts, circa 1810–1826.
   Lists of Records at Assizes, ,, ,,
   Writs of Venire, with panels attached.
   Posteas, 1807.

The collection is lodged in Bay 5 I, at the end of the Law Exchequer series of Records.

APPENDIX V.

Copy ORDER of LORDS COMMISSIONERS of the GREAT SEAL of IRELAND, 4th July, 1874.

Whereas, by the Chancery (Ireland) Act, 1867, section 29, it is enacted that whenever in the judgment of the Lord Chancellor, from the state of business in the Court, any Master whose office is by the said statute abolished, can be spared, it shall be lawful for the Lord Chancellor to release such Master from his duties as such, at such time as to him shall seem meet.

And whereas by the 2nd section of the same Act, the expression Lord Chancellor occurring therein shall mean and include the Lords Commissioners for the custody of the Great Seal of Ireland. And whereas in our judgment, having regard to the state of business in the said Court and in their respective offices, the Right Honorable William Brooke and Jeremiah John Murphy, esq., two of the said Masters, may be spared. We do hereby release the said William Brooke and Jeremiah John Murphy from their duties as such Masters from and after the 8th day of August next ensuing.

And whereas the 39th section of the said Act directs the nature of the business to be prosecuted by the then Masters of the said Court until they should be removed by resignation, death, or otherwise, or released from their duties under the said Act; and that such business if necessary should from time to time be distributed among the Masters or such of them as should then remain, and the Receiver Master in such manner as the Lord Chancellor should direct. And whereas it is enacted by the 175th section of the said Act as interpreted by the 2nd section thereof that all suits, causes, matters, or other proceedings which were pending in the said Court on the 1st day of Michaelmas Term, 1867, should be conducted or prosecuted according to the same practice as if the said Act had not passed; provided that it should be lawful for the Lord Chancellor by an order to be made upon motion or petition to direct that the whole or any part of the further proceedings in such suit, cause, or matter should thenceforth be carried on according to the practice introduced by the said Act. And whereas all the business now carried on in the offices of the said two Masters has been carried on according to the former practice. Now we do hereby direct that all the business now transacted in the offices of the said two Masters which consists in the passing of the accounts of Receivers, Guardians, and Committee of the Estates of Lunatics, and in the management of the estates wherewith they are entrusted, shall, from and after the 8th day of August next be transferred to the office of the Receiver Master and that all other business now appertaining to the said two offices shall, from and after the said 8th day of August, be transferred to the Chambers of the Lords Commissioners; and it shall be competent for any person interested in the prosecution of any suit, cause, matter or other proceeding so transferred to make application to the Lords Commissioners in Chamber touching the regulation of the course of practice to be pursued in its further prosecution.

The 4th day of July, 1874.

(Signed) JOSEPH NAPIER, C.S.
JAMES A. LAWSON, C.S.
WILLIAM BROOKE, C.S.

APPENDIX VI.

EXTRACT from REPORT of HENRY COX, Esq., on the RECORDS (prior to 1850) TRANSFERRED from the Offices of J. J. MURPHY, Esq., Ex-Master in Chancery.

The Offices consist of three rooms—viz., the Court, the Clerk's (or back) Office, and the Examiner's Office. The documents were distributed in twenty-one presses.

In consequence of the limited space, and of the rapidity of accumulation, considerable confusion existed in the dates and sequences of the documents. This necessitated a much longer time for the preparation than was anticipated. I was engaged on this duty with the assistance of two workers and a writer for a total period of about six weeks.

The following are the several classes of documents removed :—

Cause Papers.—These comprise the papers lodged in about 3,000 causes, the titles of which were, during the preparation, entered on transfer sheets. The papers in matters of a later date were found to be tied in bundles, with their proper titles attached; but no order had been observed in putting them into their receptacles. In addition to these, there were 114 bundles of papers which, owing to the confusion of their arrangement in their pigeon-holes, could not be distributed into their various causes. As nearly as possible they were grouped into bundles commencing with the same letter, and are labelled "Miscellaneous Cause Papers."

Interrogatories and Depositions.—Of these there are 118 bundles. Intermixed with these were found a few Dominicals which, at this stage, it was not deemed necessary to separate from the Interrogatories with which they were previously arranged.

Miscellaneous Deeds, Leases, &c.—Of these there are sixty-two bundles. Under this general title are included Tenants' Leases, Mortgages, Marriage Settlements, Deeds of Surrender, Deeds of Attornment, Draft Conveyances, &c.

Miscellaneous Receivers' Accounts—Nine bundles.

Miscellaneous Notes of Sale—Four bundles. These appear to be minutes of the different biddings made for various lands set out according to the order of the Court. The dates range from 1791 to 1806.

Miscellaneous Rentals—Three bundles.

Miscellaneous Bills of Costs—One bundle.

Distraining Notices—One bundle.

Miscellaneous Stockbrokers' Accounts—Seven bundles. These are accounts of stock investments brought before the Master for his approval.

There was found one bundle of Leases and Recognizances unexecuted with an index giving reasons for their non-execution.

Miscellaneous Documents—Consisting of fragments, &c., eleven bundles.

The Books comprise :

Official Day Books—Two volumes (1835-1843) with an index attached to the earlier volume.

Official Account Books—Nineteen volumes, with dates ranging from 1806 to 1839.

Masters' Note Books—Twenty-five volumes, with dates ranging from 1806 to 1846; but apparently there is a gap from 1836 to 1845. These books are not indexed, and seem to be merely rough notes for the Master's own information.

Sales and Letting Books—Three volumes, from Jan. 1818, to Oct. 1847. An index to each volume.

Summons and Attendance Books—Twenty-four volumes (1816–1845).

Guardians', Committees', and Receivers' Account Books—Two volumes, both indexed (1836-1847). Also one Receiver's Account Book (1792–1820) in cases, before Master Ellis, of minors and lunatics. Indexed.

Order Books—Two volumes, both indexed (1843–1851).

Short Cause Lists—Two volumes, commencing E. 1843.

Long Cause Lists—Two volumes, commencing E. 1843; and two volumes for 1848-9.

Merchants' Account Books Lodged as Exhibits—ninety-seven volumes.

Entry Book of Exhibits (1 vol.) in various causes, with an index of the causes. Latest entry 1806.

Besides the above were found and transferred,

A MS. copy (bound) of Report on Inquiry held by the Surveyor-General, in 1818, into the condition of the Stationery Office.

A MS. Schedule of Lettings in Examiner's Office, from 1828 to 1833 — made pursuant to Order of 21 December, 1833.

An Index to Leases remaining in the Office where Recognizances had been filed (1828 to 1833).

Two lists of Returns, from Master, of causes pending in his Office, with particulars (1833–1837).

A Report, by Masters, on their Inquiry into the state of prisoners in Marshalsea Prison (1837).

A volume of letters, probably belonging to a solicitor, but lodged in Court. The letters bear dates 1826 and 1827.

Report (bound) of Select Committee of Inquiry into the taxation of the city of Dublin, 1823.

A catalogue of law books in King's Inns Library, published 1823.

Two volumes (1810–1815 and 1821–1825) of Reports of Record Commissioners.

A printed list of Electors of county Kilkenny for year 1832.

The removal of the documents from the Court was carried out on October 13th and 14th, and of those in the Clerk's office on October 20th. The documents in the Examiner's Office remain untouched as none of them are of an earlier date than 1850.

Appendix VII.

To the Right Honorable the MASTER of the ROLLS in IRELAND.—
THE SEVENTH REPORT of SIR JOHN BERNARD BURKE, C.B., Ulster, Keeper of the State Papers in the Record Tower, Dublin Castle, dated 1st February, 1875.

SIR,—I beg leave to submit to your Honor my annual statement of the progress of the work done in the State Paper Department during the past year, viz :—1st February, 1874, to 1st February, 1875.

I.
TRANSFER OF DOCUMENTS.

The following collections have been transferred to the Public Record Office :—

1. MINUTES OF PROCEEDINGS OF THE LINEN MANUFACTURE IN IRELAND.—1711-1828 ; 139 MS. volumes.
2. RETURNS OF ALL SCHOOLS IN THE VARIOUS PARISHES OF IRELAND.—1824-1825.
3. FORM OF ANSWERS CONTAINED IN SCHEDULE to an Act, 52 Geo. III., entitled an Act for taking an account of the Population of Ireland, 1813-1814.

II.
RECEPTION OF THE STATE PAPERS.

1. THE PAPERS OF THE CHIEF SECRETARY'S OFFICE.—1853 to 1864, inclusive—twelve complete years—have been received.
2. PAPERS AND BOOKS OF THE FOUR COURTS MARSHALSEA have been, by direction of the Government, placed in the Record Tower.

III.
ARRANGEMENT, CLASSIFICATION, INDEXING, &C., OF STATE PAPERS.

1. THE PAPERS OF THE YEARS 1822, 1823, and 1824, have been arranged and placed in cartons. A Carton Catalogue has been made to each year and placed in the beginning of each Index.

An Index to the Miscellaneous Papers of these three years has been commenced.

2. THE MODERN STATE PAPERS of the years 1853, 1854, 1855, 1856, 1857, 1858, 1859, 1860, 1861, 1862, 1863, and 1864, inclusive, which have been received from the Chief Secretary's Office, are a continuation of the series already deposited here. The Papers of these years fill 257 cartons, and number at a rough calculation about fifty or sixty thousand. All these documents have been regulated by being placed in cartons and by having a Carton Catalogue added to each year's Index.

Accompanying the Indexed Papers of these years is a large mass of unindexed "Miscellaneous Papers," which have been sorted and placed in presses.

3. THE BOOKS AND PAPERS OF THE FOUR COURTS MARSHALSEA before mentioned as having been transferred to this department, have been arranged and a Press Catalogue made to the series.

4. PETITIONS ADDRESSED TO THE LORD LIEUTENANT AND COUNCIL, AND OTHER PAPERS CONNECTED WITH THEM, described in my last (6th) Report, are being carefully indexed. The progress is satisfactory, and the interest of this important collection will, when the Index is finished, be at once seen. The indexing has come down to No. 886 and the numbering to 8,123.

5. THE CALENDAR OF THE BRITISH DEPARTMENTAL CORRESPONDENCE, mentioned in my fifth Report as having been brought down to the year 1738, has been continued to 1739. The transcription of this calendar has been proceeded with from 1714 to 1718.

It will be a source of infinite gratification to me, when the current business of this Department will permit us to accomplish the task of completing the Calendar of this British Departmental Correspondence, as the collection is full of historical materials having reference to a very interesting period.

6. A draft Index has been made to the MILITARY BOOKS OF ENTRIES in this Department.

In consequence of the great mass of Papers of modern date received from the Chief Secretary's Office, there have arisen and there are continually arising searches for documents of current importance. These searches, of almost daily occurrence, involve a vast amount of investigation and cause a considerable expenditure of time, chiefly because the Papers of the various years (in incomplete bundles) are difficult of access, and also because several of the principal documents, taken out in past years for Governmental or official use, not having been restored to their proper places in the bundles, are not discoverable by means of the Indexes, and are only, if at all, to be found by an examination of the unindexed "Miscellaneous Papers." I have given this subject my earnest consideration, and have felt that it is one of the most urgent duties of this Department to make such arrangement of these State Papers as will surmount the difficulty and enable documents, when called for by Government, to be readily produced. I have consequently directed the whole of the Papers of the modern years to be sorted and placed in cartons, for, once they are so deposited, they can be referred to without trouble or delay. Good progress has been already made in the work, no less than fifteen years' arrangement under the plan having been completed; and I anticipate that within a short period the whole of these documents will be to a great extent in a state of facile reference. At this moment the remaining portion of the old Parliamentary Record Room is being adjusted for the reception of the cartons required for this purpose.

I have the honour to be, sir,

Your faithful servant,

(Signed)   J. BERNARD BURKE, Ulster,

Keeper of the State Papers in the Record Tower.

Record Tower,
Dublin Castle,
1 Feb., 1875.

APPENDIX VIII.

EXTRACT from MINUTES OF PROCEEDINGS OF TRUSTEES for the LINEN MANUFACTURE IN IRELAND.—Vol I. p. 1. (H. 54. I.)

His Grace the Duke of Ormond, Lord Lieutenant of Ireland, having (pursuant to an Act of Parliament) appointed Trustees for the Linnen Manufacture, they were by his Grace's direction summoned to meet at the Castle of Dublin on Wednesday the 10th of October, 1711, where the Deed of their appointment was read to them, which is as follows :—

WHEREAS by Act of Parliament made in this Kingdom in the Ninth Year of Her Majesties Reign, entitled an Act to enforce such Acts as have been made for the Improvement of the Linnen Manufacture, and for a further regulation of the same, it is among other things enacted that the Lord Lieutenant or other Chief Governor or Governors of this Kingdom for the time being shall and may, and is thereby enabled to Nominate and appoint certain Trustees for the disposall and Management of the Duties granted by the said Act according to the Trusts and powers thereby vested in them to consist of an Equall Number of Persons out of Each of the four Provinces of this Kingdom, as by the said Act (Relation being thereunto had) more fully may appear. Now know all men by these presents that I James Duke of Ormond Lord Lieutenant Generall and Generall Governour of Ireland, in pursuance and execution of the power vested in me by the said Act, Do by these presents appoint the Severall persons herein after named to be Trustees for the Disposall and Management of the Duties granted by the Said Act, according to the Trusts and powers thereby vested in them. That is to say the Right Honble. Sir Constantine Phipps Lord High Chancellor of the said Kingdom of Ireland, and such other person as shall be Chancellor for the time being—The most Reverend Father in God William Lord Arch Bishop of Dublin, Robert Earl of Kildare, Henry Earl of Drogheda, Arthur Earl of Anglesey, Lord Vict. Fitzwilliams, Thomas Lord Baron Howth, Robert Doyne esq. Lord Chief Justice of the Comon Pleas, Robert Rochfort esq. Lord Chief Baron of her Majesties Court of Excheqr., Charles Dering esq. her Majesties Auditor, Geull. Samuel Dopping esq., Sir Richard Levinge Knt. and Barrt. her Majesties Attorney Genll., Sir Pierce Butler Barrt., Sir William Fownes Knt., Stephen Ludlow esq., Thoms. Burgh esq., Anderson Saunders esq., John Pratt esq., all which Said persons are of the Province of Leinster.

William Earl of Inchiquin, James Earl of Barrymore, Thoms. Lord Baron of Kerry, Sir Richard Cox Knt. and Barrt. Lord Chief Justice of her Majesties Court of Queen's Bench, Lieut. Genll. Richard Ingoldsby, Lieut. Genll. William Stowart, Sir Thomas Southwell Barrt., Sir John Percivall Barrt., Sir Donat O'Bryen Barrt., Sir Robert Maude Barrt., Francis Bernard esq. her Majesties Solicitr. Geull., Coll. William Ponsonby, William Burgh esq. Accompt. Genll., Robert Fitz Gerald esq., Edward Hoare esq., Henry Pine esq., George Mathews esq., Arthur Bushe esq., all which Said persons are of the province of Munster.

The most Reverend Father in God John Lord Arch Bishop of Tuam, Arthur Earl of Granard, James Lord Visct. Lanesburrow, Michell Lord Baron of Dunkellin, Majr. Genll. Gustavus Hamilton, Sir George St. George Barrt., Sir Arthur Shaen Barrt., Coll. Henry Sandford, John Eyres esq., William Gore esq., Oliver St. George esq., William Connolly esq., Benjamin Burton esq., George Gore esq. Councillor at Law, Aldr. Ralph Gore, David Kennedy esq., John Stanton esq., John French esq., all which Said persons are of the Province of Connaught.

Hugh Earl of Mount Alexander, James Earl of Abercorne, William Lord Visct. Montjoy, Clotworthy Lord Visct. Massareens, Lord Conway, Edward Southwell esq. Principall Secretary of State for the Kingdom of Ireland, Thomas Coote esq. one of the Justices of her Majesties Court of Queen's Bench, Charles O'Neal esq., Joshua Dawson esq., Doctor Marmaduke Coghill, William Brownlow esq., Samuel Waring esq., Hawkins M'Gill esq., Mathew Ford esq., James Topham esq., Charles Campbell esq., Robert Clements esq., Michell Ward esq. Councillr. at Law, all which Said persons are of the Province of Ulster; AND I hereby Authorize and Impower the Severall persons herein before mentioned as Trustees to put the Said Act in Execution according to the true Intent and meaning thereof, In witness whereof I James Duke of Ormond Lord Lieut. of Ireland do hereunto sett my hand and Seal this Sixth day of October One Thousand Seven hundred and Eleven.

Signed, Sealed and delivered
  in the presence of   ORMOND.

  Tho. Bellew.
  James Butler.

Appendix IX.

EXTRACT from the REPORT of the ASSISTANT DEPUTY KEEPER on RECORDS RECEIVED in the Year 1874.

From the Record and Writ Office, Chancery, there were removed, on the 5th February, Cause Petitions under the Court of Chancery (Ireland) Regulation Act, 1850:—those on parchment, from 22nd August, 1850, to 9th August, 1851, and of those on paper, thirty Volumes, from 13th August, 1851, to 31st January, 1855. These latter are numbered consecutively, and each Volume contains 100 Petitions.

Also Answers (on parchment) to the Cause Petitions, from 6th January, 1851, to 31st December, 1851.

On the 4th March, 63 Volumes of the Answers and Affidavits in Cause Petition matters from 11th September, 1850, to 10th January, 1855.

NOTE.—Prior to 11th September, 1850, all Affidavits in Chancery were filed in the Chancery Affidavit Office, but on the passing of the Chancery (Ireland) Regulation Act of 1850, the Chancellor decided that the ordinary Affidavits under the Act should be filed in the Rolls Office, along with the Answering Affidavits.

In 1860 this practice was altered, and all, except the Answering Affidavits, were filed from thenceforth in the Chancery Affidavit Office. In Causes under the 15th section of the Act the practice was to file the Answering Affidavit in the Master's Office, in the nature of a Discharge to the copy of the Petition previously filed in the same office. Many, however, of the Answering Affidavits to Petitions under the 15th section have slipped in amongst these Affidavits.

There were transferred on 29th April the Cause Petition Index Books for the years 1851, 1852, 1853, 1854, the Volume for 1851 containing all Cause Petitions filed from the earliest date to that year.

On 19th May, Accounts from 22nd December, 1851, to 29th December, 1854 (Vols. 171 to 262); Petitions, 6th December, 1851, to 31st December, 1854 (Vols. 89 to 120); Reports, 18th December, 1851, to 18th December, 1854 (Vols. 109 to 144).

On 4th June the Order or Full Entry Books, from (circa) 1852 to 1854 (Vols. 485 to 522)—Vol. 489 not transferred: it is either missing, or a mistake was made in the numbering. Rolls Motion Books, 13th January, 1852, to 13th December, 1854 (Vols. 321 to 363).

Masters' Orders (a new series), 7th November, 1853, to 23rd December, 1854 (Vols. 1 to 11).

Incumbered Estates Court Certificates, 1st June, 1852, to 30th June, 1854 (Vols. 5 and 6); Attachments, 1852 to 1854 (Vols. 9 and 10); Decrees, 8th March, 1852, to 21st August, 1854 (Vols. 89 to 92); Masters' Certificates, 12th February, 1852, to 26th August, 1854 (Vols. 19 to 24); Consents, 1st January, 1852, to 14th August, 1854 (Vols. 33 to 38); Rolls Petition Hearing Books, 1852-54 (Vols. 41 to 49).

Rolls Consent Motion Books, 1852-4 (Vols. 10 to 13); Orders on Cause Petitions, 1852-4 (Vols. 3 to 6); Chancery General Hearing Books, 1852-4 (Vols. 6 to 14); Side Bar Rule Books, 21st April, 1852, to 30th November, 1854 (Vols. 51 to 55).

The above have been placed in Bay 1 P.

Also the following Indexes:—To Miscellaneous Documents, Vol. 2 to end of 1854; to Accounts, 1852 to 1854 (Vols. 12–14); to Consents for 1852 (Vol. 7); to Petitions, 1852–4 (Vols. 9, 10, 11); to Reports, 1852–4 (Vols. 7 to 9); and to Masters' Orders in Cause Petition Matters under 15th section of the Act, 1853–4 (1st Vol.) These have been lodged in the Search Room.

On 13th June were transferred the Disentailing Deeds Rolls, 1852–3 (Nos. 41 to 44), and the Patent Rolls, 1852–3 (Nos. 30 to 33)—(Bay 3 D).

On 9th July, Chancery Recognizances (Bay 3 Q); Nos. 1 to 1,913 of Roll 34, and 1 to 519 of Roll 35; Enrolments of the same, Nos. 34, Parts 1 to 4, and 35, Parts 1 and 2 (1849 to 1854—(Bay 3 D). Orders to Vacate Recognizances, 1849 to 1854—(Bay 3 Q).

I annex a Synopsis.

Former Repository.	Classes of Documents.		Number of Pieces.
RECORD AND WRIT OFFICE, COURT OF CHANCERY.	Cause Petitions,	bundles,	58
	,, Answers and Affidavits,	,,	69
	,, Index Books,	vols.	4
	Receivers' Accounts,	,,	92
	Petitions,	,,	32
	Reports,	,,	36
	Deeds Rolls,	rolls,	4
	Patent Rolls,	,,	4
	Order Books,	vols.	37
	Rolls Motions,	,,	43
	Masters' Orders,	,,	11
	Incumbered Estates Certificates,	,,	2
	Attachments,	,,	2
	Decrees,	,,	4
	Masters' Certificates,	,,	6
	Consents,	,,	6
	Rolls Petition Hearings,	,,	9
	Rolls Consent Motions,	,,	4
	Orders on Cause Petitions,	,,	4
	Chancery General Hearings,	,,	9
	Side Bar Rule Books,	,,	5
	Index Books,	,,	12
	Recognizances,	bundles,	9
	,, (Enrolments of),	rolls.	6
	,, (Orders to Vacate),	bundles,	2

APPENDIX X.

CALENDAR TO FIANTS OF KING HENRY VIII.

EXTRACT from PRELIMINARY OBSERVATIONS of J. J. DIGGES LATOUCHE, Esq., the ASSISTANT DEPUTY KEEPER of the RECORDS.

The "Fiants," or Warrants to the Court of Chancery for Grants under the Great Seal, so called from their usually commencing with the words *Fiant literæ patentes*, extend from the 12th year of Henry VIII. to the present time. They are comprised amongst the Records transferred to this department from the late Rolls Office of Chancery, where they had been deposited from time to time by the Clerk of the Hanaper, for the purpose of safe custody, and for facilitating the enrolment of the Letters Patent grounded on them.

The present practice is not to issue Letters Patent to the parties entitled to them until the enrolment has been made upon the Patent Roll, for which purpose the Fiant is treated as the original, though the enrolment directed by the Act is of the Letters themselves. This practice has, I presume, prevailed since the 17 & 18 Charles II., chap. 2, known as the Act of Explanation, the 73rd section of which enacts that all Letters Patent of titles of honor, offices, or lands shall be void, unless they contain a clause of enrolment in the Chancery of Ireland within a time to be specified. Prior to this enactment, the causes operating to such enrolments as were made, were, I apprehend, the security thereby given to the grantee, and the obtaining of their customary fees on enrolment by the officers of the Court.

The whole number of Fiants for the reign of Henry VIII. appears, by an entry in an old book entitled, "Schedule of various Records from Henry VIII. to Elizabeth" (2 Q. 144. 1), being a receipt for Records, signed by George Norton, 15th November, 1633, to have been 565. Of these I have been able to calendar 548. In the Manuscript Catalogue prepared by the Record Commissioners there are noticed only 519 ; but this number I have been enabled to augment by the addition of some which the Commissioners had by mistake included in subsequent reigns ; of some I found among the Records of the Palatinate of Tipperary; and of others found in a bundle labelled "Fiants of various dates" (1 L. 91. 1). I have also obtained the contents of a few others, which are entered as Fiants in the Books of Patents in the office of the Auditor-General.

Of the above, 365 are enrolled or marked as enrolled, but I found on the Patent Rolls only 242. This discrepancy exists chiefly in respect of Fiants for Leases.

The majority of the Fiants of Henry VIII. correspond with, and are similar in form to, the class of "Signed Bills" in the English Chancery, of which Mr. Brewer gives an example in the preface to his Calendar of "Letters and Papers, Foreign and Domestic, of Henry VIII.," p. xcix. In this country they must be divided into three classes—those signed by the King, those signed by the Lord Deputy, and those signed by other competent authority. The first class are for the most part identical with Mr. Brewer's example, a very few being without the petition, and one having the words, "Fiant litere domini Regis patentes in debita forma tenore verborum sequentium," inserted before the word "Rex" in the granting portion. I give an example of the second class, as the form is, I think, peculiar to Ireland.

W. Skeffyngton

28 (325). Fiant litere Domini Regis patentes in debita forma tenore verborum sequentium Rex &c., omnibus ad quos &c. salutem. Sciatis quod nos de gratia nostra speciali ac ex certa scientia et mero motu nostris de assensu dilecti et fidelis nostri Willelmi Skeffyngton Militis Deputati nostri ac precharissimi et dilectissimi consanguinei nostri Henrici Ducis Richmond et Somersett de prosapia nostra orti locumtenentis nostri terre et dominii nostri Hibernie ac ex avisamento consilii terro nostre predicte pardonavimus remisimus et relaxavimus ac per presentes pardonamus remittimus et relaxamus Bernardo alias Brene O'Conghor suo nationis capitaneo alias dicto Bernardo alias Brene O'Conor de Othfaly sue nationis capitaneo seu quocunque alio nomine seu cognomine censeatur, sectam pacis nostre que ad nos usque ipsum pertinet de omnibus proditionibus tam majoribus quam minoribus et de omnibus feloniis murdris roboriis incendiis depredationibus latrociniis furtis extortionibus oppressionibus transgressionibus intrucionibus abbetamentis illicitis congregationibus insurrectionibus ingressionibus manufortibus dampnis gravaminibus coyniis liberationibus riotis routis mesprisionibus contemptis ac de omnibus aliis offensis et excessibus quibuscunque per ipsum Bernardum alias Brene ante hec tempora tam contra pacem et communem legem nostram quam contra statuta de Kylkenny facta apud Kylkenny Dublin Waterford aut Drogheda dudum edita ac contra omnia alia statuta tam in Regno nostro Anglie quam in terra nostra Hibernie facta sive perpetrata unde indictus rectatus vexatus perturbatus seu appellatus existit vel non existit. Ac etiam utlagariam si que in ipsum Bernardum alias Brene occasione premissorum seu eorum alicujus promulgata fuerit Et firmam pacem nostram ei inde concedimus per presentes Ita tamen quod stet rectatus in curia nostra si quis usque ipsum loqui voluerit de premissis seu de aliquo premissorum Aliquo statuto actu ordinatione seu provisione aut aliqua alia re causa vel materia in contrarium facto in aliquo non obstante Et quod presentes litere nostre pardonationis donationis sive concessionis in commodum et utilitatum ipsius Bernardi alias Brene in omnibus intelliguntur et exprimuntur et non aliter. In cujus rei &c. Teste &c.

       JOHN DUBLYN.
       G. ARMACHANUS.
       J. RAWSON, Prior de Kyllmaynam.

Deliberatum fuit in Cancellario Hibernie decimo die Septembris Anno regni regis Henrici Octavi xxii°. ad exequendum.

On only one of the Fiants of this class is there a petition transcribed, and most of them are countersigned by some members of the Council.

The rest of the Fiants divide themselves into five common forms, of four of which I annex examples.

(1.) "Privy Seals," according to the example given by Mr. Brewer p. c.

(2.) "Indentures," of which I give an example.

265 (231). Fiant Indenture inter dominum Regem ex parte una et Willelmum Dermor ex parte altera, de Situ Ambitu precinctu et Circuitu nuper Hospitalis sive Domus sancti Johannis juxta Kenlys in Comitatu Midie Cum omnibus messuagiis edificiis columbariis pomariis gardinis terris tenementis et aliis hereditamentis quibuscunque cum pertinentiis infra precinctum ejusdem nuper hospitalis sive Domus necnon de omnibus messuagiis terris tenementis pratis pascuis pasturis molendinis aquis aquarum cursibus piscariis silvis boscis subboscis libertatibus franchesiis custumis et ceteris hereditamentis et proficuis quibuscunque cum pertinentiis in villis et campis de Kenlys Moylaghe et Saint Johns Rathe juxta Stahalmoke in Comitatu Midie predicte Ac de Ecclesiis' Rectoriis sive Capellis sancti Johannis de Kelles Dessardkeran Stonehall et Durvaghe cum pertinentiis in Comitatu predicto unacum omnibus messuagiis terris tenementis decimis oblationibus obventionibus altaragiis portionibus pensionibus Jurisdictionibus

ac omnibus aliis proficuis et hereditamentis quibuscunque cum pertinentiis eisdem Ecclesiis rectoriis sive Capellis pertinentibus sive spectantibus que nuper fuerunt accepta seu reputata ut possessiones sive hereditamenta dicti nuper Hospitalis sive Domus et de omnibus et singulis reversionibus omnium et singulorum premissorum et cujuslibet inde parcelle jam ad terminum annorum seu aliter dimissorum ac de redditis super hujus modi dimissionibus reservatis Que omnia et singula premissa cum pertinentiis in manibus dicti Domini Regis jam existunt et existere debent (grossis arboribus advocationibus ecclesiarum et feodis militum omnium premissorum tantummodo exceptis dictoque Domino Regi heredibus et successoribus suis omnimodo reservatis). Habendum &c., exceptis proëxceptis prefato Willelmo Dermor et assignatis suis a festo Pasche ultimo preterito usque ad finem termini xxi annorum proxime sequentium et plenarie complendorum. Reddendum inde annuatim dicto domino regi &c., ad receptum scaccarii sui ibidem quatuordecim libras et decem solidos legalis monete Hibernie ad festa sancti Michaelis Archangeli et Pasche equis portionibus. Et solvendum omnia redditus procurationes pensiones sinodales ac omnia alia onera quecunque extra premissa seu aliquam inde parcellam exeuntia (pensionibus nuper Prioris et personarum conventualium ejusdem tantummodo exceptis) Ac reperandum omnia domos messuagia edificia et cancelle necessaria omnium premissorum sumptibus suis propriis et expensis durante dicto termino. Cum clausula reintrationis pro non solutione redditus predicti infra xliii Septimanias &c. In cujus rei &c.

per { Johannem Alen Cancellarium. } Comissionarios
    { Willelmum Brabazon.   } Domini Regis.

Deliberatum fuit in Cancellario Domini Regis Hibernie xxi Novembris Anno regni regis Henrici viii. xxxiii ad execquendum.

Under this form are comprised all grants of leases under Commissions; chiefly two—One dated 20 May, 31 Henry VIII., being a commission to survey and value the rents and revenues of the dissolved religious houses to grant them for the term of 21 years, and to assign to their heads competent pensions. (*Vide* Mr. Morrin's Cal. Patent Rolls, pp. 54 & 55.) The other dated 3rd July, 36 Henry VIII., giving authority to Commissioners to let all manors, lands, and possessions in the hands of the Crown for 21 years. (Cal. Patent Rolls, p. 113.)

(3.) Warrants for grants of pension under the Commission of the 7th April, 30 Henry VIII. (Cal. Patent Rolls, p. 55), authorizing Commissioners to take charge of religious houses, and to assign pensions to those persons who willingly surrender.

83 (96). To all true Christen people to whome these presentes shall come John Alen the Kinges Chauncellor of his graces lande of Irlande George Archbusshop of Dublin primate of Irlande William Brabazon the Kinges maiesties Thesaurer at warres wthin the said lande. Robert Cowley mayster of the Rolls of the Kings Chauncery wthin the said lande, and Thomas Cusake gent. the Kinges highnes Commissioners sufficiently by his grace auctorised emonge other thinges for the lymyting apointing and gyving convenient lyvings or pencons unto the heades or gouvernors and religions persones of soche houses as bee or shalbe subpressed or disolved by any manere of meane wthin the said lande, sendeth greting in o^r Lord god everlasting. Knowe ye that we the said Commissioners having respect to the good conformitie inclinacon and obedience of Sr Henry Duff late Abbote of Saint Thomas Courte by Dublin of Sr James Cottrell late Abbote of the same of Sr John Brace Prior of the said place and of Sr John Butler his conbrother, and of Patricke Clyncher clerc of the organs of the said place for and unto the accomplisshing of the Kinges maiesties pleasure Doo lymite apointe assigne and gyve unto the saide Sr Henry late Abbot two and fourtie poundes to hym and his assignes during his lyfe naturall, of good and lauffull money of Irlande, unto the said Sr James Cottrell and his assignes during his lyfe naturall ten poundes of lauffull money of Irlande according the securitie

thereof made unto hym undre ther convent seale, unto S'r John Bruce aforsaid and his assignes during his lyfe naturall thre & fyftie shillings foure pence and over and besides to be curate of the parocbe churche of Saint Katherins by Dublin receyving therfor a convenient stipend of the fermo'r of the same, unto S'r John Butler and his assignes during his lyfe naturall fourtie shillinges of lauffull money of Irlande and over and besides to be curate of Saint James churche by Dublin receiving therfor a convenient stipend of the fermo'r of the same and to have his orcharde w'thin the precincte of Saint Thomas Corte aforsaide, and unto the said Patricke Clynchere and his assignes during his lyfe naturall fyve poundes of lauffull money of Irlande according the sucuritie thereof made unto hym undre the convent seale, all the said pencons of the said S'r Henry late Abbot S'r James Cottrell S'r John Brace and S'r John Butler to be had taken and yerelye perceived upon the parsonages of Grenoke, Kilsalchan Chapellmydway Ballsbyn Trewet Donamore by Grenoke Ratbtouyth and Dimsaghlen, and the said Patricke Clynchers pencion upon the tythes of Lucan w'th their appurtenances by the bandes of the lessees tenants fermors & occupiers of the same parsonages and tythes and every parte thereof for the tyme being yerelie during ther naturall lyves at the feastes of Saint Michell therebangell and Ester by even porcons. And that this o'r warraunt or plackarde shalbe accepted taken and allowed by the Barones of the Kinges exchequire and other the Kings officers and ministres for the tyme being w'thin thys his graces said lande, a sufficient warraunt acquittance and discharge aswele for and to the said S'r Henry late Abhote S'r James Cottrell S'r John Brace S'r John Butler and Patricke Clyncher and every of them for the receipt of ther said pencons or lyvings and every parte therof in maner and forme as is aforsaid as alsoo for and to the said lessees tenants fermors and occupiers and to every of them of the saide parsonages and tithes and every parte therof for the payment delyverance and satisfaccion of the same unto the said S'r Henry late Abbote and his said conbretberne & unto the said Patricke Clynchere. In witness wherof we the said Commissioners have subscribed these presentes w'th o'r propere hundes. Dated the eight & twentie daye of Julie in the one and thirtie yere of the reigne of oure moost dreade Souveraigne Lorde King Henry the eight.

JOHN ALEYN, Kings Chaunceler.
GROREIUS Dublin.
WILLM. BRABAZON.
ROBERT COWLEY, Master of the Rolls.

Deliberatum fuit in Cancellario Domini Regis Hibernie x'e Septembris Anno Henrici viii. xxxi'mo.

(4). Grants of Pensions under the Commission of 20 May, 31st Henry VIII., mentioned above; of Lands under Commission dated 1st September, 33rd Henry VIII., (cal. Patent Rolls, p. 90), giving authority to sell and dispose of the possessions of friars' houses in Ireland, reserving a rent; and of Wardship and Livery under a Commission for Wards and Liveries.

357 (451). Fiantlitere Domini Regis patentes in debita forma tenore verborum sequentium Rex omnibus ad quos &c. salutem. Cum nos per literas nostras patentes sub testimonio nostro proprio apud Westmonasterium primo die Septembris anno regni nostri xxxiii. auctorizaverimus et Dederimus Dilectis et fidelibus nostris Anthonio Sentleger militi Deputato nostro regni nostri Hibernie Johanni Alen cancellario nostro ejusdem Regni nostri Geraldo Aylmer capitali Justiciario nostro Regni nostri Hibernie predicti et Willelmo Brabazon vicethesaurario ejusdem tribus et duobus eorum, quorum predictum nostrum Deputatum unum semper fore, plenam potestatem et auctoritatem ad barganizandum vendendum et concedendum nomine nostro ad nostrum majus commodum et proficuum per eorum discretiones omnes et singulos scitus domorum fratrum infra Regnum nostrum Hibernie, cum eorum ecclesiis campanilibus plumbis campanis domibus horreis stabulis edificiis gardinis pomariis terris tenementis et aliis suis per-

tinentiis et commoditatibus quibuscunque tali persone et talibus personis heredibus et assignatis suis cui et quibus disponendos fuerunt conjunctim seu separatim habere et emere easdem pro talibus summis monete solvendis ad nostrum usum in manu et partem in manu et partem ad talem rationabilem diem et cum talibus rationabilibus conventionibus et conditionibus ut ipsi quatuor tres aut duo eorum, quorum predictum nostrum Deputatum unum fore, putaverint convenienter et apte per eorum discretiones et ulterius ut in eisdem literis nostris patentibus magis plane liquet. Sciatis quod nos pro novem libris et decem solidis legalis monete Hibernie in Hanaperio Cancellarii nostre regni nostri Hibernie predicti per Jacobum Brandon de Dundalke mercatorem ad usum nostrum solutis quequidem summa novem librarum et decem solidorum extendit ad et secundum ratam et taxam perquisionis xx^u annorum omnium et singulorum situs messuagiorum tenementorum et ceterorum hereditamentorum sequentium, De gratia nostra speciali ac ex certa scientia et mero motu nostris de assensu et consensu predictorum Anthonii Sentleger Johannis Alen Geraldi Aylmer et Willelmi Brabazon Dedimus concessimus barganizavimus et vendidimus ac per presentes Damus concedimus barganizamus et vendimus pro nobis heredibus et successoribus nostris prefato Jacobo totam Domum situm septum ambitum et precinctum nuper monasterii sive domus fratrum minorum de Dundalke in comitatu Louth ac totam ecclesiam campanile dormitorium aulam et cimitorium ejusdem nuper monasterii sive domus. Et omnia castra messuagia edificia pomaria gardina stabula prata pascua pastura terras tenementa et hereditamenta quecunque cum pertinentiis in infra aut prope situm septum ambitum et precinctum dicti nuper monasterii sive domus Necnon unum messuagium in quo nunc inhabitat Patricius O'Mulreve cum pertinentiis unam clausuram vocatam Brannane is parke cum quatuor acris terre arrabilis in Dundalke predicto ac omnia alia messuagia terras tenementa prata pascua pastura molendina aquas aquarum cursus piscarias parcas clausuras et omnia alia hereditamenta quecunque cum pertinentiis in Dundalke predicto ac alibi in comitatu Louth que nuper fuerunt accepta seu reputata aut cognita ut parcelle dicti nuper monasterii sive domus. Ac reverciones omnium et singulorum predictorum situs septus ambitus precinctus et circuitus messuagiorum terrarum tenementorum hereditamentorum ac ceterorum premissorum et cujuslibet inde parcelle cum pertinentiis Ac etiam redditus eisdem revercionibus incidentibus Habendum gaudendum occupandum et tenendum predicta Situm septum ambitum circuitum et precinctum messuagia terras tenementa redditus reverciones hereditamenta ac cetera premissa superius in presentibus expressa et specificata cum omnibus suis juribus membris et pertinentiis universis prefato Jacobo Brandon heredibus et assignatis suis ad proprium usum predicti Jacobi heredum et assignatorum suorum imperpetuum adeo plane et integre ac in tam amplis modo et forma prout omnia et singula premissa superius in presentibus expressa et specificata cum omnibus eorum juribus et pertinentiis universis ad manus nostras quocunque modo devenerunt seu devenire debuerunt. Tenendum de nobis heredibus et successoribus nostris in capite per servitium militare videlicet per vicesimam partem unius feodi militis quando scutagium currit in dicto regno nostro Hibernie Necnon reddendos et reservandos annuatim nobis heredibus et successoribus nostris apud Scaccarium nostrum Hibernie nomine vicesime partie sex denarios legalis monete Hibernie ad ffesta Pasche et sancti Michaelis Archangeli equis portionibus pro omnibus aliis servitiis exactionibus et demandis quibuscunque nobis heredibus et successoribus nostris reddendis solvendis seu faciendis Absque compoto seu aliquo alio inde nobis heredibus aut successoribus nostris reddendo solvendo seu faciendo. Eo quod expressa mencio &c. Aliquo statuto &c. In cujus rei &c. Teste &c.

Per { Antony Sentleger, Deputatum,
Johannem Alen, Cancellarium,
Gerald Aylmer, Justiciarium,
Willm. Brabazon, } Commissionarios.

Deliberatum fuit in Cancellario Domini Regis Hibernie ultimo die Aprilis Anno regni regis Henrici VIII, xxxv°. ad exequendum.

The last form in which this kind of authority appears is as an Order in Council.

By the lorde Deputie & Counsaill

ANTONY SENTLEGER.

515 (24). MEMORANDUM fforasmoche as Rayne Bell souldior one of the kings ma^{ties} Retynue wthin this his graces Realme of Ireland Hath long served his highnes very paynefully in the same. The right honorable Sr Anthony Sentleger knight of thorder and lorde Deputie of the same Realme in consideracion of that his service Hathe graunted to hym the ffarme and occupieng of the towne called the Carten in the parishe of Maynothe and parcell of the same lordshipp During the tyme of his Deputacion. Payng therefore theaccustomed Rent thereto belonging, that is to say eight pounds fyve shillings and one peny sterling. Nevertheles for that it is oncertayne how long the said lorde Deputie shall Remayne in that Rowme or otherwise being a man mortall change this present liffe whereby suche intrest as the said Rayney now hath in that ffarme were voyde and clerely extinct. Yt is therefore for his furder securyte condescended and agreid by the lorde Deputie and others of the Counsaill whose names be hereunto subscrybed that the said Rayny Bell in Recompense of his good and paynefull service And for the contynuanc of the same in the Kings affayres shall have a sure lease made to hym of the saide ffarme or towne of Carten for terme of twenty and one yeres, yelding therefore yerely suche Rent as he now paythe wthall other Duties and Customes going out of the same. And this o, concordatum shalbe unto yow the lorde chauncelo^r a suffyeient warrant to graunt the Kings ma^{ties} brode seale upon the same. Yeoven at Duhlin the xxviiith of January in the xxxviiith yere of the Raigne of o^r soverayne lorde King Henry theight.

Willm. Brabazon.
Gerald Aylmer, Justice.
Thomas Cusake, Magister Rotularum.

Nearly all these instruments have the date of their delivery into Chancery marked upon them in accordance with the Act 37°, Henry VI., cap. 1, directing that Warrants made to the Great Seal should have the day of their delivery to the Chancellor entered, and that the patents should bear the date of that day.

In the Calendar below, as most of the Fiants are written in Latin, I have in the margin marked those that are in English. The serial number is that of their present chronological arrangement, and the number in brackets gives their reference in the Record Commissioner's Catalogue. I have also added in the Record Commissioner's Catalogue the chronological serial number, that it may form a key for any person who has by him the old reference.

In conclusion, I beg to acknowledge the able assistance rendered me by Mr. Mills, on whom by much the more arduous portion of the labour has fallen.

APPENDIX X.

FIANTS.—HENRY VIII.

1521-2.

1 (26). Grant to Patrick Bermyngham, Chief Justice; of custody of the lands, and of marriage of the heir of Walter Bathe, late of Laundeston, county Dublin.—28 February, xiii.

2 (27). Grant to John Walop, knight; of the offices of constable of the castle, and receiver and bailiff of the lordship of Trym, lately held by John Rocheford, gentleman. To hold for thirty years, rendering an account to the Exchequer, with a fee of £10 for the constableship, and the usual fees for the receivership.—1 March, xiii.

1522.

3 (28). Grant to Thomas Darcy, rector of Houth; of the office of clerk or keeper of the rolls of Chancery. To hold during pleasure, with a fee of £20 of silver out of the issues of the manor of Eskyr.—7 July, xiiii.

4 (29). Grant to Rees ap Davyd; of the office of controller of the customs of Drogheda. To hold for life, with a fee of 10 marks sterling.—20 November, xiiii.

1524.

5 (3). License to James Sheffeld, prebendary of Wyklo, and vicar of Donshaghlyn; for absence from Ireland for three years.—1 April, xv.

6 (2). License to John Triguran, archdeacon of Kells, prebendary of Kilmatalway, and custos of the hospital of St. Stephen; for absence from Ireland for two months.—30 May, xvi.

7 (30). Grant to Lewis Busshe, yeoman of the guard; of the office of serjeant-at-arms. To hold for life, with such fees as John Dullard had out of the rents of the manor of Cromlyn.—15 July, xvi.

8 (170). License for Nicholas [   ] Cowley, Thomas Stewns, and Christopher White; to trade between Gascony and Ireland for one year.—21 December, xvi.

1525.

9 (481). Grant to the warden and convent of the friars minors observants in Trym; of land called the parke of Trym, valued at 20s. sterling a year. To hold for ever, in pure alms, without account.—9 August, xvii.

10 (172). License to Thomas Geralde, rector of Cloghran-Swerdes; for absence from Ireland for seven years—No date. (1 November, xvii. *in Record Commissioners Catalogue.*)

1525-6.

11 (171). Grant to Robert Cowley, of Dublin, merchant; of the fees of Galwey, which Stephan Lynche, son of Dominic Lynche, of Galwaye, lately received, viz.:—2s. sterling for every last of hides shipped there. To hold for thirty years without account, unless the fees shall exceed £8 sterling by the year, when he must account for such excess; also the office of gauger of all Ireland (not to be exercised in the counties of Dublin, Kildare, Meath, and Uriel, commonly called the English Pale), with a fee of 4d. of silver for each ton of wine or honey. To hold for thirty years without account.—26 February, xvii.

1526. FIANTS.—HENRY VIII.

12 (326). Pardon of Robert Plunket, to Kentystown, county Meath, lord of Dunsany; especially for his assistance to Charles Modder O'Reyly, in the depredation of the town of Kylskyrr, county Meath.—21 June, xviii.

13 (173). Grant to Richard Neugent, knight, Baron of Delwyn; of the manors of Belegarde and Fovyr, county Meath. To hold for fifty years, at a rent of £10.—21 September, xviii.

14 (31). Grant to Richard Newgent, knight, Baron of Delwyn; of custody of the lands of Walter Newgent, late of Multifarnan, and of wardship and marriage of Thomas Nugent, his son and heir.—10 October, xviii.

1526-7.

15 (32). Grant to John Griffith, yeoman of the guard; of the office of searcher in the ports of Dublin, Drogheda, and Dundalk, vacant by the death of Lewis Bushe. To hold for life, with the usual fees.—6 February, xviii.

1527.

16 (36). Grant to Edward Lencey, gentleman; of the office of serjeant-at-arms. To hold for life, with the accustomed fees payable from the issues of the manor of Cromlyng.—12 June, xix.

17 (4). Nomination of Milo, prior of the house of canons of the order of St. Augustin of Ynysteoke; to be Bishop of Ossory.—8 August, xix.

18 (407). Charter to the bailiffs and commons of the burgh of Dundalk. Recites charter of Richard II. Grants liberty to buy, sell, and export salted hides and other goods of the staple, and all merchandize growing in Ireland, or brought to Dundalk from England or other foreign country, as fully as the men of Dublin and Drogheda may; also to have a cocket seal as in Dublin and Drogheda.—28 August, xix.

19 (406). License for the abbot and convent of the B.V.M. of Trym; to acquire lands, &c., to the value of £20 beyond reprises.—2 September, xix.

20 (33). Grant to James le Butler, esquire of the king's body; of the manors of Dyamor and Derver, county Meath. To hold for life, from the expiration of a term of nine years, previously granted to John Fitzgerald, knight.—14 September, xix.

21 (35). Grant to William Busshe, esquire, serjeant of the king's pantry, and Thomas Bathe, of Dublin, gentleman (a previous grant dated 15 April, xv, to Busshe only, being cancelled); of the office of chief chamberlain of the Exchequer. To hold to them and the longest liver, with the accustomed fees, out of the rents of the manor of Cromlyn, or from the Exchequer.—26 September, xix.

22 (34). Grant to Richard Fitzwilliam, esquire; of the office of seneschal of the manors of Newcastell by Lyonys, Eskyr, Tassagart and Cromlyn, county Dublin. To hold for life, with the accustomed fees.—14 October, xix.

1528.

23 (504). License to George Seyntleger, knight, son and heir of Anne, daughter and co-heiress of Thomas, late Earl of Ormond, and to Anne, wife of said George; of absence from Ireland, for their lives. Also pardon of all intrusions.—25 June, xx.

24 (37). Grant to John White; of the office of serjeant-at-arms, vice Edward Lense, deceased. To hold for life, with the accustomed fees out of the issues of the manor of Crumlyng.—6 July, xx.

1528. FIANTS.—HENRY VIII.

25 (508). Grant to Gerald Aylmer; of the office of second justice of the Common Bench.—[ ] September, xx. [*Fiant wanting. Contents taken from Record Commissioners Catalogue.*]

1528–9.

26 (408). Grant to mayor, sheriffs, burgesses, and commonalty of Drogheda; of a piece of ground called Myllmote, alias Windmyllmote, with an orchard adjoining, in Drogheda. To hold for ever in fee-farm, at a rent of 4s.—23 February, xx.

1530.

27 (1). Restitution of temporalities to Edward Bishop of Meath.—26 March [xxi.]

28 (325). Pardon of Bernard, or Brene O'Conghor alias O'Conor, of Othfaly, captain of his nation.—10 September, xxii.

1532.

29 (38). Grant to Richard de la Hyde; of the office of chief justice of the Common Bench. To hold during pleasure, with a fee of £20 out of the fee-farm of the city of Dublin, and £20 out of the issues of the counties of Meath, Dublin, and Louth, and all profits enjoyed by Robert Dowdall in the same office.—20 August, xxiv. *(Cal. P.R., p. 5, art. 23.)

30 (39). Grant to Gerald Aylmer: of the office of second justice of the Common Bench. To hold during pleasure, with such fees as he already had.—23 August, xxiv. (Cal. P.R., p. 4, art. 8.)

31 (41). Grant to Patrick White; of the office of second baron of the Exchequer. To hold during pleasure, with such fees as he already had.—25 August, xxiv. (Cal. P.R. p. 4., art. 15.)

32 (482). Grant to John Barnewell, knight, lord of Trimileston; of Dunlwyrs alias Donlwrus, Balenebonrich alias Bwnryscheston, and Cabraght, county Meath. To hold in tail male, at the fee-farm rent of £6 6s.; and within four years to erect certain houses for the support of the castle of Killyncrosse against the O'Conors.—1 December, xxiv. (Cal. P.R., p. 7, art. 43.)

1532–3.

33 (511). Grant to Jonet Lynche of Galway, widow, and Stephen Lynche (confirming a previous grant to said Jonet and Anthony Lynche); to have three nets upon the water of Galway, between the bridge and the sea, for catching salmon and other fish, one near the great stone, another near Panrise, and the third near Porteres-place; also a mill and bakehouse. To hold to them and the heirs of the body of Stephen, remainder to the heirs of the body of Jonet; at a rent of 13s. 4d.—15 January, xxiv.

1533.

34 (40). Grant to Christopher Delahyde; of the office of second justice of the Chief Place, vice Bartholomew Dyllon, knight. To hold during pleasure, with the accustomed fees out of the customs of Drogheda.—1 April, xxiv.

(Cal. P.R., p. 5, art. 19.)

1534.

35 (57). Grant to Thomas Cusake; of the office of second justice of the Common Bench. To hold during pleasure with a fee of £20 English, as fully as Gerald Aylmer held the same.—
24 May, xxvi. (Cal. P.R., p. 12, art. 5.)

* Calendar of the Patent and Close Rolls of Chancery in Ireland of the reigns of Henry VIII., Edward VI., Mary and Elizabeth. Vol. I. By James Morrin, Dublin, 1861.

. 1534. FIANTS.—HENRY VIII.

36 (42). Grant to Thomas Fynglas; of the offices of Prothonotary, and keeper of the records, and of chirographer, of the Common Bench. To hold for life, with the accustomed fee.—
2 June, xxvi. (Cal. P.R., p. 7, art. 44.)

37 (505). Licence to John Travers, to export within seven years 33 sacks of wool (each sack containing 26 stones 1 pound) to the ports of Weschester, Lyrpole, or Brystow in England.—
15 June, xxvi. (Cal. P.R., p. 12, art. 4.)

38 (43) Grant to Gerald Aylmer; of the office of chief baron of the Exchequer, vice Patrick Fynglas. To hold for life, with a fee of £40 of silver.—25 June, xxvi. (Cal. P.R., p. 12, art. 2.)

1534-5.

39 (48). Grant to Robert Casy; of the office of controller of the great and small custom, tonnage, poundage, and subsidy of Dublin. To hold for life, with a fee of ten marks sterling.—
26 January, xxvi. (Cal. P.R., p. 14, art. 22.)

1535.

40 (47). Grant to Nicholas Stanyhurst and Thomas Alen; of the office of clerk or keeper of the hanaper, held by William Fitzwilliam. To hold to them and the longer liver, with such fees as Nicholas Wycombe or Richard Nangle had.—11 August, xxvii. (Cal. P.R., p. 16, art. 50.)

41 (162). Grant to John Alen, clerk or master of the rolls of Chancery; of the office of chancellor of the Exchequer or chancellor of the green wax of the Exchequer. To hold for life, with such fees as Patrick Bremyngham or Richard Delahide had.—
No date.—[11 August, xxvii.] (Cal. P.R., p. 16, art. 47.)

42 (165). Grant to Thomas Alen, son of Warin Alen; of the office of second chamberlain of the Exchequer. To hold for life, with the accustomed fees.—11 August, [xxvii.]
(Cal. P.R., p. 16, art. 48.)

43 (157). Grant to Walter Goldynge, clerk; of the office of second engrosser of the Exchequer. To hold for life, with such fees as Thomas Hakete had.—12 August, [xxvii.]
(Cal. P.R., p. 16, art. 46.)

44 (163). Grant to Thomas de St. Laurence alias Howth, gentleman; of the office of second justice of the Chief Place or Bench. To hold during pleasure, with a fee of forty marks.—12 August, [xxvii.] (Cal. P.R., p. 16, art. 44.)

45 (166). Grant to Walter Kerdiff, gentleman; of the office of second justice of the Common Bench vice Thomas Cusacke, gentleman. To hold during pleasure, with a fee of £20.—
12 August, [xxvii.] (Cal. P.R., p. 16, art. 45.)

46 (151). Grant to John Rogers; of the office of constable of the castle and manor of Wykeloo lately held by Richard Hansard. To hold for life, with the accustomed fees.—No date.—[12 August, xxvii.]

47 (46). Grant to John White, knight; of the office of constable of the castle of Dublin. To hold for life, with a fee of twenty marks from the customs and subsidy of Dublin.—28 August, xxvii. (Cal. P.R., p. 25, art. 14.)

48 (158). Grant to Owen White; of the office of serjeant-at-arms, vice John White, knight. To hold for life, with a fee of £10 out of the issues of the manor of Crumling.—28 August, [xxvii.]
(Cal. P.R., p. 18, art. 66.)

1535.   FIANTS.—HENRY VIII.

49 (44). Grant to Hugh Holgrave; of the office of summonister of the Exchequer. To hold for life, with such fees as Robert Houth had.—26 November, xxvii. (Cal. P.R., p. 18, art. 67.)

1535-6.

50 (161). Grant to Robert and Walter Cowley, of Kilkenny, gentlemen; of the office of clerk of the crown of Chancery. To hold to them and the longer liver, with such fees as Nicholas Stanyhurste had.—No date.—[11 January, xxvii.]
(Cal. P.R., p. 14, art. 28.)

51 (45). Grant to Walter Cowley; of the office of customer and collector of the customs of Drogheda, vice Robert Delman alias Yans. To hold for life, with a fee of £10.—3 February, xxvii. (Cal. P.R., p. 25, art. 12.)

52 (160). Grant to Robert and Walter Cowley; of the office of customer, and collector and receiver of the customs of Dublin. To hold to them and the longer liver, with a fee of £10.—No date.—[xxvii.]

1536.

53 (49). Grant to Richard Savage, yeoman of the crown; of the office of chief serjeant of all the baronies of the county Dublin, and of the cantred of Newcastell near Lyons. To hold for life, with a fee of £4 10s., sterling, and such other fees as Bartholomew Fitzgerald or John Egyr alias Pety John had.—20 June, xxviii.
(Cal. P.R., p. 25, art. 13.)

54 (159). Grant to John Prowse; of the office of constable of the castles of Carlingford and Grenecastell, and of all woods around Carlingford, with the custom of fish taken there called the castelmese or castelfishe. To hold for life, with the accustomed fees. Also sixty acres of land adjoining the castle of Carlingford. To hold for life, without account.—No date.—[28 August, xxviii.]
(Cal. P.R., p. 25, art. 15.)

55 (479). Grant to Peter Butler, earl of Ossory; of the custody of the lands of James Butler, knight, late baron of Donboyn, and the wardship and marriage of Edmund his son and heir.—No date.—[16 October, xxviii.]

56 (50). Grant to Robert Casy, yeoman of the crown; of the offices of gauger and searcher in the ports of Dublin, Drogheda, and Dundalke. To hold for life, with the accustomed fees.—18 November, xxviii. (Cal. P.R., p. 25, art. 11.)

57 (409). Grant to John Alen of Cowteshale, county Norfolk, (English.) Master of the Rolls; of the priory of St. Wulstans, county Kildare, and the manor of Kyldroght, with their appurtenances. To hold for ever, by the service of two knights' fees. Also a direction for the issue of a commission to suppress the priory.—1 December, xxviii. (See Cal. P.R., p. 40, art. 47.)

1536-7.

58 (512). Charter to the mayor, sheriffs, and commonalty of Drogheda. The mayor and recorder to be keepers and justices of the peace. No sheriff, escheator, or coroner, other than those of the town, to have authority there. The town to have a prison, the mayor and recorder being justices of gaol delivery, to erect a gallows and inflict punishment on felons. All existing rights confirmed.—Westminster, 5 March, xxviii. (Cal. P.R., p. 37, art. 15.)

1537. FIANTS.—HENRY VIII.

59 (174). License to Richard Forster, gent.; to transport annually during 6 years, 200 stones of wool from Ireland to any port in England.—Richmount, 7 December, xxviii. Delivered into Chancery, 20 April, xxviii. (Cal. P.R., p. 27, art. 34.)

60 (53). Grant to Richard Goodyn; of the office of a gunner in the Castle of Dublin. To hold for life, with 8d. sterling a day.—Grenewiche, 1 May, xxix. Delivered into Chancery, 29 August, xxix.

61 (164). Grant to Walter Cowley; of the office of principal or chief solicitor. . To hold during good behaviour, with a fee of £10.—No date.—[7 September or Dec'., xxix.] (Cal. P.R. p. 37, art. 17.)

62 (52). Grant to William Hand, gunner; of the office of a gunner in the castle of Dublin. To hold for life, with 8d. sterling a day.—Hamptoncort, 3 October, xxix. Delivered into Chancery, 11 November. xxix. (Cal. P.R., p. 38, art. 22.)

63 (54). Grant to James Sherloke, gent.; of the offices of treasurer, general receiver, and bailiff of the lordship of Wexford, lately belonging to George Earl of Shrewsbury. To hold during good behaviour, with the accustomed fees, returning the issues to the Exchequer. Also of the office of receiver and bailiff of all other manors and lands in the county Wexford. To hold during good behaviour, with a fee of 5 marks.—7 December, xxix.
(Cal. P.R., p. 37, art. 16.)

1537-8.

64 (51). Grant to Patrick Colley; of the place of a soldier in the castle
(English.) of Dublin. To hold for life, with 8d. sterling a day—Westminster, 21 January, xxix. (Cal. P.R., p. 38, art. 25.)

1538.

65 (327). Pardon to Bernard O'Connor, of Dengyn, in Offaly.—10 August, xxx.

66 (413). Grant to Gerald Aylmer, Chief Justice; of the manor, castle and watermill of Dullardeston, the lands of Dullardeston, Thurstenston, Shensyaleston, Rolanston, Tancardeston, Ardgalf, Faganston, Brayston alias Raieston, Peperton, county Meath, Staffordeston, Cnokdromyn and Luske, county Dublin, which belonged to William Bath, attainted; and the reversion of the castle and lands of Kilbride, with a rent of £8, and of the castle and lands of Nanger, with a rent of £3 10s., county Dublin, leased, 24 December, xxix, to Finian Basnette, of Nanger, and John Gibbons, of Kilbride, for twenty-one years. To hold in tail male, by knight service, at a rent of £20 sterling.—23 September, xxx.
(Cal. P.R. p. 37, art. 21.)

67 (410). Grant to Peter Talbote, of Kylmahioke, gent.; of the manors and castles of Powerscourte, Fasaghe Roo, and Rathdowne, county Dublin, the lands of Powerscourte, Fasaghe Roo, Rathdowne, Cookeston, Teample Cargye, Kyllegrye, Kylgarran, Cowlneskeaghe, and all other lands in the king's hands by the attainder of Richard Fitzgeralde, and all lands in Farcolyn. To hold for ever, at a rent of 40s.—30 October, xxx.
(Cal. P.R., p. 38, art. 28.)

1538-9.

68 (56). Grant to Robert Cowley; of the office of clerk or master of the rolls and records of Chancery. To hold for life, with a fee of 50 marks sterling out of the customs of Dublin and Drogheda.—2 January xxx.

1538–9.   FIANTS.—HENRY VIII.

69 (55). Grant to Egidia Wale, Abbess of the late house of St. Mary of Grane; of a pension of £4.—14 January, xxx.
(Cal. P.R., p. 60, art. 12.)

70 (412). Grant to the mayor, bailiffs, citizens and commonalty of Dublin, in consideration of their services during the rebellion of Thomas Fitzgerald; of the site of the priory of All Saints near Dublin, with all appurtenances in the counties of Dublin, Meath, Kildare, Louth, Tipperary, Kilkenny, and elsewhere. To hold for ever, at a rent of £4 4s. 0½d. Recites grant of 2 Ric. III., remitting the payment of £49 6s. 8d. a year for sixty years; and of 2 Hen. VIII., of £20 for forty years, both portions of the fee-farm of the city; and confirms these remissions for ever.—4 February, xxx.   (Cal. P.R., p. 48, art. 1.)

71 (411). Grant to Leonard Grey, knight, Lord Grey; of the priory of nuns of Grayn, county Carlow, with appurtenances. To hold in tail male, by knight service.—7 February, xxx.

72 (478). Grant to William Wise, Esquire of the King's body; of
(English.) the site of the priory of St. John beside Waterford, and its possessions in the said city, and the lands of Krydan, Ballymabyn, and Lyssent, county Waterford, and in the city and county of Cork. To hold in tail male, by the service of one knight's fee. Also a direction for the issue of a commission to suppress the priory.—No date.—[xxx.] (Cal. P.R., p. 38, art. 23.)

1539.

73 (62). Grant to William Seyntloo, esq.; of the castle and manor of Roscarlon, the water mill of Ballanon, the lands of Mountayntowne, Loughton, Globbeston, Maudelenton, Ballysynan, Ballydon by Killeoke, and Little Ballydon, Kilmahanoke, the Hoke of St. Imoch, Clonamen, the Long Graunge, Rispoylle and Rathtown, county Wexford, parcel of the possessions of David Nevyle, esq., attainted; Kilkowan, Rathtowne, Newton, Rahowle, Great Colic, Old Colic, Shanno, Bastardeston, Churcheton, Slecoulter alias Whitechurche and Kilcowanmore, in the Fassough of Bentre, county Wexford, parcel of the possessions of James Ketyng, gent., attainted; the Parke parcel of the manor of Carge, with the ferry of Wexford, lately belonging to George Earl of Shrewsbury; the islands called the Salteys and the rectory of Kilmore, parcel of the possessions of the abbey of Tynterne in England—a lease dated 20 December, xxix, for twenty-one years, to said William being surrendered. To hold for life, by fealty only.—Westminster, 28 January, xxx. Delivered into Chancery, 6 June, xxxi.   (Cal. P.R., p. 49, art. 2.

74 (87). Warrant by Commission for a pension of £10 to Sir Laurence
(English.) White, prior of the late hospital of St. John Baptist beside the Newton of Tryme; also of 26s. 8d., to Sir Patrick Donugan his "conbrother," issuing from the parsonages of Fynnor and Tolaghnoge.—18 July, xxxi.   (Cal. P.R., p. 64., art. 51.)

75 (79). Warrant by Commission for the pensions following :—To Sir
(English.) Geffre Dardes, abbot, and other canons of the late abbey of the B.V.M. of Tryme—The abbot, £15; Sir William Harte, 26s. 8d.; Sir John Ashe, 26s. 8d.; Sir Water Caddell, 20s.; Sir Robert Laurence, 26s. 8d.; Sir Patrick Smarte, 20s.; Sir Patrick Fynglas 20s.; Sir David Yonge, 20s.; Domynyke Longe, 26s. 8d.; issuing out of specified possessions of the abbey. 19 July, xxxi.
(Cal. P.R., p. 64, art. 50.)

1539.   FIANTS.—HENRY VIII.

76 (88). Warrant by Commission for the pensions following :—To
(English.) Sir Thomas Wafre, abbot of the late abbey of the B.V.M. of the
Nawan, and his "conbretherne".—The abbot, £15 ; Sir Thomas
Cahill, £3 6s. 8d. ; Sir Thomas Folame, 26s. 8d. ; Sir John
Betaghe, 20s., and to be parish priest of the church of our Lady
of Nawan ; Sir William Orche, 26s. 8d. ; issuing from the par-
sonages of Novan and Smermor and lands of Smermora and
Horlestona.—21 July, xxxi.   (Cal. P.R., p. 64, art. 48.)

77 (97). Warrant by Commission for the pensions following :—To
English.) Richard Countor, abbot of the late abbey of the B.V.M. of
Melyfount, and his "conbrethern".—The abbot, £40 ; Sir John
Byrrell, £3 6s. 8d., and to be curate of Tolaghalen ; Sir
Thomas Bagote, £4 ; Sir Peter Rewe, 40s., and to be curate of
Knockamoghan ; Sir Thomas Alen, 53s. 4d., and to be curate of
Newton ; Sir John Prowte, 40s., and to be curate of Donnowre ; Sir
William Norreys, 40s., and to be curate of Callan and Uncheoke ;
Sir Robert Nangle, 40s., and to be curate of Graungeithe ; Sir
Patrick Contowre, 53s. 4d., and to be curate of Barleys and Salt-
house ; Sir William Veldon, £3 6s. 8d. ; Sir Patrick Lawles, 40s. ;
also to John Ball, 40s. ; Clement Bartholomew, 20s. ; and Felym
O'Neyll, 20s. ; issuing from the parishes of Cnockmahan, Don-
owre, and Monkenewton.—26 July, xxxi.
                            (Cal. P.R., p. 60, art. 6, and p. 59, art. 2.)

78 (95). Warrant by Commission for a pension of £4 to Sir Cornell
English.) Duff, prior of the late hospital of St. John the Baptist by Kenlis ;
and of 20s. to Sir Thomas Corregan his "conbrother ;" issuing
out of the churches of Stonhall and Tristelkeran.—27 July,
xxxi.   (Cal. P. R., p. 65, art. 62.)

79 (181). Lease to Robert Delman, of Dublin, gentleman ; of the
site of the monastery of the B.V.M. of Tristirnaghe, the lands of
Tristirnaghe, Abbayton, the Grang, Templeforan, Milne Townfforan, Cargestown, Cargestown alias Ballynecargetown, Mounctown, Syffyn,
and Racorbally, county Meath, and Balrothry, county Dublin ; the
rectories of Tristirnaghe, Kilbycksy, Templefforan, Shandonaghe,
Sonnaghe, and Killoghe, county Meath, and Balrothry, county
Dublin, and the advowsons of Killoghe and Balrothry. To hold
for twenty-one years from the 10th July, at a rent of £60. (See
141.)—27 July, xxxi.

80 (182). Lease to Thomas Alen, gentleman ; of the site of the
hospital of St. John the Baptist of Naas, the lands of Naas,
Johnston, Siggenston, Waltereston, Tristeldermot and Edeston ;
the rectories of St. Johns in the Naas, and Whitechurch, county
Kildare. To hold for twenty-one years, at a rent of £39 3s. 4d.—
28 July, xxxi.

81 (176). Grant to Thomas Fynglas, gentleman ; of custody of the
lands of the late Robert Barnewall, of Dromnagh, and of the
wardship and marriage of Edward, his son and heir ; also of
custody of the lands of the late Richard Fitzwilliam, of Baggot-
rath, and of the wardship and marriage of Thomas, his son and
heir.—Westminster, 4 October, xxx. Delivered into Chancery,
7 August, xxxi.'

82 (90). Grant for Thomas Possike, prior of the late hospital of St.
John the Baptist of Naas ; of a pension of £9 ; and for Laurence
Byrlyc, religious person of the same ; a pension of 40s. ; issuing
from the rectory of Whitchurche, county Kildare.—23 August,
xxx.   (Cal. P. R., p. 59, art. 5.)

1539.   FIANTS.—HENRY VIII.

83 (96). Warrant by Commission for a pension to Sir Henry Duff,
(English.) late abbot of St. Thomas Courte by Dublin of £42 ; to Sir
James Cottrell, late abbot, a pension of £10 (in confirmation of
a grant from the convent) ; to Sir John Brace, prior, a pension of
53s. 4d., and to be curate of the church of St. Katharin by
Dublin ; to Sir John Butlar, his "con-brother," a pension of 40s.,
to be curate of St. James by Dublin, and to have his orchard
within the precinct of Thomas Court ; issuing from the parsonages
of Grenoke, &c. ; and to Patrick Clyncher, "clerc of the organs,"
a pension of £5 (vide post 84).—Dated 28 July, xxxi. Delivered
into Chancery, 10 September, xxxi.
(Cal. P. R., p. 59, art. 1 & 3 ; p. 60, art. 9.)

84 (91). Grant to Patrick Clyncher ; of a pension of £5, issuing from
lands in the parish of Donaghmore by Grenoke, and from the rectory
of Lucan ; confirming a grant of the said pension with certain
casements, made by the abbot and convent of St. Thomas the
Martyr by Dublin.—10 September, xxxi.

85 (178). Lease to Edmund Redman, surgeon ; of the site of the
hospital of St. John the Baptist without the Newgate of Dublin.
To hold for twenty-one years, at a rent of 43s. 4d.—27 September,
xxxi.

86 (74). Warrant by Commission for the pensions following :—To
(English.) Sir John Willie, prior, and the canons of the late house of the
B.V.M. of Louth—The prior, £16 13s. 4d. ; Sir John Saundre,
£4. and to be curate of Loutbe ; Sir Thomas Verdon, 40s. ; and
John Gernon, 40s.—23 November, xxxi.

1539-40.

87 (78). Warrant by Commission for a pension to Sir Richard
(English.) Plunket, abbot of the late house of the B. V. M. in Kells, of
£10 : to Sir Henry White, canon of the same, a pension of 20s.
and to be curate of Emlaghe ; and to Sir John Rone, canon of
the same, a pension of 20s. and to be curate of the church of
Killeaghe ; issuing out of the parsonage of Killeaghe, county
Meath.—20 January, xxxi.   (Cal. P. R., p. 60, art. 11.)

88 (92). Grant for William Cottrell, conventual person of the late
abbey of the B. V. M., by Dublin ; of a pension of £3 6s. 8d.,
issuing out of the lands of Robockeswalls, parish of Portmarnoke.—20 January, xxxi.   (Cal. P. R., p. 63, art. 44.)

89 (84). Grant for Matilda Hancoke, conventual person of the late
abbey of St. Brigide of Odder, county Meath ; of a pension of
26s. 8d. ; issuing from the rectory and lands of Odder.—
20 January, xxxi.   (Cal. P. R., p. 64, art. 54.)

90 (85). Grant to Margaret Sylke, late abbess of St. Brigide of
Odder ; of a pension of £6 : to Margery Mape, conventual
person of the same, a pension of 40s. : and to Johanna Tancy,
conventual person, a pension of 40s. ; issuing out of lands in
Odder.—1 March xxxi.   (Cal. P. R., p. 64, art. 53.)

91 (175). Lease to Thomas Cusake of Cossingeston, knight ; of the
site of the priory of Lesmollyn, lands of Lesmollen, Pouderloghe,
Henryeston, Claterston, Claghan, Betaghton and Ballymolan,
county Meath ; Belgrawe, Dunsinke, Skybbreston, Balmacar-
nano, Kelleston, Corneliscourte, Bellautre and Irishton, county
Dublin ; Poncheston, county Kildare ; Payneston, county
Louth ; 26s. 8d. rent from Hollyvodrathe, county Dublin ; 54s.
from Mollaghcurre ; 13s. 4d. from Termonfeghen, county Louth ;

1539–40.   FIANTS.—HENRY VIII.

10s. from [   ] (sic); 2s. from Platen; £3 6s. 8d. from Blondeston; 13d. from Loghton; £10 15s. 8d. from Henryeston; 20s. from Claghan; 18s. from Donameston; 23s. 4d. from Tutealand; 16s. 6d. from Morton; 13s. 4d. from Corfanton; 26s. 8d. from Ethelton, county Meath, and the rectory of Kylpatrike, county Meath. To hold for 21 years, at a rent of £100.—1 March, xxxi.

92 (59). Warrant by Commission for a pension of £3 to Sir John (English.) Carroll, abbot of the late house of St. Peter of the Cnocke; and of £1 6s. 8d. to Sir Henry Lucoke, canon of the same. Dated 23rd Nov. xxxi.—Delivered into Chancery, 10 March, xxxi.
(Cal. P. R., p. 65, art. 58.)

93 (60). Grant for Walter Esmonde, conventual person of the late monastery of the B. V. M., by Dublin; of a pension of 40s., issuing out of Drysshoke, in the parish of St. Glanokes by Dublin. —10 March, xxxi.   (Cal. P. R., p. 61, art. 20.)

94 (68). Grant for conventual persons of the late abbey of the B. V. M., by Dublin; of the pensions following:—Thomas Walsche, 40s.; John Tirrell, 40s.; John Whitrell, 40s.; William Ley, 40s.; William Walsche, 40s.; Robert Lide, 40s.; William Loghan, 40s.; issuing from Morraghan and other possessions.— 10 March, xxxi.   (Cal. P. R., p. 63, art. 47.)

95 (75). Grant for conventual persons of the late abbey of the B. V. M., by Dublin; of the pensions following:—Henry Veisen, £3 6s. 8d.; James Barret, 53s. 4d.; Patrick Bennet, 40s.; John Festame, 53s. 4d.; Seth Pecoke, 40s.; John Barret, 53s. 4d.; issuing out of the Grange of Balgeth and other possessions.—Dated 20 January, xxxi.—Delivered into Chancery, 10 March, xxxi.   (Cal. P. R., p. 63, art. 46.)

96 (63). Grant for Alison Whyte, late prioress of the B. V. M. of Gracedieu; of a pension of £6, issuing out of Gracedieu and other possessions.—10 March, xxxi.   (Cal. P. R., p. 63, art. 43.)

97 (80). Warrant by Commission for a pension of £3 to Sir Thomas (English.) Davy, prior of the late hospital of St. John, in Drogheda; issuing out of Priorton and Kilartre. Dated 1 Aug., xxxi.— Delivered into Chancery, 10 March, xxxi.
(Cal. P. R., p. 65, art. 57.)

98 (83). Grant for Nicholas Corbally, late prior of the B. V. M. de Urso, of Drogheda; of a pension of £5, issuing out of possessions in Drogheda and Killaneyr.—10 March, xxxi.
(Cal. P. R., p. 60, art. 10.)

99 (153). Grant to Thady M'Gillernowe, prior, and to other conventual persons of the late abbey of Granarde; of the following pensions:—The prior, 4 marks; Thomas O'Ferrall, 13s. 4d.; Eugene M'Gyllananewe, 13s. 4d.; Maurus O'Hyrraghti, 13s. 4d.; Fergall Crossan, 13s. 4d.; Oonacius Gillananewe, 13s. 4d.; issuing out of the rectory of Strade Innybrecray.—No date.— [10 M [   ] xxxi.]   (Cal. P. R., p. 61, art. 14.)

100 (93). Grant for William Launde, late abbot of the B. V. M., by Dublin; of a pension of £50, issuing out of the manors and rectories of Ballybaghill and Portmarnoke.—13 March, xxxi.
(Cal. P. R., p. 63, art. 45.)

101 (65). Grant for Richard White, conventual person of the late priory of St. Katherine, of Waterford; of a pension of 53s. 4d.; and for Philip Moran, conventual person of the same, a pension of 53s.; issuing out of the rectory of Dungarwan, diocese of Ossory.—20 March, xxxi.   (Cal. P. R., p. 62, art. 24.)

1539-40. FIANTS.—HENRY VIII.

102 (81). Grant for conventual persons of the late priory of the B. V. M. of Gracedieu; of the pensions following:—Margaret Coscrowe, 50s.; Thomasina Dermyn, 50s.; Katherine Wstace, 50s.; Alison FitzSimon, 50s.; issuing out of Gracedieu, &c.— 20 March, xxxi. (Cal. P. R., p. 64, art. 52.)

103 (86). Grant for conventual persons of the late priory of the Holy Trinity of Lasmullen; of the pensions following:—Geneta Barnewall, 40s.; Alison Wstace, 40s.; Anne Weldon, 40s. Issuing out of Lasmullyng, &c., county Meath,—20 March, xxxi. (Cal. P. R., p. 63, art. 42.)

104 (89). Grant for Edmund Nugent, Bishop of Kilmore, late commendatory of the priory of B. V. M. of Trysternaghe; of a pension of £26 13s. 4d., issuing out of Templefforan, &c., county Meath.—20 March, xxxi. (Cal. P. R., p. 64, art. 55.)

105 (82). Grant to conventual persons of the late priory of the B. V. M. of Tristernaghe; of the pensions following:—Walter Twit, 26s. 8d., with the service of the church of Rathaspike; Galfrid Hyll, 26s. 8d., with the church of Kylbysky; Cornelius Note, 26s. 8d., with the church of Tristernaghe; Patrick Note, 26s. 8d., with the church of Sonnaghe; Thomas Barnewall, 26s. 8d., with the church of Impere; issuing out of Kargiston, &c., county Meath.—20 March, xxxi.
(Cal. P. R., p. 64, art. 56.)

106 (94). Grant for conventual persons of the late priory of the B. V. M. of Mollingar; of the pensions following:—John Kelly, 40s.; Thomas Reling, 26s. 8d.; John Ledwitche, 26s. 8d.; issuing out of Dunboyne.—20 March, xxxi.
(Cal. P. R., p. 65, art. 61.)

107 (67). Grant to Milo, bishop of Ossory, late commendatory of the priory of St. Columbe, of Enestioke, county Kilkenny; of a pension of £20.; issuing out of the manor of Enestioke, &c.— 20 March, xxxi. (Cal. P. R., p. 62, art. 27.)

1540.

108 (58). Grant to John Griffyn *alias* M'Morchowe, conventual person of the late priory of St. Columbe, of Enystioke, county Kilkenny; to be curate of the church of St. Columbe, Enystioke, with a messuage and orchard, and the ultarages and oblations of the parish.—27 March, xxxi.

109 (77). Grant for Patrick Stakpoll, late abbot of the B. V. M. of the Rock of Casshel; of a pension of £4; and for Maurice Mannan, conventual person of the same, a pension of 13s. 4d.— 4 April, xxxi. (Cal. P. R., p. 62, art. 31.)

110 (66). Grant to Dionysius O'Mulryan and John Donati, conventual persons of the late house of the B. V. M. of Cahyr; of pensions of 13s. 4d. each.—6 April, xxxi.
(Cal. P. R., p. 63, art. 36.)

111 (72). Grant to conventual persons of the late abbey of the B. V. M. of Inyslawenaght; of the pensions following:—William Cahill, 40s.; Mathew Cahill, 40s.; Maurice Keyrry, 20s.; and Edmund Cahill, 20s.; issuing out of Enislawnaght, &c., county Tipperary.—10 April, xxxi. (Cal. P. R., p. 62, art. 26.)

1540.   FIANTS.—HENRY VIII.

112 (73). Grant for Katherine Mothing, late abbess of St. Kilkin, of Kilkelyn; of a pension of £5, issuing out of Kilkelyn, &c., county Kilkenny.—15 April, xxxi.   (Cal. P. R., p. 61, art. 22.)

113 (76). Grant for conventual persons of the late priory of SS. Peter and Paul, of Selskyr; of pensions following:—Richard Lawles, 53s. 4d.; John Flemyng, 5 marks; Patrick Mason, 40s.; issuing out of the manor of Ballyreily, &c.—16 April, xxxi.
(Cal. P. R., p. 63, art. 40.)

114 (61). Grant for Edmund Moldony, conventual person of the late priory of St. Katherine, by Waterford; of a pension of 26s. 8d.; and for John Konowe, conventual person of the same, a pension of 26s. 8d.; issuing out of premises in Waterford, &c.—17 April, xxxi.   (Cal. P. R. p. 61, art. 21.)

115 (64). Grant to Thomas Shortall, late abbot of the B. V. M. of Kilcoule, county Tipperary; of a pension of £5; issuing out of Kilcoule:—18 April, xxxi.   (Cal. P. R., p. 63, art. 38.)

116 (71). Grant for conventual persons of the late abbey of St. Kilkin, of Kilkellyn; of the pensions following:—Elicia Gaall, 40s.; Egidia FitzJohn, 40s.; Anastacia Cantwell, 46s. 8d.; Anne Clere, 40s.; Elicia Butler, 43s. 4d.; issuing out of Kilkellyn, &c., county Kilkenny.—18 April, xxxi.
(Cal. P. R., p. 61, art. 23.)

117 (69). Grant for Edmund Laghnan, conventual person of the late priory of the B. V. M. of Kenles, county Kilkenny; of a pension of 40s.; and for Nicholas Lahy, conventual person of the same, a pension of 26s. 8d.; issuing out of possessions in Kenles.—20 April, xxxi.   (Cal. P. R., p. 63, art. 37.)

118 (177). Lease to Thomas Tobyn, of Killaghe, gentleman; of the rectories of Mondassell and Kilmenynenan, late possessions of the priory of Kenlys. To hold for twenty-one years, at a rent of £13 6s. 8d.—20 April, xxxi.

119 (179). Lease to Thomas Alen, of Dublin, gentleman; of the site of the monastery of the order of Preachers, by the Mote of Nase, with its appurtenances, county Kildare. To hold for twenty-one years, at a rent of £6 9s.—20 April, xxxi.

120 (180). Lease to Thomas Alen, of Dublin, gentleman; of the site of the hospital of St. John the Baptist of the Naas, lands in Naas, Herberteston, Johnston, Waltereston, and Whitechurch, county Kildare, and Trestelderinot, county Carlow. To hold for twenty-one years, at a rent of £35 18s. 2d.—20 April, xxxi.

121 (328). Pardon of Edmund Brenaghe, of Knockmelan, gentleman. Fine 6s. 8d.—20 [   ] xxxi.   (Cal. P. R., p. 52, art. 49.)

122 (155). Grant for Walter Dece, conventual person of the late priory of SS. Taurin and Feghin, of Fower; of a pension of 33s. 4d.; and to Richard Harfford, conventual person of the same, a pension of 33s. 4d.—No date.—[xxxi.]
(Cal. P. R., p. 60, art. 13.)

123 (100). Grant for Edmund Powere, prior of the late priory of St. Katherine, by Waterford; of a pension of £20, issuing out of the rectories of Carricke, Kilcohne, and Killowran.— 26 April, xxxii.   (Cal. P. R., p. 61, art. 18.)

124 (156). Grant to Edmund Lonorgane, late prior of Cahyr, county Tipperary; to be curate of Cahyr, with the altarages and oblations of the parish, and a pension of £3 6s. 8d.—26 April, xxxii.
(Cal. P. R., p. 61, art. 16.)

1540. FIANTS.—HENRY VIII.

125 (193). Lease to Martin Pellis of Athie, gentleman; of the manors of Athie and Wodstoke, possessions of Gerald, earl of Kildare, attainted. To hold for twenty-one years, at a rent of £10 10s. 8d.—26 April, xxxii.

126 (199). Lease to Martin Pellis, of Athy, gentleman; of the site of the priory of Friars Preachers of Athy, with a mill near Tulmacarre, and other appurtenances, county Kildare. To hold for twenty-one years, at a rent of 40s.—26 April, xxxii.

127 (202). Lease to Thomas Casey, of Athboy, merchant; of the site of the priory of Carmelite Friars of Athboy, with appurtenances, in Athboy and Adenston, county Meath. To hold for twenty-one years, at a rent of 40s.—Dated 14 December, xxxi. Delivered into Chancery, 26 April, xxxii.

128 (392). Lease to Mathew Kyng, of Kilmaynane, gentleman; of the site of the priory of SS. Feghin and Taurin of Fowre, lands of Fowre, Mylcastell, Carpinderestowne, Comoylestowne, Lyerkyll, Hyltowne, Gylbertestowne, Drumawry, Fayron, Kylnaylaghe, Betogheston, Nynche, and Neweraithe by Kellys; the rectories of B.V.M. of Fowre, St. Feghin of Fowre, St. Ornata of Archideorum, B.V.M. of Lighbla, St. Edane of Fayron, St. Bridget of Ouldecastell, St. Germane of Faghlyn, St. Patrick of Dorniskyll, St. Michael of Ragarff, St. Patrick of Balmagarvey, and divers rectories in the Breny. To hold for twenty-one years at a rent of £140.—26 April, xxxii.

129 (396). Lease to David Floyde, of Dublin, soldier; of the site of the priory of preachers, or black friars, of Trym, with appurtenances in Trym, Toullgharde and [   ]. To hold for twenty-one years at a rent of 40s.—26 April, xxxii.

130 (390). Lease to Thomas Nugent, of Dublin, gentleman; of the site of the abbey of the B.V.M. of Strowill, with its appurtenances. To hold for twenty-one years, at a rent of 13s. 4d.—Dated 9 May, xxxi. Delivered into Chancery, 26 April, xxxi. (sic.)

131 (110). Grant to David Bossher, conventual person of the late priory of St. Columbe of Enestioke, county Kilkenny; to be curate of the parish of St. Columbe alias Columkille, county Kilkenny, with the altarages and oblations, and a pension of 40s. issuing out of the rectory of Dunkit.—27 April, xxxii.
(Cal. P R., p. 62, art. 28.)

132 (70). Grant for James Baren and David Dobyn, conventual persons of the late priory of St. Columbe of Enestioke, county Kilkenny; of pensions of 40s. each, issuing out of the rectories of Dunkitte, &c.—27 April, xxxi. (recte xxxii.)
(Cal. P. R., p. 92, art. 29.)

133 (112). Grant for Oliver Grace, late abbot of the B.V.M. of Jeripount; of a pension of £10, issuing out of Jerepounte, &c., county Kilkenny.—28 April, xxxii. (Cal. P. R., p. 62, art. 30.)

134 (99.) Grant for James Grace, conventual person of the late abbey of the B.V.M. of Jerepount; of a pension of 40s., issuing out of Jerepount, &c., county Kilkenny.—28 April, xxxii.
(Cal. P. R., p. 62, art 25.)

135 (115). Grant for conventual persons of the late abbey of the B.V.M. of Jerepount; of the pensions following: Patrick Brenane, 40s.; Nicholas Fynne, 40s.; Richard Croke, 40s.; Thomas Croke, 40s.; issuing out of Woldgrang, &c., county Kilkenny.—28 April, xxxii. (Cal. P. R., p. 62, art. 32.)

1540. FIANTS.—HENRY VIII.

136 (108). Grant to Richard Cantwell, late prior of St. John the Evangelist of Kilkenny; to be curate of the church of St. John the Baptist, of Kilkenny, with a third part of the rectory, tithes, &c., and a messuage and orchard in Kilkenny.—28 April, xxxii.
(Cal. P. R., p. 60, art 7.)

137 (107). Grant to James Bicton, conventual person of the late priory of St. John the Evangelist of Kilkenny; to be curate of the church of S. Colman, of Claraght, with the altarages and oblations, and a pension of 40s. issuing out of premises in Kilkenny, and the rectory of Claraght.—28 April, xxxii.
(Cal. P. R., p. 62, art. 35.)

138 (114). Grant for conventual persons of the late priory of St. John the Evangelist of Kilkenny; of the pensions following:—Thomas Marshall, 40s.; Robert Purcell, 40s.; Robert Rothe, 40s.; issuing out of premises in Kilkenny, &c.—28 April, xxxii.
(Cal. P. R., p. 62, art. 34.)

139 (109). Grant to Nicholas Tobyn, late prior of the B.V.M. of Kellys, county Kilkenny; to be curate of the parish church of the B.V.M. of Kellys, with a third of the rectory, tithes, &c., and a house and orchard in Kellys.—28 April, xxxii.

140 (509). Grant to James Butler, late abbot of the B.V.M. of Inyslawnaghe; to be vicar of the church of S. Patrick, of Inyslawnaghe, with the altarages and oblations, and a pension of £5 6s. 8d.—30 April, xxxii. (Cal. P. R., p. 62, art. 33.)

141 (198). Lease. Same lessee and premises, &c., as 79. To hold for twenty-one years, from Easter last.—1 May, xxxii.

142 (393). Lease to Laurence Newell, gentleman; of the site of the priory of Augustin friars of Clomyn, with appurtenances, county Wexford. To hold for twenty-one years, at a rent of 13s. 4d.—1 May, xxxii.

143 (113). Grant to John Colodan, conventual person of the late monastery of the B.V.M. of Kilcowle; of a pension of 40s.—2 May, xxxii. (Cal. P. R., p. 63, art. 39.)

144 (167). Grant to John Colton, conventual person of the late abbey of the B.V.M. of Kilcoule, county Kilkenny; to be curate of the parish church of the B.V.M. of Kilcoule, with the altarages and oblations; also for John Bryte, conventual person, of the same, a pension of 20s. issuing out of tenements in Kilcoule. No date.—[2 May, xxxii.]
Enrolled as to pension. (Cal. P. R., p. 61, art. 15.)

145 (194). Grant for John Petit, late prior of the B.V.M. of Mollingar; of a pension of £20, issuing out of Slewin, &c.; also a lease of the lands of Slevin and Graunge, and the rectory of Vastina. To hold for twenty-one years at a rent of £14.—7 May, xxxii. (Cal. P. R., p. 65, art. 60.)

146 (154). Grant for Margaret Habarde, late prioress of Tarmafoghen; of a pension of 26s. 8d.; and for Anne Gaydon, conventual person of the same: a pension of 13s. 4d.; issuing out of Tarmafeghen, &c.—No date.—[10 May, xxxii.]
(Cal. P. R., p. 61, art. 17.)

147 (101). Grant for Robert Wessley, late prior of the B.V.M. of Connall, county Kildare; of a pension of £13 6s. 8d., issuing out of the rectories of Rathernan, &c.—12 May, xxxii.
(Cal. P. R., p. 65, art. 59.)

1540. FIANTS.—HENRY VIII.

148 (111). Grant for conventual persons of the late priory of the B.V.M. of Conall; of the pensions following:—Walter Blake, 40s.; Hugh Doyne, 40s.; Philip Blake, 26s. 8d.; Walter (or Patrick) Rocheford, 26s. 8d.; Patrick Newell, 20s.; Patrick More, 20s.; Nicholas Doyne, 20s.; issuing out of the rectory of Carbre.—13 May, xxxii. (Cal. P. R., p. 64, art. 49.)

149 (286). Charter for the abbey of the B.V.M. of Wothonia, diocese of Emly, of the Cistercian order, with assent of James, earl of Ormond and Ossory, its founder and patron; transforming it to a secular provostry (prepositura); John Ryane, late abbot, to be provost.—20 May, xxxii.

150 (183). Lease to Leonard Gray, knight, Lord Gray, viscount of Grane; of the site of the abbey of the B.V.M. of Eneslawnaghe, four weirs and a several fishery there, lands of Enislawnaghe, Graunge, Balleorcley, Kilmalashe, Graungharvey, Loghkeraghe, Kilmaviaghe, the rectory of S. Patrick of Inislawnaghe, county Tipperary, lands of Kilm°., lands and rectory of Glanwidan alias Ferrynnemannaghe, county Waterford. To hold for twenty-one years, at a rent of £24.—Dated 8 April, xxxi. Delivered into Chancery, 20 May, xxxii.

151 (187). Lease to Walter Cowley, of Browueston, gentleman; of the rectory of Blanchevilleston, county Kilkenny, parcel of the possessions of the abbey of Jeripount. To hold for twenty-one years, at a rent of 4 marks.—20 May, xxxii.

152 (195). Lease to James White, of Waterford, gentleman; of the site of the monastery of preachers, or black friars, of Waterford, with appurtenances in the city, and land by Kylbary, county Waterford. To hold for twenty-one years, at a rent of 5 marks. —20 May, xxxii.

153 (395) Lease to James White, of Waterford, gentleman; of the rectory of Killowran. To hold for twenty-one years, at a rent of £5.—20 May, xxxii.

154 (397). Lease to James White, of Waterford, gentleman; of the rectory of Dunkyt. To hold for twenty-one years, at a rent of £9 6s. 8d.—20 May, xxxii.

155 (394). Lease to Walter Cowley, of Browneston, gentleman; of Johnston, county Meath, and the rectories of Mogowre and Colman, county Tipperary, parcel of the possessions of the hospital of St. John the Baptist, without the Newgate of Dublin. To hold for twenty-one years, at a rent of 40s.—20 May, xxxii. Delivered into Chancery, 26 May, xxxii.

156 (5). Grant to Robert Dyllon, of Phulpotiston, county Meath, gentleman, the king's attorney, in consideration of the sums of £360 and £380 7s. 3d. sterling (reciting a lease to him for twenty-one years, dated 23 December, xxix., of the site of the priory of St. Peter of the Newton, near Trym, the lands and tithes of Newton, Kyllthombe, Cloyneboynaghe, Shirlokeston, and Rathnally); of the said site and lands, the tithes being excepted; Dunkenny, and Hunteslando, possessions of the monastery of St. John the Baptist of the Newetowne, near Trym; one messuage, and Robenrath, in Novan, parcel of the possessions of the abbey of St. Mary of the Novan; Branganston, parcel of the possessions of John Burnell, attainted; Dalltonston, county Meath, parcel of the possessions of Christopher Ewstace, attainted. To hold for ever by the service of a twentieth part of a knight's fee,

1540. FIANTS.—HENRY VIII.

and a rent of 28s. 5d., also from 1558, 4 marks out of Dunkenny, formerly payable to Gerald earl of Kildare, attainted. [Much defaced.—See Aud. Gen. pat. books, vol. i., p. 9].—22 July, xxxii.

157 (190). Lease to Edmund, archbishop of Cashel; of the site of the monastery of friars minor of Cashell, with appurtenances. To hold for twenty-one years, at a rent of 56s. 8d.—24 August, xxxii.

158 (102). Grant to Robert Shortall, late prior of Fertnekeruglio; of a pension of 5 marks.— 31 August, xxxii. (Cal. P. R., p. 60, art. 8.)

159 (105). Grant to William Higham, one of the yeomen of the (English.) Crown; of the office of serjeant or bailiff of the county Kildare. To hold for life.—Westminster, 20 June, xxxii. Delivered into Chancery, 9 September, xxxii.

(Cal. P. R., p. 67, art. 6.)

160 (104). Grant to John Alen, master of the rolls, and Thomas Alen, gent.; of the offices of constable of the castle of Maynoth, seneschal of the court and surveyor of the manor of Maynoth and Maynothesley, and keeper of the park of Maynoth. To hold to them and the longest liver, with a fee of £10 sterling, and all other rights.—1 October, xxxii.

(Cal. P. R., p. 67, art. 7.)

1540-1.

161 (414). Grant to James Butler, earl of Ormond and Ossory; of the site of the priory of Kenlis, county Kilkenny, lands, &c., of Kenlis, le Grange, Killensth, Desart, and le Grow, and the rectory of Konlis. To hold in tail male, by the service of a third part of a knight's fee, paying annually £5, or the third of the said rectory, to the vicar of Kenlis.—4 January, xxxii.

162 (329). Pardon to William Furlonge, of Greseton, county Wexford, horseman, Philip, Nicholas, and John, his sons; Mayas Furlonge, of Daveston, same county, horseman; Thomas Furlongo, of Bulganriaghe, same county, horseman; Thomas, Henry, John, and James Furlonge, of the same county, footmen, sons of Patrick Furlonge.—Fine, £5 10s.—13 January, xxxii.

(Cal. P. R., p. 69, art. 31.)

163 (200). Lease to Edmund Duffe, gent.; of the site of the priory of friars preachers of Arclow, with appurtenances. To hold for 21 years, at a rent of 20s.—15 February, xxxii.

164 (106). Grant to Stephen Fitzwilliam, of Jopeston, gent.; of the office of a gunner in the castle of Dublin. To hold for life, with a fee of 8d. sterling a-day out of the manors of Trym and Moygar.—23 February, xxxii.

165 (193). Lease to Thomas Butler, of the Cahir, knight; of the site of the priory of the B.V.M. of Cahir, a fishery, lands of Cahir-doneiske, Manistyr no Cahir, Mouche Graunge, Little Graunge, and Kilemlaghe, rectories of Cahir-doneiske, Loghlwyr, Donohill, and Corroke, county Tipperary, and Feddamore, county Limerick. To hold for 21 years, at a rent of £14 4s. 8d.— 27 February, xxxii.

(See Cal. P. R., p. 94, art. 46.)

166 (189). Lease to Edmund Bray, of Clonmell, merchant; of the tithes of the Grange and Kylleliaghe, county Tipperary, late possessions of the abbey of the B.V.M. of Enyslawnaghe. To hold for twenty-one years, at a rent of £4.—1 March, xxxii.

1540-1.   FIANTS.—HENRY VIII.

167 (483). Livery to Thomas Nugent, son and heir of Christopher, son and heir of Lavalin Nugent, of Braclyn.—9 March, xxxii.
(Cal. P.R., p. 70, art. 40.)

168 (391). Lease to George, Archbishop of Dublin; of the site of the priory of St. Augustin of Fethirde, with appurtenances in Fethirde and Clowanston, county Tipperary. To hold for twenty-one years, at a rent of £3 6s. 8d.—13 March xxxii.

169 (186). Lease to the Mayor, &c., of the city of Waterford; of the site of the priory of friars minor or grey friars of Waterford, with appurtenances in county Waterford, and a meadow at the Pyle of Dunkyt, county Kilkenny. To hold for twenty-one years, at a rent of £5 9s. 8d.—14 March, xxxii.

170 (98). Grant to Donogh Brene, esquire, in consideration of his good service; of an annuity of £20 English. To hold during good behaviour.—20 March, xxxii. (Cal. P.R., p. 70, art. 43.)

171 (330). Pardon of Edmund Asshebolde or Asbolde, of Maynothe, yeoman, servant of Lord Leonard Gray, late Deputy; for having raised Kedogh Omore, of Stradballi, in Lex, gent., Schan M'Coyn of Kylclene, horseman, Neyll O'Lyallorde of Disert, horseman, and other Irish, to make war upon Peter Butler, earl of Ormond and Ossory, Alexander FitzTyrrelagh, of the Great Grange, and other English; and for all other offences.—24 March, xxxii.
(Cal. P.R., p. 70, art. 42.)

1541.

172 (196). Lease to Thomas Butler, of Cahyr, knight; of the site of the abbey of the B.V.M. of Enoslawnaghe, and other premises as in No. 150. To hold for twenty-one years, at a rent of £28 during the first four years, and of £30 thereafter.—26 March, xxxii.

173 (191). Lease to Dermot Ryan, of Cashel; of the site of the monastery of Franciscans of Kyllally, with appurtenances, county Tipperary. To hold for twenty-one years, at a rent of 40d.—26 March, xxxii.

174 (188). Lease to David Sutton; of the site of the house of Franciscan friars of Clane, county Kildare, with appurtenances. To hold for twenty-one years, at a rent of £5 3s. 2d. (defaced).—29 March, xxxii.

175 (197). Lease to Walter Cowley, of Brownestowne, gent.; of the site of the hospital of St. John the Evangelist, by Kilkenny, lands in Kilkenny, a mill in the Magdelen street by Kilkenny, Chanons Growe alias Lowes Wodde, Drakeland, Brownestowne, Cottresboly, Sellerstowne, the rectories of St. John, Claraghe, Tybbride, Kildreynaghe, Castlecomer, Scaricke, Newton of Jeripounte, Mockully, Kilmadoe, county Kilkenny, rectories of New Rosse alias Rospont alias Rossincrowne, the Ilande Rely, and Ernestowne, county Wexford, the tithes of a carucate by St. Patrick's stepe, the altarages and tithes of Jenkynstowne, and the altarages of Downfert, county Kilkenny. To hold for twenty-one years, at a rent of £66 6s. 8d.—6 April, xxxii.

176 (201). Lease to David Sheghan, of Cork, merchant; of the site of the monastery of friars minor, by Cork, with a fishery, a weir, and land in Cork and land in Tempelmymruth. To hold for twenty-one years, and a rent of 42s. 4d. sterling.—10 April, xxxii.

D

1541. FIANTS.—HENRY VIII.

177 (103). Grant to Walter Hussey and John Ryan; of the office of chief engrosser of the Exchequer. To hold to them, and the longer liver, with a fee of £10, and other fees, as fully as Walter Hussey had.—13 April xxxii.

178 (338). Pardon to Peter Walsche, of Derconnor, Arnemallan or Unane, gentleman, yeoman, horseman, or kerne, son of Walter Walsche.—26 April, xxxii. (Cal. P.R., p. 71, art. 53.)

179 (209). Lease to Edmund Sexten, of Limerick, gent.; of the site of the house of St. Peter in Limerick, lands in Limerick, Balleneg [allaghe alias] Templenegallaghe and Ballenegallaghe by Loghgyre. To hold for twenty-one years, at a rent of 20s. sterling.—27 April, xxxiii.

180 (210). Lease to Robert Casey, of Dublin, gent.; of the site of the priory of Augustinian friars by Dublin, with appurtenances in Dublin and Tybberboyne. To hold for twenty-one years, at a rent of £6 0s. 9d.—6 May, xxxiii.

181 (222). Lease to William Hande, of Dublin, gent.; of the site of the monastery of Franciscans by Dublin, with appurtenances in Saint Francis street and Clondolcan. To hold for twenty-one years, at a rent of 30s.—6 May, xxxiii.

182 (127). Grant to Nicholas Stanyhurst; of the office of clerk of the Parliament. To hold during pleasure, with a fee of £10 during the continuance of the Parliament.—13 May, xxxiii.
(Cal. P.R., p. 71, art. 49.)

183 (129). Grant to Patrick Mole; of the office of second remembrancer of the Exchequer. To hold during pleasure, with the accustomed fees.—20 May, xxxiii. (Cal. P.R., p. 68, art. 20.)

184 (225). Lease to Walter Trott, vicar of Rathemore; of the manor and castle of Rathemore, county Kildare, lands, Rathmore, Phillippiston, Edeston, Rallytas, Cullenshill, Adamston, Ballycan and the ploweland, Firrehill, Skeyockes and Oolde Poinsheton, Rathnekill, Monfynn, Boieston, Russelleiston, Umfreiston, Tullaghferreis, Knockynym, Butlerscourte, parcel of the possessions of Gerald, earl of Kildare, attainted. To hold for twenty-one years, at a rent of £40. Also Ladie Castell, parcel of the possessions of the said earl; Heyneston, Agarret and Litle Newton, county Kildare; Rathowle, Rathesallaghe and Ballyodns, the Three Castles by the mountain side, Ballore alias Ballygoro, county Dublin, and Comyngston, parcel of the possessions of James FitzGeralde, knight, attainted. To hold for twenty-one years, at rents amounting to £18 19s.—20 May, xxxiii.

185 (288). Presentation of Dubtag O'Digenagh, clerk, to the rectory of Gesell, in Offaly, diocese of Kildare, vacant by the death of Gerald Walshe.—21 May, xxxiii. (Cal. P.R., p. 71, art. 50.)

186 (340). Pardon to Thomas Kyng alias M'Ynry, of Blakhall, county Meath, horseman.—23 May, xxxiii.
(Cal. P.R., p. 71, art. 51.)

187 (348). Pardon to Thady Raynolde alias M'Raynylde, chaplain, upon surrendering his bulls of appointment to the bishopric of Kildare.—23 May, xxxiii. (Cal. P.R., p. 92, art. 17.)

188 Grant of English liberty to Sawe Ny Doyn, of Bodnamiston, county Meath, widow, and her issue. Fine 13s. 4d.—25 May, xxxiii. (Cal. P.R., p. 71, art. 52.)

1541.   FIANTS.—HENRY VIII.

189 (116). Grant for Thomas Tute, late prior of the B.V.M. of Loughsewdy; of a pension of £4, issuing out of the rectories of S. Patrick of Mymor and Clonkyshe in the Annall.—28 May, xxxiii. (Cal. P.R., p. 63, art. 41.)

190 (337). Pardon to Richard Hurste, of Poynton, county Chester, yeoman, a soldier in Ireland; especially for the death of Robert Strongintharme, soldier.—29 May, xxxiii.
(Cal. P.R., p. 71, art. 54.)

191 (221). Lease to William Bermyngham, of Dunfert, knt.; of the rectories of Kyllaghan, Clondalye, Tyenane, Toboyne, and Kylreyny, parcel of the possessions of the late abhey of Clonardo. To hold for twenty-one years, at a rent of £10.—30 May, xxxiii.

192 Grant of English liberty to Edmund Kerulan, chaplain of the parish of Syddan, county Meath. Fine, 13s. 4d.—9 June, xxxiii. (Cal. P.R., p. 71, art. 55.)

193 (6). Grant to Bernard M'Gillepatricke, esq., and the heirs male of his body; of the dignity of baron of Upper Ossory.—11 June, xxxiii. (Cal. P.R., p. 71, art. 56.)

194 (10). Grant to Edmund Butler, esquire, and the heirs male of his body; of the dignity of baron of Dunboyne.—11 June, xxxiii.
(Cal. P.R., p. 71, art. 57.)

195 (341). Pardon to Gerald Hey, of the county Wexford, horseman (especially for the death of Philip Chever, kerne); James Ketin (especially for the death of Thady O'Doule), Edmund Hey, John Hey, Patrick Hey, horsemen; Mathew Hey, husbandman; Walter Ketin, clerk; Thomas Siggens and Robert Stafford, horsemen, all of the county Wexford. Fine, £3.—13 June, xxxiii. (Cal. P.R., p. 71, art. 59.)

196 (9). Grant to Oliver Pluncket, knight, and the heirs male of his body; of the dignity of baron of Louth; also the site of the priory of Louth, lands of Louth, Corder, Colcryedan, Petro Canonicorum alias Chanonsroke, Iniskyne, Feraghes, Rosmagha, Kilcronie, Rabrest, Dundalke, Drommyskyn, Canonton by Termonfeghen, Donelston, Castelcowe, Termonfeghen, Larnghmynse, Lyme, Riagheston, and Stakerenan. To hold in tail male, by the service of a fifth part of a knight's fee, and a rent of £9 10s. 2d.—15 June, xxxiii.

197 (7). Grant to William Bermyngham, knight, and the heirs male of his body; of the dignity of baron of Carbrie; also the site of the monastery of Ballybogan, county Meath; the site of the abbey of Clonard, county Meath; lands of Ballybogan, Henrieston alias Ralnekyll, Knockangowle, Kylnedoboraghe, Kyloskilling, Ballokestie, Cardonston, Clonard, Kylclashe, Ballinlug, Ballyensagha, Kilreuey, Kiltaleyn, and Toboyne, and the tithes of Toboyn. To hold in tail male, by the service of a fifth part of a knight's fee, and a rent of £4 3s. 4d.—17 June, xxxiii.

198 (339). Pardon to Walter Nugent, of Balinshelot, county Meath, gentleman.—18 June, xxxiii. (Cal. P.R., p. 71, art. 58.)

199 Grant of English liberty to Thady O'Ferall, of Tullaghe, in the Annall, gentleman, and his issue.—18 June, xxxiii.
(Cal. P.R., p. 72, art. 61.)

200 Like grant to Richard O'Ferall, formerly abbot of Granard. Fine, 13s. 4d.—18 June, xxxiii.
(Cal. P.R., p. 72, art. 62.)

1541. FIANTS.—HENRY VIII.

201 (17). Grant to John Rawson, knight; of the dignity of Viscount of Clonetarf. To hold for life. Also of an annuity of £10 sterling issuing out of the manors of Tassagard and Rathtowith; and of 500 marks sterling out of Droggs, by Kylmaynam, and other possessions of the hospital of St. John of Jerusalem in Ireland.—20 June, xxxiii.

202 Grant of English liberty to Mora Enckarwell, wife of the earl of Desmond, and her issue.—21 June, xxxiii.
(Cal. P.R., p. 72, art. 63.)

203 (11). Order of Lord Deputy, nobility, and council in the Upper (English.) House of Parliament assembled, for safe conduct for James Gernoon, son and heir of Sir Patrick Gernoon, of Gernoonstowne, attainted, and Janet Plunkete, until he receive a pardon from the King.—22 June, xxxiii. (Cal. P.R., p. 71, art. 60.)

204 (485). Livery to John, son and heir of Richard Cusake, late of Ballymolghan, gentleman. And to Christopher Gret, son and heir of Katherine Caryck, daughter and heir of Katherine Bryane, sister and heir of Richard Bryane, feoffee of said Richard Cusake.—[22 June] xxxiii. (Cal. P.R., p. 84, art. 18.)

205 Grant of English liberty to Keadaghe O'More, gentleman, and his issue.—27 June, xxxiii. (Cal. P.R., p. 72, art. 65.)

206 (349). Pardon to Kedaghe More, of Lexin, gentleman.—28 June, xxxiii. (Cal. P.R., p. 72, art. 66.)

207 Grant of English liberty to Egidia ny Mulryan, wife of Maurice Desmond, and her issue.—28 June, xxxiii.
(Cal. P.R., p. 72, art. 64.)

208 (13). Order of the Lord Deputy and council, at the petition of (English.) the earl of Ormond, that, in consideration of its situation among the Irishry, the abbey of Tome in Ormounde be not dissolved. Donald O'Meare, the custos, and his brethren, to adopt a secular habit.—28 June, xxxiii. (Cal. P.R., p. 73, art. 75.)

209 Grant of English liberty to John O'Meare, chief captain of his nation, and his issue.—29 June, xxxiii.
(Cal. P.R., p. 72, art. 67.)

210 (215). Lease to James, earl of Desmond; of the site of the monastery of friars preachers of Kylmalloke, with appurtenances. To hold for three years, at a rent of 26s. 8d. sterling.—29 June, xxxiii.

211 (8). Grant to Thomas Wstace, lord of Kilcullen, and the heirs male of his body; of the dignity of viscount of Baltinglas; also the site of the abbey of Baltinglas, lands of Baltinglas, Granggodloy, Kylmoreth, Hilstonstone, Sleorath, Newgrang, Cargyn, Taghnewran, Rayhou, Branarghton, Newton, Monkwod, the chapel and grange of Newhouse, the castle and grange of Graugcon, Crokwrrke, Baronston, Gyffynston, Newhouse, Rodton, Rathbrene, Ballehoke alias Hokiston, Cokmyll, Mangertorlaght, and Millerston. To hold in tail male, by the service of a fifth part of a knight's fee and a rent of £5 19s. 8d.—30 June, xxxiii.

212 (122). Grant to Eneas Hernan, late preceptor of Anee; of a pension of £28 17s. 8d. sterling.—30 June, xxxiii.
(Cal. P.R., p. 65, art. 64.)

1541.   FIANTS.—HENRY VIII.

213 (350). Pardon to Edward Nugent, of Stonehall or of Mylcastell, gentleman or horseman; especially for the murder of Edmund Nugent, of Multyfernane, gentleman.—30 June, xxxiii.
(Cal. P.R., p. 72, art. 72.)

214 (333). Pardon to Thady O'Karwell, of Leymybanan, gentleman. —1 July, xxxiii.

215 (294). Mandate for the investiture and consecration of Richard Ferall, late abbot of Granarde, as bishop of Ardagh. By virtue of King's letter, at Grenewiche, 2 May, xxxiii.—1 July, xxxiii.

216 (203). Lease to Edmund Sexten, of Limerick, gentleman, Patrick Gowle, of Kylmalloke, and Nicholas Fannyng, of Limerick, merchants; of the preceptory or manor of Anee, county Limerick, with its appurtenances. To hold for twenty-one years, at a rent of £6 13s. 4d. sterling, and paying his pension of £28 17s. 4d. sterling to the late preceptor.— 4 July, xxxiii.

217 (11c). Order of the Lord Deputy and council; that the house of
(English.) Augustin friars of Downemore be not dissolved. Moryardar Flen, with three or four of the brethren, to adopt a secular habit. (Partly defaced).—[7 July] xxxiii.
(Cal. P.R., p. 84, art. 19.)

218 (15). Order of the Lord Deputy and council; that the monastery
(English.) of friars of Athenry, being situated amongst the Irishry, be not dissolved. Adam Copynger, the custos, and his brethren to adopt a secular habit.—7 July, xxxiii.

219 (216). Lease to Nicholas Cowley, of Kilkenny, gentleman; of the site of the priory of St. Kevin of Fertnekeraghe, county Kilkenny, with appurtenances. To hold for twenty-one years, at a rent of £10 3s. 4d.—7 July, xxxiii.

220 (346). Pardon to Edward Staple alias Stakboll, of Ardbraccan, bishop of Meath.—7 July, xxxiii.

221 (117). Grant to Nicholas Plunket, late preceptor of Killerge, county Carlow; of a pension of £25 4s. 7d., issuing out of Killerge, &c.—9 July, xxxiii.   (Cal. P.R., p. 65, art. 63.)

222 (214). Lease to Christopher Dowedall, of Artureston, county Louth, Oliver Werdon, of Kiltalaght, same county, gentlemen; and Jenico Chamerlayne, of Drogheda, merchant; of the preceptory or manor of Killergie, county Carlow; lands of Killergie, Russelston, Moygane, Courtt of Killergie, and Tulleofelme, in the counties Carlow, Kildare, and Kilkenny; rectories of Killergie, Kilmekaill, and Powerstowne. To hold for twenty-one years, at a rent of £4, and paying his pension of £25 4s. 7d. to the late preceptor.—10 July, xxxiii.

223 (417). Grant to Gerald Flemyng, knight; of the site of the abbey of Kenlys, county Meath, lands in Kenlys, Emlebogan, Corbally, Grangeston, Cnocknerbury, Kylbrede, Maghlendone, Kyldrum, Urier, and Gyanston; rectories of Kyllaghe and Emlobegan. To hold in tail male, by the service of a fifth part of a knight's fee, with a rent of £6 6s. 8d. Paying also yearly 26s. 8d. to the bishop of Meath; 20s. to the archbishop of Armagh; 7s. to the archdeacon of Meath, and 11s. to the archdeacon of Kenlys. —10 July, xxxiii.

224 (291). Presentation of Richard Herford, chaplain, to the vicarage of the B.V.M. of Lyckblaye, diocese of Meath.—12 July, xxxiii.

1541.   FIANTS.—HENRY VIII.

225 (218). Lease to William Gerbarde, gent.; of the grange of Kilmore, county Wexford, parcel of the possessions of the late abbey of Tynterne, county Wexford. To hold for twenty-one years, at a rent of 43s. 4d.—13 July, xxxiii.

226 (118). Grant to John Walyngton, late sub-prior of the hospital of St. John of Jerusalem in Ireland, and preceptor of Tullie, county Kildare; of a pension of £16 13s. 4d.—14 July, xxxiii.
(Cal. P.R., p. 65, art. 65.)

227 (298). Restitution of temporalities to Richard Ferall, bishop of Ardagh. By King's letter, at Grenewiche, 2 May, xxxiii.—14 July, xxxiii.

228 (287). Presentation of Patrick Whyte, clerk; to the vicarage of St. David of Naas, diocese of Kildare.—15 July, xxxiii.

229 (219). Lease to Laurence Dowedall of Shalthousse, gent.; of the site of the priory of the B.V.M. of Termonfeghin, county Louth, lands of Termonfeghen, Kyleloghyr, and Kellagbtoun, tithes of Kellaghton. To hold for twenty-one years, at a rent of £6 13s. 4d.—17 July, xxxiii.

230 (130). Grant to William Ketynge, late preceptor of Kilclogan and Ballikeiocke, county Wexford; of a pension of £18, out of the preceptories of Kilclogan and Ballikeiocke.—18 July, xxxiii.
(Cal. P.R., p. 65, art. 66.)

231 (207). Lease to Martin Scryne, of Dundalke, merchant; of the site of the monastery of preachers or black friars of Carlingford, county Louth, with appurtenances. To hold for twenty-one years, at a rent of £5.—18 July, xxxiii.

232 (217). Lease to Martin Pelles, of Athye, gent.; of Oldragh and Percyvalston, in the marches of the county Kildare, parcel of the possessions of Gerald earl of Kildare, attainted. To hold for twenty-one years, at a rent of 40s. during the first three years, and 53s. 4d. subsequently.—20 July, xxxiii.

233 (220). Lease to Richard Keatyng, of the county Wexford, gent.; of Ballycrosse, with Polllenton, Ballyboughte, and Casteletowne, parcel of the possession of the abbey of Tynterne, county Wexford. To hold for twenty-one years, at a rent of £4.—20 July, xxxiii.

234 (334). Pardon of William Stanton, of Rathnemanagbe, husbandman; especially for the death of John Croke, cottier.—26 July, xxxiii.

235 (205). Lease to Patrick Barnewall, of Foldeston, gent.; of lands of Luske, Swerds, Cromlyn, and Dologht, county Dublin; Loghshallaghe, Grenoke, and Dardieston, county Meath; and in Drogheda; rectories of Gracedieu, Portrarne, Lambaye, Wespelleston, Balmadon, Newcastell M'Gyngane, and Tobhyr, county Dublin; possessions of the late priory of [Gracedieu]. To hold for twenty-one years, at a rent of £40.—29 July, xxxiii.

236 (230). Lease to Robert Butler, of Dublin, gent.; of the site of the nunnery of Moylaghe, with appurtenances in Moylaghe, a messuage in Clonmell, and the rectory of Moylaghe, county Tipperary. To hold for twenty-one years, at a rent of £3 6s. 8d. —29 July, xxxiii.

237 (290). Presentation of Thomas Oref, chaplain; to the vicarage of the B.V.M. of Gawran, diocese of Ossory, vacant by the resignation of Thomas Morchow.—29 July, xxxiii.

238 (513). Lease to John Alen, chancellor, Gerald Aylmer, knight,

1541.   FIANTS.—HENRY VIII.

chief justice, and others; of the site of the monastery of friars preachers, beside Dublin, messuages in St. Mighan's parish, St. Patrick's-street, and Newe-street, and a moiety of Helen Hores Meade alias Gybbetes Meade, county Dublin. To hold for twenty-one years at a rent of £6—see State Papers, Hen. VIII, 1834, vol. 3, p. 321—31 July, xxxiii.

239 (224). Lease to Richard Butler of Fernes, esq.; of the site of the priory of St. Columbe of Enistiok, lands of Enistioke, Bolaghe, Kilcrosse, Leiscanouaghe, and Rosseshynnan, county Kilkenny, and Ardekerneis, county Wexford; rectories of Enistioke, Rosseshynnan, Kilbecoke, Killaghe, Kilcoghan, Thomaston, Columkyll, Taghanschurche, Shankill, Dunkitt, Newtown of Lynnam, Agheteart, St. Michael's in the country of Compsy, and Killyn, county Kilkenny, Ballyernan and Ardekerneis, county Wexford, Stradbally and Ballykilly, county Waterford. To hold for twenty-one years, at a rent of £64.—1 August, xxxiii.

240 (293). Union of the vicarage of the B.V.M. of Gawran, to the prebend of Tyscoffyn, in the cathedral of St. Kanice, Kilkenny, during the life of Thomas Cref the prebendary. Thomas Cref to find a fit priest to hold service in the church of Gawran.— 2 August, xxxiii.

241 (227). Lease to James, earl of Ormond and Ossory, treasurer of Ireland; of the site of the abbey of the B.V.M. of Jerypounte, lands of Jerypounte, Ballylenche, Bawne, Wollgrange, Stanyslande, Morehouselande, Crosseteoke, Smythestowne, Gibbons shopehouse, Jackestowne, Shrowliswodd, Kylgrallan, Thomastowne, Newtown of Jerypounte, Grangliegan, Blakrathe, Foroughmore, Dunbilly, grange of Kylrye, Madokestowne, Kylkenny, grange of Clorane and Gawran, grange of Mokhownne alias Rathlyn, county Kilkenny, and in Rosse, county Wexford, rectories of Rowre and Blaunchfeldestowne, county Kilkenny, and tithes in Kilkenny. To hold for 21 years, at a rent of £86. —11 August, xxxiii.

242 (506). Lease to James Butler, earl of Ormond and Ossory, treasurer; of Ardlowe, county Kilkenny, Tullyleyce, county Cork, and Cleynglays, county Limerick; rectories of Tullyleyce and Grenocwonagh, county Limerick, Knocktoffre, Ballynegeraghe, Howelliston, Kylmoyeanny, Tullyhaght, Beallaghe, and Cahirleyak, Kylry, Kylkneddy, Whitchurche, Erliston, Ardylley, Drimem'veyran, Garrangibbon, and Kyryhill, county Kilkenny; Bearnanely and Fymoayn, county Tipperary; Ballyen, county Wexford; and Kelliston alias Kyllasney, county Carlow, possessions of the late monastery of the B.V.M., of Kenlis, county Kilkenny. To hold for twenty-one years, at a rent of £68 13s.—12 August, xxxiii.

243 (228). Lease to James Butler, earl of Ormond and Ossory, treasurer; of the site of the monastery of Augustin friars of Callan, county Kilkenny, with appurtenances; also the site of the monastery of Carmelite friars of Thurles, county Tipperary, with appurtenances. To hold for twenty-one years, at rents of 20s. 8d. and 13s. 4d. respectively.—12 August, xxxiii.

244 (229). Lease to James Butler, earl of Ormond and Ossory, treasurer; of the site of the monastery of Carmelites of Leghlynbridge, county Carlow; also the site of the monastery of Augustin friars of Tullaghfelym, same county, with their appurtenances. To hold for twenty-one years, at rents of 46s. 8d. and 26s. 8d. respectively.—12 August, xxxiii.

1541.   FIANTS.—HENRY VIII.

245 (208). Lease to Thomas Alen, gent.; of the manor of Kyll, county Kildare; lands of Kill, Hartwell, Arteston alias Artureston, and Ballybroige, county Kildare; St. Katherine's and Alenston, county Dublin; rectories of Kyll, Alasty, Hartwell, Artareston, and Ballybroige, county Kildare, and St. Katherine's, county Dublin; possessions of the late abbey of Thomascourt, by Dublin. To hold for twenty-one years, at a rent of £25 18s. 8d.—16 August, xxxiii.

246 (223). Lease to William Walsohe, of Carrickmayne, gent.; of Kilpeter, in O'Byrne's country, parcel of the possessions of the hospital of St. John of Jerusalem. To hold for twenty-one years, at a rent of 26s. 8d.—17 August, xxxiii.

247 (232). Lease to Richard Savage, of Chapel Isoulde, gent.; of the site of the monastery of Augustin friars of Rosse, with appurtenances in Rosse and Pollcapill, county Wexford. To hold for twenty-one years, at a rent of 26s. 8d.—19 August, xxxiii.

248 (213). Lease to Thomas Cope alias Baker, of Dublin, yeoman; of the site of the monastery of Augustin friars of Drogheda, with appurtenances in Drogheda. To hold for twenty-one years, at a rent of 10s. 8d.—19 August, xxxiii.

249 (206). Lease to Walter Dowedall and Edward Becke, merchants; of the site of the monastery of Friars Preachers of Drogheda, with appurtenances in Drogheda and Phillippeston. To hold for twenty-one years, at a rent of 47s.—20 August, xxxiii.

250 (211). Lease to William Blechington, gent.; of the manor of Ardemulghan, lands of Ardemulghan, Carnulfe, Elenstonred, Heyeston, Kingeston, and Ooldetowne, county Meath, possessions of Gerald, earl of Kildare, attainted. To hold for twenty-one years, at a rent of 40 marks during the first four years (in consideration of the premises having been wasted by O'Neile and O'Donell, and of his re-building a mill on the Boyne), and of £37 subsequently.—20 August, xxxiii.

(In dorso) Mem. that Marten Skreene had a lease of the same for xxxvii¹. sealed, which was never taken out of the hanaper, but after cancelled.

251 (16). Order of the Lord Deputy and council; for a commission to (English.) the earl of Desmond, Mr. Thomas Agarde, Eneas O'Hernan, late master of Any, and Edmund Sextan, to take inventories of, dissolve, and put in safe custody, all religious houses in the counties of Limerick, Cork, Kerry, and Desmond.—24 August, xxxiii.

(Cal. P.R., p. 73, art. 76.)

252 (212). Lease to John Brokes, of Novan, gent.; of the site of the abbey of the B.V.M., of Novan, county Meath; lands of Novan, Angevilston, the grange by Foghanhill, Knockamore, Deraneston, Ballynevan, Rathloghe, Athlomney, Slane, Balreske, Ardbrackan, Fynokeston, Donamore, Ardmulghan, and Kenles; rectories of Novan, Clamadiffe, Ardbrackan, and Kilshynne, county Meath. To hold for twenty-one years, at a rent of £92.—31 August, xxxiii.

253 (119). Grant to Gerald Ketynge, one of the brethren of the hospital of St. John of Jerusalem in Ireland; of a pension of £6 13s. 4d., issuing out of Kilmaynan Wodde, county Meath.—6 September, xxxiii.   (Cal. P. R., p. 65, art. 67.)

254 416). Lease to Laurence Townley, of Dublin, gent.; of the site of the abbey of the B.V.M., of Mellifunt, county Louth; the manor of

1541. FIANTS.—HENRY VIII.

Mellifunt, lands of Mellifount, Tullaghallon, Denerayhe, Molle, Ballynuner, Shepgrang, Litlegrange, Boyrathe, Colbuge, Balgatheran, Saltehouse, Stalebone, Unshoke, Moraghe, Belpatrik, Coldreynold, and Callan, and a fishery of the Boyne, with the weir of Staling, Brows weir, Moncken weir, county Louth; Oldbrige, Shepehouse, Rathmolane, Stalinge, Donore, Doo, Glashalyn, Grangeithe, Crewodd, Balranny, Kardoragh, Ranyskyn alias Monknewton, Newgrange, Ballyfadoke, Knoythe, Kelliston, Cracamothan, Rosynry, Gilton, Dromynhaull, Radronoghe, Cullyn, and Starenaghe, and a fishery of the Boyne, with the weirs of Stalinge, Brows, Monckenwerr, and Oldbrigge, county Meath; manor of Ballyscanlan, county Louth; messuages in Drogheda; rectories of Crucerathe, Balregan by Donore, Donore, Knocamohan, Rossynry, Monknewton, and Grangeithe, county Meath; Monamore, county Drogheda; Bareleston, Tullaghalen, Staleban, Nelliston, Callan, Ballypatrik, Unshoke, Saltehouse, and Ballyscanlan, county Louth. To hold for twenty-one years, at a rent of £316 13s. 4d.—11 September, xxxiii. See No. 470.

255 (120). Grant to conventual persons of Thomascourte by Dublin; of the pensions following:—John Rocheforde, 53s. 4d.; Thomas Browne, 53s. 4d.; and Thomas Sarswell, 53s. 4d.; issuing out of Letercorr and Kilmore, co. Meath.—12 October, xxxiii.
(Cal. P.R., p. 66, art. 69.)

256 (121). Grant to conventual persons of Thomascourte, by Dublin; of the pensions following:—Nicholas Casey, 53s. 4d.; William Owen, 53s. 4d.; Nicholas Wogan, 53s. 4d.; and John Quyne, 53s. 4d.; issuing out of Lexlyp, &c., co. Kildare—12 October, xxxiii. (Cal. P.R., p. 66, art. 68.)

257 (297). Presentation of John FitzEdmund Lysart, chaplain; to the vicarage of the B.V.M. of Belaghtobyn, diocese of Ossory (lately belonging to the abbey of Kenlys), vacant by the death of William Toben.—13 October, xxxiii.
(Cal. P.R., p. 84, art. 22.)

258 (12). Safe conduct, for 40 days, for John Naune and his company, Egyptians, driven from Scotland by stress of weather.—20 October, xxxiii. (Torn.) (Cal. P.R., p. 83, art. 3.)

259 (345). Pardon to Bernard O'Connor, of Dengyn, esq., captain of Offaly. By King's letter, at York, 23 September, xxxiii.— 20 October, xxxiii. (Cal. P.R., p. 73, art. 79.)

260 (347). Pardon to Roland de Burgo, bishop of Clonfert.— 20 October, xxxiii. (Cal. P.R., p. 82, art. 2.)

261 (344). Pardon to William Hande alias Foteman, of Dublin, gunner.—23 October, xxxiii. (Cal. P.R., p. 82, art. 4.)

262 (296). Grant to Florence [Gerawan], bishop of Clonmacnoise, upon the surrender of his bulls for the same; of the bishopric of Clonmacnoise, the rectory of Balleloghriaghe, diocese of Clonfert, and the vicarage of Lymanaghan, diocese of Clonmacnoise. To hold for life. By King's letter, at York, 23 September, xxiii. (sic).—23 October, xxxiii. (Torn.) (Cal. P.R., p. 82, art. 1.)

263 (292). Grant to Roland, bishop of Clonfert, upon the surrender of his bulls for the same; of the bishopric of Clonfert, the deanery of Clonfert, the vicarages of Balleloghry, Theacneac, Kyllarmair, Wolga, Lycomolassy, in the diocese of Clonfert; the vicarage of Ballenocerthy and the rectory of Uranmor, diocese of

1541.   FIANTS.—HENRY VIII.

Enaghdune. To hold for life. By King's letter, at York, 23 September, xxxiii.—24 October, xxxiii. (Torn.)
(Cal. P.R., p. 82, art. 5.)

264 Order of the Lord Chancellor and council (on reference from the
(English.) Lord Deputy upon a petition to Parliament by Powyll Fayoff, of Lytle Egypt, his captain and company, Egyptians sojourning in Dublin) discharging the said Powyll from an indictment in the King's Bench, alleging that he had stolen newe color sarsnet, blacke satten, and blacke damaske, at Swerds, the goods of Richard Russell, of Drogheda, merchant.—11 November, xxxiii.

265 (231). Lease to William Dermor; of the site of the hospital of St. John by Kenlys, county Meath; lands of Kenlys, Moylagh, and St. John's Rathe by Stahalmoke; rectories of St. John of Kelles, Dessardkeran, Stoneball, and Durvaghe, county Meath. To hold for twenty-one years, at a rent of £14 10s.— 21 November, xxxiii.

266 (343). Pardon to John Mahon and Tyrlagh Conor, of Ardsallaghe, county Meath, yeomen.—28 November, xxxiii.
(Cal. P.R., p. 82, art. 6.)

267 (502). Livery to Thomas, son and heir of Richard Fitzwilliam, late of Baggot Rathe; and license to John Sutton of Tipper to alienate to him the manors of Dondrom and Thorncastell, and the lands of Dondrom, Thorncastell, Balliboter, alias Boteriston and Oveniston, county Dublin; and to Thomas Fitzwilliam to alienate the same to Thomas Fynglas, John Bath, Walter Goldinge, and John Bellinge.—20 December, xxxiii.
(Cal. P.R., p. 82, art. 7.)

268 (342). Pardon to Thomas Stephins, of Dublin, alderman, late customer of Dublin and Drogheda, constable of the castle of Trym, constable of the castle of Wiclowe, and constable of the gaol of Trym. Also to Richard Stanley, gent., undergaoler of the castle of Trym.—23 December, xxxiii.
(Cal. P.R., p. 82, art. 8.)

1541-2.

269 (289). Presentation of Thomas Bernarde, chaplain; to the rectory of Oldrosse, diocese of Ferns, lately belonging to Thomas, duke of Norfolk.—2 January, xxxiii.   (Cal. P.R., p. 83, art. 10.)

270 License to Patrick Barnewall, of Feldiston, esq.; to alienate to Robert Ewstace, prebendary of Rathmyghell, William Pentney, vicar of Morechurch, William Hamlen, vicar of St. Peter's, of Drogheda, Andrew Barnwall, clerk, John Tyrrell, vicar of Rathkeny, Robert Faran, of Chapelmydway, chaplain, and Robert Caddell, of Twrvey, gent.; the manors of Feldiston and Gracediewe, and the lands of Feldiston, Gracediewe, Donganston, Irishton, Newton, Browneston, Rathstall, Mych Meniscorte, Litle Meniscorte, Ballybaghull, the grange of Ballybaghull, Drisshoke, Belingiston, Woleston, Portnernoke, and Robbockiswallis, county Dublin. To be held for ever. A further license to Robert Ewstace and the others, to alienate to any other persons.—28 January, xxxiii.   (Cal. P.R., p. 83, art. 11.)

271 Grant of English liberty, to Thady M'Kennedy M'Brene, of Ballytarsney, gent., and his issue. Fine 13s. 4d.—30 January, xxxiii.   (Cal. P.R., p. 84, art. 21.)

272 (486). Livery to George, son and heir of Richard Delahide, of Loghchynney; of his possessions in Pheypoweston, Irysshton,

1541-2. FIANTS.—HENRY VIII.

Gallaneston, Loghbran, Tunckardiston, Donabate, Loghchynney, Thomaston, Croten, Lainlotter, Balibetagh, county Dublin; Donshaghlen, Boneston, Donmowe, and Flemyngton, county Meath. Fine £13 6s. 8d.—7 February, xxxiii.

273 (123). Grant to Thomas Ewerarde, prior of the late hospital of St. John the Baptist, without the New Gate of Dublin; of a pension of £15, issuing out of its possessions in county Tipperary. —10 March, xxxiii.

274 (128). Grant to John Goldsmith, gent.; of the office of searcher in the port of Galway. To hold during pleasure, with the accustomed fees.—17 March, xxxiii.

(Cal. P.R., p. 83, art. 13.)

275 (331). Pardon to Roland Scurloke, of Wexford or Dublin, bachelor of physic; for heresies published about six years previously.—18 March, xxxiii. (Cal. P.R., p. 83, art. 15.)

276 (332). Pardon to Thady M'Raynylde, alias Reynolde, chaplain. —20 March, xxxiii. (Cal. P.R., p. 84, art. 16.)

277 (126). Grant to Robert Westby, gent.; of the offices of gauger and searcher of the port of Limerick. To hold during pleasure, with the accustomed fees.—20 March, xxxiii.

1542.

278 (125). Grant to Robert Lewes and Laurence Hamond; of the offices of controller of the customs, subsidy, tonnage, and poundage of Dublin, and of gauger and searcher of Dublin, Drogheda, and Dundalk. To hold to them and the survivor, with a fee of £10 for the office of controller, and all other fees as fully as Robert Casye had.—28 March, xxxiii.

(Cal. P.R., p. 84, art. 17.)

279 (295). Presentation of William Kahekan, priest; to the archdeaconry of Ferns, to which the prebend of Marnevin, diocese of Ferns, is annexed.—28 March, xxxiii.

(Cal. P.R., p. 83, art. 14.)

280 (484). Livery to Thomas, son and heir of Nicholas Vicombe, late of Dreynam, and brother and heir of John Vicombe. Fine £3 6s. 8d.—31 March, xxxiii. (Cal. P.R., p. 84, art. 20.)

281 (336). Pardon to John Kelli, of Dundalke, merchant.—3 April, xxxiii.

282 (204). Lease to Robert Adams, gent.; of the site of the abbey of Cnocke, county Louth, lands of Knocke, Grange by Mylton, Rathdowne, Clancarwill, Lattywe, Louth; rectories of Castehring, Knocksmyll, Grange by Allardeston, and Grange by Mylton. To hold for 21 years, at a rent of £7 6s. 9½d.—3 April, xxxiii.

283 (415). Grant to Peter Talbot, gent. (upon his surrender of the manor of Powerscourt, lands of Powerscourte, Cokeston, Killegrye, and Kylgarran, and in Fercolyn); of Bloyke, Balmachorus, Glanmunder alias Balymany; Teghbrodan alias Kilmaynanbege, county Dublin. To hold for ever, at a rent of 2d. (See No. 546).—6 April, xxxiii.

284 (1099 Edward VI.) Grant of English liberty, to Patrick Kelly, clerk. Fine 6s. 8d. No date.—[xxxiii].

(Cal. P.R., p. 72, art. 69.)

285 (1100 Edward VI.) Like to Eneas O'Hefernaen, master of Aney, and his issue. No date.—[xxxiii.] (Cal. P.R., p. 72, art. 70.)

1542.   FIANTS.—HENRY VIII.

286 (753 Edward VI.) Pardon to James Pursell, of Garran, gent., and Galfrid and William, his sons. Fine 6s. 8d. from each. No date.—[xxxiii.] (Cal. P.R., p. 72, art. 71.)

287 (754 Edward VI.) Pardon to William Roche alias Etlee, Nicholas Roche, Philip Roche, sons of Patrick Roche alias M'Ne Whittey, David Keting alias M'Ne Whittey, son of Philip Keting, Walter and Gerald, sons of Patrick Roche, of Barneton, and Moriertaghe More O'Konowan, kerns. No date.—[xxxiii.]
(Cal. P.R., p. 73, art. 73.)

288 (324). Presentation of Thomas Fitzgerald, clerk; to the rectory of the B.V.M. of [Gessell], in Offally, diocese of Kildare, vacant by the death of Gerald Walche. No date.—[xxxiii.]
(Cal. P.R., p. 73, art. 74.)

289 (322). Presentation of Lewis Tidder, clerk, to the vicarage of Dromysgen, diocese of Armagh. No date.—[xxxiii.]
(Cal. P.R., p. 73, art. 77.)

290 (335). Pardon to William Ketynge, of Castell Dermot, gent., captain of the Kern.—22 April, xxxiii. (recte xxxiiii.)

291 (132). License to Elienor Nugent, widow of Gerald Flemyng, knt.; to marry whom she will.—25 April, xxxiiii.

292 (299). Presentation of Dermot O'Conliske, priest; to the archdeaconry of Killaloe.—26 April, xxxiiii.

293 (305). Presentation of Odo O'Hawrde, priest; to the rectory of Douro and vicarage of Kilbarran, diocese of Killaloe.—26 April, xxxiiii.

294 (304). Presentation of Robert Johns, priest; to the vicarage of Kelleeston, diocese of Leighlin.—29 April, xxxiiii.

295 (306). Presentation of Simon Geffray, priest; to the vicarage of the B.V.M. of Downegarven, diocese of Lismore.—29 April, xxxiiii.

296 (310). Presentation of Richard M'My, chaplain; to the vicarage of Dromiskin, diocese of Armagh, vacant by the resignation of Lewis Tidder.—29 April, xxxiiii.

297 (136). Grant to John Morton, gent.; of the offices of gauger and searcher, in the port of Rosse, Ballihacke, and Downecannan. To hold during pleasure, with the accustomed fees.—29 April, xxxiiii.

298 (300). Presentation of Richard Nangle, professor of theology; to the rectory of Ardrayne, diocese of Kilmacduagh, vacant by the death of Theobald Bourke.—[1 May] xxxiiii.
(Cal. P.R., p. 91, art. 1.)

299 (134). Grant to Ninyan Brackenbery, gent.; of the offices of gauger and searcher in the port of Waterford. To hold during pleasure, with the accustomed fees.—2 May, xxxiiii.
(Cal. P.R., p. 91, art. 2.)

300 (133). Grant to Johanna Power, late prioress of St. Brigid of Moylaghe, county Tipperary; of a pension of 20s.—2 May, xxxiiii.

301 (351). Pardon to Leshaghe Ley O'Connor, horseman. Fine 6s. 8d.—3 May, xxxiiii. (Cal. P.R., p. 91, art. 3.)

302 (401). Grant of English liberty to David FitzIncroghe and Katherine Incroghe and their issue. Fine, 10s.—4 May, xxxiiii.
(Cal. P.R., p. 91, art. 5.)

1542. FIANTS.—HENRY VIII.

303 Like to Cornelius MacBriain, gent., and his issue. Fine, 20s.—4 May, xxxiiii. (Cal. P.R. p. 91, art. 6.)

304 (437). Grant to Anthony Sentleger, knight, lord deputy; of the site of the priory of Grane, county Carlow; the manor of Grane; lands of Grane and other places in the parish of Grane, Litle Daveston, Plankeston, Brodeston, Horeganeston and Galrygiston; rectories of Grane, Aghirbally, Hacket, Kiltegan, Kilcorny, Kylmore, Kilcashell, Kilpype, and a third of the rectory of Dunlekor, county Carlow; Kyllallan and Carne, county Wexford; Kilwanton, Kilrogan, Bacbelliston alias Neghwan, Ballynliegan, and Rynny, county Cork; Donabate, Kylmahod, and Brey, county Dublin; Bally[c]ottlan and Tristildermot, county Kildare. To hold for ever, by the service of a twentieth part of a knight's fee, with a rent of 66s. 8d.—4 May, xxxiiii.

305 (398). Grant of English liberty to Dorothy O'Moro and her issue, she being about to marry the son of Thomas Ewsace (sic.), lord of Kilkolen.—5 May, xxxiiii. (Cal. P.R., p. 91, art 7.)

306 (424). Grant to John Stridche the sovereign, and the commonalty, of Clonmell; in consideration of £12 paid and £12 to be paid at Michaelmas; of a moiety of the site of the monastery of friars minors of Clonmell, and a moiety of the appurtenances in Clonmell, Newton of Annor, near Annor's Bridge and elsewhere in county Tipperary. To hold for ever, by the service of an eighth part of a knight's fee, and a rent of 12d.—9 May, xxxiiii. (Cal. P.R., p. 88, art. 2.)

307 (435). Grant to David Balieff, of Waterford, citizen; of the great garden of the friars minors of Waterford, and a new quay outside the city walls, with appurtenances to the water of the Swir, and all shops, &c., built by said David or his assigns upon the premises; parcel of the possessions of the late monastery of friars minors of Waterford. To hold for ever in fee farm, at a rent of 10s. during the life of the grantee, and 20s. subsequently.—10 May, xxxiiii. (Cal. P.R., p. 96, art 59.)

308 (423). Grant to James Butler, earl of Ormond and Ossory; in consideration of the sum of £24; of a moiety of the site of the monastery of friars minors of Clonmell, and a moiety of the appurtenances in Clonmell, Newton of Annor, near Annor's-bridge and elsewhere in county Tipperary. To hold for ever, by the service of an eighth part of a knight's fee, with a rent of 12d.—15 May, xxxiiii. (Cal. P.R., p. 88, art. 3.)

309 (430). Grant to Thomas Cusake, of Coussingeston, knt., in consideration of £168 13s. 4d. to be paid; of the lands of Londreston, county Meath, parcel of the possessions of the late monastery of friars preachers by the bridge of Dublin; the site of the priory of friars preachers of Trym, with appurtenances, county Meath; and the site of the priory of Augustin friars of Scryne, with appurtenances, county Meath. To hold for ever, by the service of a twentieth part of a knight's fee, and a rent of 8s. 5d.—24 May, xxxiiii. (Cal. P.R., p. 88, art. 5.)

310 (234). Lease to John Travers, esq.; of Carrickbrenan alias Monckenton, and the rectory of the same, county Dublin, parcel of the possessions of the late abbey of the B.V.M., by Dublin. To hold for 21 years, at a rent of £24 5s. 2d.—2 June, xxxiiii

1542.   FIANTS.—HENRY VIII.

311 (226). Lease to Edmund Sexten, of Lymeryke, gent., Patrick Gowle of Kyllmalloke, and Nicholas Fannynge, of Lymeryke, merchants; of the preceptory or manor of Anee, county Limerick, lands of Anye, Ballynocloghire, Lymerike, Killmalloke, Adare, Croghe, Askeyny, Ratlikilly, Ardaghe, Casshell, Carryke, Ardarty, and Dengille, rectories of Anee, Loynge, Kylfrusse, Kayrcorney, Kayrfussoke, Kylcalane, Morton, Owlys, Browe, Carnowsy, Rochiston, Ardarre, Newton by Ardarre, Narlaghe, Kylville, Kylleny, Kyllyno, Kyllume, Kyltome, Rathronan, Arcffynan, Mortelston, Cnograffyn, and Carrintoбhyr, in the counties Limerick, Kerry, Tobhyrare (Tipperary), and Clare. To hold for 21 years, at a rent of £6 13s. 4d. sterling, and paying £28 17s. 4d. sterling to the late preceptor.—5 June, xxxiiii.

312 (139). Grant to Thomas Cusake, of Cousingiston, knight; of the office of Clerk or Master of the Rolls of Chancery. To hold for life, with a fee of 50 marks sterling out of the customs of Dublin and Drogheda, and all other fees, as fully as John Alen or Robert Cowley.—10 June, xxxiiii.   (Cal. P.R. p. 93, art. 29.)

313 (418). Grant to Robert Eustace and others, to the use of Thomas Lutrell, of Lutreleston, knt, in consideration of £88 11s. 8d. paid and a like sum to be paid; of the site of the monastery of friars minors or grey friars of Clane, county Kildare, lands, Clane, Newton of Clane, Muchrath, Flesheston, and Langton, county Kildare; the site of the monastery of friars preachers of Naas, with appurtenances, county Kildare; the lands of Rathynnycluge, county Dublin, parcel of the possessions of the late monastery of Augustin friars of Dublin. To hold to the use of him his heirs and assigns, by the service of the twentieth part of a knight's fee, and a rent of 9s. 4d.—15 June, xxxiiii.
                                       (Cal. P.R., p. 90, art. 14.)

314 (422). Grant to Thomas Lutrell, of Lutrelliston, knt., Chief Justice of the Common Bench; of the lands of Kellieston and Ballistrowan, county Dublin, parcel of the possessions of the late priory of Lasmulling, county Meath. To hold for ever in fee-farm, at a rent of £3 18s.—15 June, xxxiiii.
                                       (Cal. P.R., p. 90, art. 18.)

315 (428). Grant to Thomas Lutrell, knt., Chief Justice of the Common Bench, in consideration of the sum of 10 marks; of the lands of Brewyn alias Bohirnybryuee, near Glaschymoky, parcel of the possessions of the late house of friars minors of Dublin, and already in his possession. To hold for ever, by fealty, and a rent of 12d.—15 June, xxxiiii.   (Cal. P.R., p. 90, art. 16.)

316 (1 a). Order of the Lord Deputy and Council, for Sir James (English.) Dowedall of Balliscanlan, knt., to have freedom of one ploughland from all exactions, and £10 from the county Louth; he giving security to build within a year a castle in Upper Casteltoun in Coule in the marches of the Irish.—19 June, xxxiiii.
                                       (Cal. P.R., p. 291, art. 201.)

317 (429). Grant to Thomas Casey, of Athboy, merchant, in consideration of the sum of £38, being at the rate of 20 years profits; of the site of the priory of Carmelite friars of Athhoy, county Meath, with appurtenances in Athboy and the Friars mead in Adenston, county Meath. To hold for ever, by the service of a twentieth part of a knight's fee, and a rent of 2s.—21 June, xxxiiii.

1542. FIANTS.—HENRY VIII.

318 (236). Lease to Thomas Agarde, of Bectyff, gent. ; of lands in Trym, Ladyrathe, Grange of Trym, Rathnally, Creroke, Freffane, Richardeston, Ardcragho, Chanonton, Stonehall, Rocheton, Ryngelston Rathkenny, and Wodton, rectories of B.V.M. of Trym, [Kildalke], Cloynard, the Grange alias West Grange, and Balnecloighe, county Meath, possessions of the late abbey of the B.V.M. of Trym. To hold for 21 years, at a rent of £111.— 29 June, xxxiiii.

319 (352). Pardon to Arthur juvenis O Thole, of Castelkewin, gent.— 5 July, xxxiii. (Cal. P.R., p. 93, art. 31.)

320 (124). Grant to William Cottrell, conventual person of the late abbey of the B.V.M. by Dublin, reciting surrender of a previous grant; of a pension of £3 6s. 8d., issuing out of Ballybaghull, &c. —7 July, xxxiiii.

321 (138). Grant to William Laundey, late abbot of the B.V.M. by Dublin, reciting surrender of a previous grant ; of a pension of £50, issuing out of Ballybaghull, &c.—8 July, xxxiiii.

322 (432). Grant to Dermot Ryan, of Tipperare, gent., in consideration of £10 paid and £10 to be paid ; of the site of the priory of friars of St. Augustin of Tipperare, with appurtenances in Tipperary and Cloghfade, county Tipperary. To hold for ever, by the service of a fortieth part of a knight's fee, and a rent of 8d. —8 July, xxxiiii. (Cal. P.R., p. 89, art. 7.)

323 (431). Grant to Walter Tyrrell, of Dublin, merchant, in consideration of the sum of £114 13s. 4d. ; of the site of the monastery of friars of St. Augustin by Dublin, a messuage and gardens in the parish of St. Andrew, land near Hoggyn green, messuages and gardens in St. Patrick st. and St. Michan's parish by the said city, and land in Tybberboyne, county Dublin. To hold for ever, by the service of a twentieth part of a knight's fee, and a rent of 6s. 1d.—10 July, xxxiiii. (Cal. P.R. p. 89, art. 8.)

324 (419). Grant to Thomas Stephins, of Dublin, merchant, in consideration of the sum of £36 10s. ; of the site of the monastery of friars minors by Dublin, with appurtenances in Saint Fraunces street, Clondolkan, and elsewhere in county Dublin, Brune alias Borbrune by Glasnymycky excepted. To hold for ever, by the service of a twentieth part of a knight's fee, with a rent of 2s.— 10 July, xxxiiii. (Cal. P.R., p. 89, art. 12.)

325 (436). Grant to Lewis Tudyr and others, to the use of Anthony Sentleger, knt., Lord Deputy ; in consideration of the sum of £56 ; of the site of the monastery of friars minors observants of Trym, a garden without the Portchgate, the Mawdlen chapel, the Mawdlen church yard, an eel weir on the Boyne, a park extending from the weir to Lynces park, land extending from the river to Saint Thomas' Park, near the Mawdlen chapel, between the bishop of Meath's land and Brownisland, by the Saleparke, and between Saint Thomas' land and the land of Peter Lynce, of Knocke by Forstereston, also the King's park alias the park of Tryme, county Meath. To hold for ever, by the service of a twentieth part of a knight's fee, and a rent of 2s. 10d.—10 July, xxxiiii.

326 (235). Lease to Walter Tirrell, of Dublin, merchant; of the site of the priory of Lowghsewde, lands, Lowghsewdie, Colloghton, Bravyn Ibryn, Icoyne, and Sayre ; rectories of Moyaghir, Srure, Kyllocammoke, Clongysse, Kyslie, Ballacormyke, Moygowe,

1542. FIANTS.—HENRY VIII.

Tessynort, Tessynuye, Kilglasse, St. Michael Babutt, and Moymore, county Meath. To hold for 21 years, at a rent of £23 14s. 4d.—26 July, xxxiiii.

327 (421). Grant to Edmund Sexten, one of the chamberlains; of £8 sterling a year, being the fee-farm of the city of Limerick. To hold for life, without account. Remission of 200 marks the amount of a recognizance by the said Edmund for the payment of the arrears of the said fee-farm. And a grant of £20, which he had paid to the Exchequer on account of these arrears.—1 August, xxxiiii. (Cal. P.R., p. 94, art. 38.)

328 (302). Presentation of Thomas Clynche, chaplain; to the vicarage of St. Movinoge, diocese of Cashel, the incumbent being of the Irish nation.—1 August, xxxiiii.
(Cal. P.R., p. 94, art. 39.)

329 (309). Grant to Eneas Hernan, late preceptor of Anee; of the custody of the possessions of the vacant bishopric of Emly. To hold as long as they remain in the king's hands, rendering to the king the true yearly value.—19 August, xxxiiii.

330 (370). Pardon to Thomas Cusake, of Cousingeston, county Meath, knight, Master of the Rolls.—21 August, xxxiiii.
(Cal. P.R., p. 94, art. 41.)

331 (400). Grant of English liberty to Donogh [O'Ryan]—21 August, xxxiiii. (Cal. P.R., p. 94, art. 40.)

332 (308). Presentation of Donogh Ryan, chaplain; to the deanery of Emly, the incumbents, Richard MacBrien and William O'Hurnley, occupying by authority of the bishop of Rome.—22 August, xxxiiii. (Cal. P.R., p. 94, art. 42.)

333 (399). Grant of English liberty to Edmund O'Cahan, of Casteltown of Delvyn, yeoman, and his issue. Fine, 3s. 4d.—26 August, xxxiiii. (Cal. P.R., p. 94, art. 43.)

334 (135). Grant to William Hande, gunner; of the place of a gunner in the castle of Dublin. To hold for life, with a fee of 8d. sterling a day.—7 October, xxxiiii.

335 (420). Grant to Robert Ewstace and others, to the use of Patrick Barnewall, of Feldiston, esquire, in consideration of the sum of £88 13s. 4d.; of the site of the monastery of Carmelite friars of Knocktoffer, county Kilkenny; lands, Madanston, Knocktoffer, Ophane, Ballywodan, Ballyhode, Gragyn, Garran-O'Dowgeade, and Ballygyrdery alias Grang, county Kilkenny. To hold for ever, by the service of a twentieth part of a knight's fee, and a rent of 4s.—24 October, xxxiiii.

336 (307). Presentation of Andrew Barnewall, clerk, to the vicarage of Fydowne, diocese of Ossory.—27 October, xxxiiii.
(Cal. P.R., p. 94, art. 44.)

337 (323). Presentation of Onorius Coffe, chaplain, to the vicarage of Ballaloghlowe, diocese of Clonmacnoise. No date.—[27 October, xxxiiii.] (Cal. P.R., p. 94, art. 45.)

338 (438). Grant to Thomas Butler, of Chaier, knight; of the dignity of baron of Chaier alias Chairedowneyske, county Tipperary. To hold to him and his heirs. Also of a rent of £15, issuing out of Inyslawnaghe, Grange of Inyslawnaghe, Ballihortclye, Kilmolache, Grangehirweye, Loghekyraghe, Kilmawsaghe, and Clonmell, county Tipperary; Kilmack and Glanwedan, county Waterford, belonging to the late monastery of Inyslawnaghe; and Chaier, Kylmslagh, New grange, Great

1542.   FIANTS.—HENRY VIII.

grange, and Knockheleye, county Tipperary, belonging to the late monastery of Chaier. To hold to him and his heirs for ever, without account.—10 November, xxxiv.

(Cal. P. R., p. 94, art. 46.)

339 (439). Grant to George Dowedall, prior of the late hospital of St. John the Baptist "de Atrio Dei" (Ardee) county Louth; of a pension of £20 English, issuing out of possessions of said hospital.—10 November, xxxiv.

340 (434). Grant to Anthony Sentleger, knight, lord deputy, in consideration of the sum of 100 marks; of the site of the abbey of the B. V. M. of Trym, and the lands of Porchefeldes, near the abbey. To hold for ever, by the service of a twentieth part of a knight's fee, and a rent of 3s. 4d.—14 November, xxxiv.

341 (353). Pardon to James Gernon, gent., son and heir of Patrick Gernon, late of Gernonston, county Louth, knight.—16 November, xxxiv.

342 (11ᵇ). License of absence to Roger Dorehan, clerk, rector of Ardmulkan, county Meath, for life.—24 November, xxxiv.

(Cal. P. R., p. 95, art. 47.)

343 (233). Lease to John Parker, gent.; of the site of the priory of SS. Peter and Paul of Shelsker, county Wexford; the manor of Ballyrelike; lands, Shelsker, Wexford, Ballyrelike, Cairge, Newabay, Isermon, St. Margaret's town, Kylmo[cre], Kyllean, little Ballyla, Arkewan, Kylcury, Slane, Balwenston, Kyllnsky, Kylmolege, St. Nicholas, and Kyllyllin; rectories of Shelsker, St. Tullogs, St. Peter the Less by Wexford, Karricke, Kyllean, Kylmoore, Isermon, St. Ewera, St. Margaret, Ballymen, Kyllurin, Slane, Taykillin, Kylmolloge, Ratharle, Kyllnsky, Ballywalden, Ardcolme, Ardkewan, St. Nicholas, Kyllyllin, and Scryne. To hold for twenty-one years, at a rent of £98.—10 December, xxxiv.

1542-3.

344 (137). Grant to Hugh Dale, conventual person of the late priory of the B. V. M. of Loghsewde; of a pension of 26s. 8d. out of the possessions of the priory. Dated 30 January, xxxiii.—Delivered into Chancery.—20 January, xxxiv.

345 (433). Grant to David Sutton, of Tullie, gent., in consideration of the sum of £52 6s. 8d.; of the site of the monastery of Friars Minors of Kildare, with appurtenances in Kildare and Collyerlande, county Kildare; also the site of the priory of Carmelite Friars of Kildare, with appurtenances in county Kildare. To hold for ever, by the service of a twentieth part of a knight's fee and a rent of 2s. 3d.—31 January, xxxiv.

346 (237). Lease to Edmund Sexten; of the site of the monastery of Franciscan friars by the city of Lymerick, with a school-house and other appurtenances. To hold for twenty-one years from 23 March, xxxii., at a rent of 43s. 2d. sterling.—9 February, xxxiv.

347 (239). Lease to Edmund Sextene, of Lymerick, gent.; of the site of the house of St. Peter in Lymerick; lands in Lymerick, Ballenegelaghe alias Templenegallagh, and Ballynegallaghe by Loughyr. To hold for twenty-one years, at a rent of 20s. sterling.—9 February, xxxiv.

348 (487). Livery to Edward, brother and heir of Thomas Plunket, late of Rathmore, knight. Fine, £30.—10 February, xxxiv.

(Cal. P. R., p. 95, art. 48.)

E

1542-3. FIANTS.—HENRY VIII

349 (238). Lease to Walter Cowoley of Browneston, gent.; of the rectory of Aghtinagh alias Agheninagh, manors of Ballybroke and Grenan, county Kilkenny, or country of Ossory; lands, Aghtinagh, Ballybroke, and Grenan, parcel of the possessions of the late abbey of Thomas court, by Dublin. To hold for twenty-one years, at a rent of 13s. 4d.—13 February, xxxiv.

350 (426). Grant to Gerald Aylmer, knight, in consideration of £14 17s. 3d. paid, and £40 to be paid; of the site of the monastery of Friars Minors of Drogheda; land by the Bebocke, in the franchise of Drogheda; a messuage in Swerds, county Dublin; and appurtenances in counties Drogheda, Meath, and Dublin. To hold for ever, by the service of a twentieth part of a knight's fee, and a rent of 3s. 6d.—16 February, xxxiv.

351 (427). Grant to James White of Waterford, gent., in consideration of the sum of £90 8s.; of the site of the monastery of Friars Preachers of Waterford, with appurtenances. To hold for ever, by the service of the twentieth part of a knight's fee, and a rent of 4s.—16 February, xxxiv.

352 (301). Presentation of Thomas O'Harnan, bachelor of theology, to the rectory of Ardrahen, diocese of Kilmacduagh, vacant by the death of Richard Nangle, doctor of theology.—Dublin, 24 February, xxxiv.

Note in Sentleger's hand.—" *My lord chanceler thys ys geven att instance off my lord off Dublyne, byffor owr tyme. I wold be glad to speke w' you and trust ye wylbe her att Sent patryks. I have dyferryd my jurney for thay say the fords be hy we may nott well pas.*"

353 (14). Presentation of William Copland, one of the king's chaplains; to the church of St. Patrick of Trymo, diocese of Meath.—12 March, xxxiv.

354 (303). Presentation of Uriel O'Hegan, clerk; to the vicarage of Hariston, diocese of Kildare, vacant by the death of Thady McDonel reagha.—14 March, xxxiv.

1543.

355 (503). Grant to John Goldsmyth; of the office of clerk of the council, vice John Alen. To hold for life, with the accustomed fees.—13 April, xxxiv. (Cal. P.R., p. 96, art. 58.)

356 (131). Grant to George Karry, gent.; of a fee of 12d. sterling a day. To hold for life.—16 April, xxxiv.
(Cal. P.R., p. 95, art. 50.)

357 (451). Grant to James Brandon of Dundalke, merchant; in consideration of the sum of £9 10s., being at the rate of twenty years' profits; of the site of the monastery of friars minors of Dundalke, Branane's park; land in Dundalk; and other appurtenances, county Louth. To hold for ever, by the service of a twentieth part of a knight's fee, and a rent of 6d.—30 April, xxxv.

358 (140). Grant to Stephen Roche, late prior of the hospital of St. Laurence by Drogheda; of a pension of £4, issuing out of the possessions in Drogheda.—1 May, xxxv.

359 (23). Lease to Robert Wesby, of Kilmoynam, gent.; of the site of the hospital of St. Laurence of Drogheda, with appurtenances in Drogheda and Mollare, county Louth. To hold for twenty-oneyears, at a rent of £6 13s. 4d.—1 May, xxxv.

360 (488). Livery to James Nugent, kinsman and heir of Edmund Nugent, late of Multyfernan. Fine £6 13s. 4d.—2 May, xxxv.

1543.   FIANTS.—HENRY VIII.

361 (454). Grant to Walter Flemynge of Caisshell, merchant, in consideration of the sum of £46; of the site of the monastery of friars preachers, of Casshell, county Tipperary, with appurtenances. To hold for ever, by the service of a twentieth part of a knight's fee, and a rent of 2s. 6d.—5 May, xxxv.

362 (445). Grant to James FitzGerald, Earl of Desmond, in consideration of £96 16s. 8d. English, to be paid; of the site of the monastery of friars preachers observant or black friars of Limerick, with land called Cortbrekke and other appurtenances. To hold for ever, by the service of a twentieth part of a knight's fee and a rent of 5s. 2d. English.—7 June, xxxv.

363 (447). Grant to William Walshe of Yoghull, esq.; in consideration of £34 10s. English, to be paid; of the site of the monastery of friars preachers observants by Yoghull, county Cork, with appurtenances. To hold for ever, by the service of a twentieth part of a knight's fee, and a rent of 22d. English.—8 June, xxxv.

364 (21). Lease to William Keting of Trysteldermot, gent. or kern; of the site of the hospital of St. John the Baptist of Tristeldermot, lands, Tristeldermot, Graungefoure, Huyston, Tomenston, Colenston, Kilcaa, and Braye, county Kildare. To hold for twenty-one years, at a rent of £5 10s. 2d.—15 June, xxxv.

365 (357). Pardon of alienation to Thomas Fitzwilliam of Baggotrathe, esq., Edward Sutton of Richardeston, gent., Walter Golding of Portmarnoke, gent., Bartholomew More of Athcarne, gent., William Byrt of Tulloke, gent., Richard More of Nowan, merchant, John Clerke of the same, chaplain, and Robert Foster of the same, merchant; of the manor of Churcheston, lands, Churcheston and Finianston, county Meath; by Thomas Waring of Nowan, merchant, George Bedlewe, or Bellewe, of the same, chaplain, Patrick Mann, vicar of Kylmessan, John Dowding, Nicholas Wafyr, gentlemen, and James Lyname, merchant, or by Walter Golding, of Churcheston, gent.—26 June, xxxv.
(Cal. P. R., p. 101, art. 1.)

366 (440). Charter incorporating the Cistercian abbey of the B.V.M. and St. Patrick of le Nyvorie (Newry), as a secular college, by the name of the warden and vicars choral of the college of the B. V. M. and St. Patrick of le Nyvorie; with a common Seal. John Prowte, abbot, to be first warden. Also confirmation of its possessions, paying yearly four marks in satisfaction of first fruits and twentieth parts.—28 June, xxxv.
(Vide Cal. P.R., p. 79, art. 105.)

367 (242). Lease to John Ryan of Dublin, clerk; of the tithes of Iryshton, in the parish of Palmereston, by Anilyffy, county Dublin, and the rectory of Palmereston, parcel of the possessions of the late hospital of St. John the Baptist without the Now gate of Dublin. To hold for twenty-one years, at a rent of 47s. —14 July, xxxv.

368 (425). Grant to Edmund Sexten of Lymcrike, gent., in consideration of the sum of £42 English; of the site of the monastery of friars minors in Lymerick, with appurtenances. To hold for ever, by the service of a twentieth part of a knight's fee, and a rent of 2s. 2d. English.—25 August, xxxv.

369 (450). Grant to Walter Archer, the sovereign, and the burgesses

1543.   FIANTS.—HENRY VIII.

and commonalty of Kilkenny, in consideration of £200 10s. paid, and £222 to be paid; of the site of the monastery of preachers or black friars of Kilkenny, with "the King's Chambre" and other appurtenances, lands in Kilkenny, Irishton by Kilkenny, Aldranwodde by Keppaghe, Glassanaghe, Ketingeston, Carrickellir, Cowlyshill, Brownistonwaring, Lysnefunchin, Ballynolan, and Ferynbroke, county Kilkenny; the site of the monastery of Franciscans or grey friars, lands in Kilkenny, Iryshton by Kilkenny, Donnore alias Troeswodd, Ardaghnegran, Wonteston, Kyldyr, Brownestonwaring, Ketyngeston by Dromedelgen, Kilferaghe, Ballygowin, and Cowlishill, county Kilkenny. To hold to them and their successors for ever, by the service of a twentieth part of a knight's fee, and a rent of 22s. 4d. Reserving to the lord deputy for the time being the use of certain apartments in the monastery of friars preachers, and of firewood from the wood of Troeswodde as often as he shall stay at the town.—25 August, xxxv.

370 (465). Grant to John Parkar, in consideration of £44 1s. 8d. to be paid; of the site of the monastery of friars preachers of Rosbarcan, county Kilkenny, with appurtenances; the site of the monastery of Augustin friars of Clomene, tenements by Saint Kerans Pyll, and 2s. chief rent out of Collens lands in Clomene, county Wexford. To hold for ever, by the service of a twentieth part of a knight's fee and a rent of 2s. 4d.—25 August, xxxv. See No. 471.

371 (491). Livery to James Ketyng, cousin and heir of Philip, son and heir of John Keting, late of Baldonston, county Wexford, gent., brother of said James. Fine £8.—3 September, xxxv.
(Cal. P. R., p. 101, art. 3.)

372 (355). Pardon to Robert Walsche, gent., son of William Walsche, late of Tegchroan, county Meath, gent.—22 September, xxxv.
(Cal. P. R., p. 101, art. 5.)

373 (141). Grant to Bartholomew Russell, of Seeton, county Dublin, gent.; of the offices of clerk of the crown, and of clerk of the pleas and keeper of the writs and rolls in the Chief Place, vice James Cusake. To hold for life, with such fees as Cusake had.—23 October, xxxv.   (Cal. P. R., p. 102, art. 16.)

374 (466). Lease to Thomas Lutrell, of Lutrelliston, knight; of the site of the hospital of St. John the Baptist, without the New gate of Dublin, lands in Dublin and suburbs, Palmereston by Grenoke, Jordanston, Cottrelliston, Grallaghe, little Newton, Ayshton, Saint John's Leyes, Lucan, Churchton by Wicklowe, Nowan, Johniston, Grenoke, Ballydowde, Grangelare, Kylbeled, Drogheda, Almonston, Corke, Bolike, Ballylackyn, Skadeston, Colaghe, Peperton, Meganar, Drongan, Clonyng, Athforthe, Cromston, Fetherde, Ratboowithe, Colman, Kylconyll, Ballynra, Cloghir, Mylton, Cordagen, Ballylentie, Kyltayne; rectories of Palmeriston, Gyrly, Ardristell, Tempulmorre, Rathtowthe, Straffan, Grangelare, Donarde, Bolike, Clonynga, Ragowle, Ballylakan, Mogare, Colman, Drongan, Fetherde, Athfathe, Kilkaishe, Raylieston, Peperton, Coloughe, Ballynare, Kylshiane, Clonepethe, Skadeston, Cromeston, Clogher, and Cordangon, and all appurtenances, except the services and rents out of the manor of Palmeriston by Aniliffe, and the lands of Palmeriston by Ani-

1543.   FIANTS.—HENRY VIII.

liffe, and Irishton in the parish of Palmeriston, Whitiston in the parish of Palmeriston by Grenoke, and Newton in the parish of Luske, Dardieston, Ballydowde, and a meadow by Hoggen green. To hold for twenty-one years, at a rent of £110. A memorandum states that £9 is allowed for the repair of the chancels and the collection of rents.—8 November, xxxv.

375 (453). Grant to James Flemyng, knight, baron of Slane, in consideration of the sum of 30s.; of the site of the monastery of friars minor of Slane, county Meath, with appurtenances. To hold for ever, by the service of a fortieth part of a knight's fee and a rent of 1d.—12 November, xxxv.

376 (240). Lease to Owen O'Morinu of Moltyfernan; of the site of the abbey of St. Beccan, of Kilbegan, county Westmeath, with appurtenances. To hold for twenty-one years, at a rent of ten marks.—16 November, xxxv.

377 (489). Livery to John, son and heir of Christopher Bedlowe, by Katherine Flemyng (formerly of Dweleke, widow), his wife; said Christopher having been son of Walter Bedlowe, knight. Fine £50.—16 November, xxxv.

378 (19). Confirmation to Roland de Burgo, bishop of Clonfert, of the bishopric and deanery of Clonfert, and the vicarages of Killamairve, Licmolassie, Theacneaghe, Ballyloghreagh, Uroumore, and Ballynecorthie (see No. 263). And grant of the site and possessions of the monastery of regular canons of the order of St. Augustin, "de Portu Pura," (sic) in Clonfert; to be united to the bishopric of Clonfert for ever—without account.—24 November, xxxv.

379 (460). Grant to Dermot Ryane, of Tipperarie, gent., in consideration of the sum of £6 13s. 4d.; of the site of the monastery of Franciscan friars of Kyllalle, county Tipperary, with appurtenances. To hold for ever, by the service of a twentieth part of a knight's fee, and a rent of 4d.—27 November, xxxv.

380 (311). Mandate for investiture and consecration of Master George Dowedall, clerk, as archbishop of Armagh.—28 November, xxxv.
(Cal. P. R., p. 103, art. 17.)

381 (461). Grant to Walter Dowdall, of Drogheda, and Edward Becke, of Merrynerton, county Meath, merchants, in consideration of the sum of £41 3s. 4d.; of the site of the monastery of friars preachers in Drogheda, a messuage in Bowestreet inhabited by Robert Keres, junior, a messuage, &c., in Dwelekestreet, the Colverhouse park, a garden in the Fayrestreet occupied by Richard Russell, a messuage in Saint Laurence street and a garden and orchard in Irishstreet occupied by Patrick Russell, land by Philippiston, county Drogheda, and by Bedloweston, county Meath. To hold for ever, by the service of a twentieth part of a knight's fee, and a rent of 2s. 2d.—30 November, xxxv.

382 (354). Pardon to Margaret Guynan of Wexforde, singlewoman.—3 December, xxxv.

383 (402). Grant, under King's Letter, 9 July, xxxv., to Dermot O'Sheaghyn, knight, captain of his nation, upon his submission; of the manors and lands of Gortenchegory, Dromneyll, Dellyncallan, Ballyhide, Monynean, Ardgossan, Ballyegyn, Kepparell, Clonehagh, Tolonegan, Lycknegaish, Crege, Karrynga, Tyrrelaghe, Rathvilledown, Ardmylowan, a third part of Droneskenan,

1543. FIANTS.—HENRY VIII.

a third part of Rathe, half of Flyngiston, Ardvillegoghe, Dromle, Ballyhwe, Cowle, and Behe, previously held by him and his ancestors. To hold in tail male by the service of one knight's fee.— 3 December, xxxv. (Enrolled Pat. Rolls, 35 Henry VIII., m. 2 d.

384 (449). Grant to Bernard FitzPatrick, knight, baron of Upper Ossory, under King's Letter, 9 July, xxxv.; of the reversion of the grange of Balgeyth alias the Graunge in the Marche alias Harrold's Graunge, county Dublin, held by Walter Pypparde, of Kilca, gent., under lease dated 20 June, xxxv., for twenty-one years, and valued at £10 9s. 8d. a year. To hold in tail male by the service of one knight's fee.—5 December, xxxv.

(Cal. P. R., p. 104, art. 32.)

385 (20). License to Edward, bishop of Meath, to unite the archdeaconry of Kellys and the rectory of Nobbar, to the see of Meath for ever.—17 December, xxxv.

(Cal. P. R., p. 103, art. 21.)

386 (403). Grant to James, earl of Desmond, under King's Letter, 9 July, xxxv.; of the reversion of premises leased 20 July, xxxv., for twenty-one years to Walter Peppard, of Kilca, gent.— the hospital and other messuages, the grange of Cloneliffe, and all lands in the suburbs of Dublin belonging to the demesne land of St. Mary's Abbey, and the Fyrris of St. Marie Abbay (the church, abbot's lodging, the Aish parke, the Ankisters parke, and other premises excepted). To hold in tail male, by the service of a fifth part of a knight's fee.—20 December, xxxv.

(Cal. P. R., p. 103, art. 22.)

387 (448). Grant to Edmund Butler, archbishop of Casshell, in consideration of £11 paid and £45 to be paid; of the site of the monastery of friars minors of Casshell, with appurtenances, county Tipperary. To hold to him, his heirs and assigns for ever, by the service of a twentieth part of a knight's fee, and a rent of 2s. 10d.— 20 December, xxxv.

388 (456). Grant to William Boureman, gent., in consideration of £127 10s. sterling to be paid; of the site of the monastery of friars preachers by Cork, with appurtenances, the half Skeaghbegge, land in Rathmyny and Galveiston, county Cork. To hold for ever, by the service of a twentieth part of a knight's fee, and a rent of 6s. 9d. sterling.—20 December, xxxv.

389 (245). Lease to Edward Basnet, dean of St. Patrick's, Dublin; of Newcastell M'Kingan alias the King's Castle, in the O'Byrns's country, in the marches of Dublin, in the county Dublin. To hold for twenty-one years, at a rent of 26s. 8d. The lease to be void if the King determine to place a garrison there.— 26 December, xxxv.

1543-4.

390 (241). Lease to Owen O'Doyn alias Grene; of the tithes, &c., of Oregan and Russenall, in the country of O'Duyn, parcel of the possessions of the hospital of St. John of Jerusalem in Ireland. To hold for twenty-one years, at a rent of £8 13s. 4d. —3 January, xxxv.

391 (452). Grant, under King's Letter, 9 July, xxxv., to Denis O'Grada, knight, captain of his nation, upon his submission; of the manors and lands of Thoymcreny, Fynnaghe, Kylluchuly-

1543-4.   FIANTS.—HENRY VIII.

begg, Kylluchulymore, Seanboycronayn, Kyllokendy, Clony, Kylchomvrayn, Enocke (Cnock) in Prechayn, and half Kiltula, previously held by him and his ancestors. To hold in tail male, by the service of one knight's fee. The grant not to extend to any possessions on this side of the Shannon.—5 January, xxxv.
(Cal. P. R., p. 104, art. 30.)

392 (443). Grant to Anthony Sentleger, gentleman of the privy chamber, lord deputy, in consideration of £60 sterling to be paid; of two water mills, with their appurtenances, on the Boyne, by Trym, county Meath, belonging to the late monastery of the B. V. M. of Trym; also the water, water-courses, soil, and fishing of the Boyne, from the mill of Newhaghard to the bridge of St. Peter's near the Newton of Trym. To hold for ever, by fealty only.—6 January, xxxv. (Cal. P. R., p. 104, art. 31.)

393 License to Edward, bishop of Meath, to alienate, with consent of his clergy; to Philip Pentney, of Tauraghe, and Edmund Felde, of Cossyngeston, gent.; the manor of Ardcathe, county Meath, lands, Ardcathe, Balgeithe, Portereston, Prensparke, Clony, Irishton, Boynardiston, Corriston, Largwy alias Largay, Pronston, Rowlston, Denanston, Moreton, and Bertrameston, and elsewhere in the parish of Ardcath, and the mill of Kylberde. Also to Thomas Stephins of Dublin, merchant; William Cockes, rector of Rathwere; Roger Durran, rector of Ardmulghan; and Richard Gray of Drogheda, chaplain; the manors of Scurlokiston, Newton, Killeane, and Clonarde, county Meath, and all his lands in those parishes. To be held for ever.—13 January, xxxv.
(Cal. P. R., p. 105, art. 33.)

394 (243). Lease to Osborn Echingham, knight; of the site of the abbey of Mayo alias " de Fonte Vivo," county Cork; lands, Mayo, Lyslyvan, Carraghewryn, Leynaghe, Gradge, and the cell called Manyster In Horry; rectories of Mayo and Lysle. To hold for twenty-one years, at a rent of £18 18s. 4d. English.—15 January, xxxv.

395 (459). Grant to William Dickson of Ballyskeaghe, yeoman, in consideration of the sum of £12; of the site of the monastery of Carmelite friars of Clonecurry, county Kildare, with appurtenances. To hold for ever, by the service of a twentieth part of a knight's fee and a rent of 8d.—15 January, xxxv.

396 (457). Grant to Richard Butler, of Dormerston, esq., in consideration of the sum of £25 13s. 4d.; of the site of the monastery of Augustin friars of Rosse, county Wexford; tenements in Rosse held by James Courcy, Edmund Hopper, Denis Couly, James Travers, and John Browne, and land in Pollcapyll, county Wexford. To hold for ever, by the service of a twentieth part of a knight's fee, and a rent of 16d.—16 January, xxxv.

397 (462). Grant to Edmund Butler, knight, baron of Donboyne, in consideration of the sum of £110 of silver; of the site of the monastery of Augustin friars of Fyddert, county Tipperary; land, &c., in Fyddert, Ballyclowan, and Crosarde. To hold for ever, by the service of a twentieth part of a knight's fee, and a rent of 5s. 4d.—16 January, xxxv.

398 (458). Grant to John Desmond, gent., in consideration of £15 to be paid; of the site of the monastery of friars minors of Mowre alias Galbally, in Arlagh, county Tipperary, with

1543-4.   FIANTS.—HENRY VIII.

appurtenances. To hold for ever, by the service of a twentieth part of a knight's fee, and a rent of 4d.—20 January, xxxv.

399 (444). Grant to Martin Pelles of Athye, gent., in consideration of £13 paid and £30 to be paid; of the site of the monastery of friars preachers of Athie, messuages in More by the Barrowe near Athie, land in Athie, Ardrie, the Ilande on the Barrowe, two fishing weirs on the Barrowe, Tolloghnorre, and Mollonsgrange, county Kildare. To hold for ever, by the service of a twentieth part of a knight's fee, and a rent of 2s. 8d.—24 January, xxxv.

400 (442). Grant to Murrogh, earl of Tomond, under King's Letter, 9 July, xxxv.; of the reversion of the site of the hospital of St. John the Baptist without the Newgate of Dublin, leased to Edmund Redman, of Dublin, surgeon (vide No. 85), and to Thomas Lutrell, of Lutrelleston, knight (vide No. 374); and of Culmyne and Ranvelleston, county Dublin, parcel of the possessions of St. Mary's Abbey, leased 20 July, xxxv., for twenty-one years to Walter Peparde, of Kylcaa. To hold in tail male, by the service of one knight's fee and paying yearly 3s. 4d. to the heirs of Walter Hussey. In full satisfaction for all possessions claimed in Oynaghe or elsewhere on this side of the Shanon.—24 January, xxxv. (See No. 446.)

401 (441). Grant to Donogh O'Breane, knight, baron of Ibrackane, under King's Letter, 9 July, xxxv.; of the reversion of Drisshoke near Dublin, Kilmacodrike, and Newgrange alias the grange of Ballichelmer, county Dublin, parcel of the possessions of St. Mary's Abbey, leased 20 July, xxxv., to Walter Pipperte, of Kilka, for twenty-one years. To hold in tail male, by the service of one knight's fee. In full satisfaction for all possessions claimed in Oynagh or elsewhere on this side of the Shanon.—30 January, xxxv.

402 (464). Grant to Jenico Preston, knight, viscount of Gormaneston, in consideration of the sum of £6 13s. 4d.; of a messuage and close in Drogheda, held by John Ywe, carter, parcel of the possessions of the friars preachers of Drogheda. To hold for ever, by the service of a twentieth part of a knight's fee, and a rent of 4d.—31 January, xxxv.

403 (244). Lease to John Travers of Dublin, esq.; of the manor of Enescortie, lands of St. John's by Enescortie, and the rectory of Kilcorhre. To hold for twenty-one years, at a rent of 43s. 4d.—3 February, xxxv.

404 (446). Grant to John Travers of Dublin, esq., in consideration of the sum of £41; of the site of the monastery of friars preachers of Arclowe, with appurtenances, county Wexford; also the site of the monastery of friars observants of Enescortie, with appurtenances, county Wexford. To hold for ever, by the service of a twentieth part of a knight's fee, and a rent of 2s. 2d.—4 February, xxxv.

Attached are extents of the possessions of the two houses.

405 (455). Grant to Robert Browne, late of Baltynglas, yeoman; in consideration of £19 to be paid; of the site of the monastery of friars minor by Logliger alias Ballynybrahir, county Limerick, with appurtenances; also the site of the monastery of friars preachers of Ballynwillyn in Gonaght, county Limerick, with

1543-4. FIANTS.—HENRY VIII.

appurtenances. To hold for ever, by the service of a twentieth part of a knight's fee, and a rent of 12d.—4 February, xxxv.

406 (18). Lease to Robert Browne, soldier; of the site of the monastery of Ballyandreyhett, county Cork, lands, Ballyandreyhett, and the grange of Cayledowle, rectories of Rahan, Carycklom Lo Heyler, Temple Rowan, Castelton, Ballaghaha, Ballynanlanaghe and Chaple Robyn, county Cork. To hold for twenty-one years, at a rent of 40s. English.—4 February, xxxv. Attached are an order of council and an extent. The order imposes the condition that the lessee shall assign such portion of land to William Walshe, the late prior, as the deputy and council shall think requisite.

407 (356). Pardon to David Sutton, of Tully, gent.; of all alienations of the site of the priory of Grane alias Granne, the manor of Grane, lands, Grane, Organston alias Horganston alias Ballyorgan, Brodeston alias Ballywrode, Little Grane alias Granevegg, Little Davieston alias Ballygruvegge, Plonkiston alias Plankiston alias Ballysowke, counties Carlow and Kildare.—4 February, xxxv.

408 (490). Livery to Robert, son and heir of James Darcye, late of Clonem'gillemant, county Meath. Fine £6.—8 February, xxxv.

409 (463). Grant to Paul Tornor and James Dewerouse, of Wexforde, merchants, in consideration of the sum of £15 3s. 4d.; of the site of the monastery of friars minor of Wexford, with appurtenances. To hold for ever, by the service of the twentieth part of a knight's fee, and a rent of 10d.—20 February, xxxv. Added in Sentleger's hand: *Take ane oblygatyone for asmyche stone off the churche ther as schall suffyce for the repayr off the kyng's castell ther.*

1544.

410 (467). Lease to Philip FitzDavid Barry, late abbot; of the site of the abbey "de Choro Benedicti" (Midleton), county Cork, with appurtenances. To hold for twenty-one years, at a rent of £3 13s. 4d., English.—10 April, xxxv.

411 (142). Grant to Thady, son of Fergananym O'Keroyll; of the captaincy of the country of Ely Ikeroyll, during good behaviour, with such jurisdictions and profits as other captains in the marches of the kingdom.—13 May, xxxvi.

(Cal. P.R., p. 105, art. 1.)

412 (314). Presentation of James Magray, chaplain, to the vicarage of Comyr, in Odoghe, diocese of Ossory.—15 May, xxxvi.

413 (146). Grant to William Nugent, late prior of SS. Taurin and Feghin, of Fower, county Meath; of a pension of £50 issuing out of possessions of said house.—20 May, xxxvi.

(Cal. P.R., p. 109, art. 31.)

414 (358). Pardon to Oswald Banbrego, cook, and Gregory Tweydall, yeoman, of Ballydowde, soldiers.—23 May, xxxvi.

(Cal. P.R., p. 105, art. 2.)

415 (359). Pardon to Thomas Rudleche, soldier.—23 May, xxxvi.

(Cal. P.R., p. 105, art. 3.)

416 (367). Pardon of alienation to Meiler Hussey, of Moylusse, county Meath, gent., Alienor Barnewall, his wife, formerly wife of Patrick Kynton, late of Laspopell, county Dublin, and Jenet Kynton, daughter and heiress of said Patrick; of the manor of Derver, county Louth, lands, Derver, Donmoghan,

1544.   FIANTS.—HENRY VIII.

Adamiston, Philipiston, Lawleston, Carikeshinagbe, Huhiston, Gibbiston, Tarfeghen, Callan, Baggotiston, Stabanan, county Louth, and Laspopel, county Dublin; by said Patrick, or by Patrick Kynton, late of Trymlctiston, and by any other. Fine £6 13s. 4d.—26 May, xxxvi.   (Cal. P.R., p. 106, art. 4.)

417 License to George, Archbishop of Dublin, with consent of the chapters of the cathedrals of the Holy Trinity and St. Patrick, to alienate to Silvester Genyngs, Laurence Townley, and Andrew Wise, of Thomascourt, gentlemen; the town and land of Rathland, lying to the south of Thómascourte Wodde, occupied by Thomas Bathe. To be held for ever, at a rent of 13s. 4d.— 8 June, xxxvi.   (Cal. P.R., p. 106, art. 6.)

418 (257). Lease to Edward Basnet, Dean of St. Patrick's, Dublin; of Ballydowde, county Dublin, parcel of the possessions of the abbey of the B.V.M., by Dublin. To hold for twenty-one years, at a rent of 16s., and paying 23s. 9d. yearly to John Alen, farmer of Esker.—10 June, xxxvi.

419 (366). Pardon to Robert Browne, of Malrankan, kern, son of John Browne.—13 June, xxxvi.   (Cal. P.R., p. 106, art. 7.)

420 (365). Pardon to Thomas Stephens, of Dublin, alderman and merchant, constable of the castle and of the gaol of the castle of Trym.—20 June, xxxvi.   (Cal. P.R., p. 106, art. 8.)

421 (362). Pardon to Nicholas Pluncket, of Lutreleston, county Dublin, yeoman; especially for the death of John Kelle.—25 June, xxxvi.   (Cal. P.R., p. 106, art. 9.)

422 (312). Presentation of George Roohe, clerk, to the archdeaconry of Cork.—5 July, xxxvi.

423 (361). Pardon to Ferdorgbe, and Donald M°Gynnos, sons of the late Prior M°Gynnos.—20 July, xxxvi.
(Cal. P.R. p. 106, art. 10.)

424 (313). Presentation of Edmund Karlane, to the vicarage of Syddan, diocese of Meath, vacant by the death of [Henry] Telin[ge]. —22 July, xxxvi. (Torn.)   (Cal. P.R., p. 106, art. 11.)

425 (360). Pardon to Richard Stephenson, soldier or yeoman.— 24 July, xxxvi.   (Cal. P.R., p. 106, art. 13.)

426 (363). Pardon to Patrick Plunket, of Gybbeston, gent., and Alexander Plunket, of Fostneston, gent.—24 July, xxxvi.
(Cal. P.R., p. 106, art. 12.)

427 (364). Pardon to Robert boye Plunket, of Iryshton, gent., and Thomas Plunket, of Armaughe-breganghe, gent.—24 July, xxxvi.
(Cal. P.R., p. 106, art. 14.)

428 (246). Lease to John Wackley, of Dublin, gent.; of the site of the hospital of St. [John the Baptist] of Kilkenny, county Westmeath, lands, Kilkeny, Byrtas, Walteriston, Ballnekyll, Lewed, Balnecloy, Killensaghne, Tullaghne[car]de, and Tullaghmore, county Westmeath; rectories of Walteriston, Ballynekill, Lowed, Balnecloy, Kilnesaghne, Tullaghnecard, and Tullaghmore. To hold for twenty-one years, at a rent of £16 6s. —25 July, xxxvi.

429 (389). Pardon to George [Roche], Archdeacon of Cork.—[3 August, xxxvi.] (Torn.)   (Cal. P.R., p. 106, art. 15.)

430 (22). Confirmation of the perpetual union of the archdeaconry of Kenlys and the rectory of Nobbar, to the see of Meath. See No. 385.—5 August, xxxvi.   (Cal. P.R., p. 108, art. 27.)

1544. FIANTS.—HENRY VIII.

431 (514). Charter incorporating the master, brethren, and poor of the hospital of the Holy Ghost, in the late monastery of grey friars, of Waterford. Henry, son of Patrick Walshe, of that city, merchant, to be the first master, with three or four secular priests as brethren, and at least sixty sick and infirm poor of both sexes of the city.—15 August, xxxvi. (Much defaced.)
(Cal. P.R., p. 108, art. 28.)

432 (507). Grant to the dean and chapter of the cathedral of St. Patrick, Dublin, for the glory and honor of God, the Blessed Virgin, and S. Patrick, and for the keeping of hospitality there; of license to absent themselves from their cures, while residing within the precinct of the cathedral, they finding fit curates for their churches.—20 August, xxxvi. (Cal. P.R., p. 109, art. 29.)

433 (147). Grant to Henry Draycott; of the offices of treasurer, general receiver, and bailiff, of the lordship of Wexford, and of the whole county of Wexford. To hold for life, with a fee of £20, as fully as James Sherloke, rendering the profits to the Exchequer.—20 August, xxxvi. (Cal. P.R., p. 106, art. 16.)

434 (470). Grant to Henry Walshe, son of Patrick Walsh, the master, and the brethren and poor of the hospital of the Holy Ghost, of Waterford, in consideration of the sum of £151 13s. 4d.; of the site of the monastery of friars minors, or Franciscans, of Waterford, with appurtenances, and a meadow by the pyll of Donkytt, county Kilkenny, and a rent of 10s. during the life of David Bayly, and of 20s. after his death, out of the great garden of the friars minors of the said city, and all buildings erected thereon. To hold to them, their heirs and successors for ever, by the service of a twentieth part of a knight's fee, and a rent of 8s.—[1] September, xxxvi. (See No. 431.)
(Cal. P.R., p. 107, art. 22.)

435 (144). Grant to John Margetts; of the office of clerk of the first fruits. To hold for life, with a fee of £10, and other profits. —20 September, xxxvi. (Cal. P.R., p. 107, art. 24.)

436 (472). Grant to Con, Earl of Tyrone; of Balgryffyn, county Dublin, valued at £16 17s. 11d. a year. To hold for life, remainder to Mathew O'Neile, Baron of Dungennyn, in tail male, remainder to the heirs male of the earl. To hold by the service of a twentieth part of a knight's fee, and a rent of 57s. 11d.— 20 September, xxxvi. (Cal. P.R., p. 109, art. 30.)

437 (145). Grant to Henry Draycott; of the office of king's remembrancer of the Exchequer. To hold for life, with such fees as Thomas Howeth alias de St. Laurence had.—23 September, xxxvi. (Cal. P.R., p. 107, art. 25.)

438 (143). Grant to James Dyllon, late prior of Kilkeny, county Westmeath; of a pension of £10. "Grauntyd unto the said prior considering his blood and good hospatilitie he kepts and that he here after intendethe to kepe."—26 September, xxxvi.
(Cal. P.R., p. 109, art. 35.)

439 (473). Grant to Francis Harbbart, gent.; of the manor of Ballioutland alias Ballycutlane, county Kildare, lands, Ballycutland, Donawde, and Syggenston, county Kildare, Ballymore, and Ardnought alias Ardnothe, county Dublin, late possessions of Christopher Eustace, of Ballycoutlande, attainted. To hold in tail male, by the service of one knight's fee, and a rent of £13 7s. 1¼d. sterling.—27 September, xxxvi. (Cal. P.R., p. 107, art. 26.)

1544.   FIANTS.—HENRY VIII.

440 (255). Lease to Ranulph Brereton, of Castelton of Moylaghe, gent. ; of the site and castle of the manor of Castelton of Moylaghe, county Meath, with the land appertaining, parcel of the possessions of Gerald, Earl of Kildare, attainted, and leased to said Brereton for 21 years, 16 November, xxix. To hold for 10 years, from 1558, at a rent of £12.—28 November, xxxvi.

441 (254). Lease to Ranulph Brereton, of Castelton of Moylaghe, gent. ; of Rathmolian, Cloncurrye, Johneston, Ardynewe, Cullydraghe, Tupertymnin, Troman, Rathflyske, Coulere, Isottiston, Corbally, Malynataghe, Stranawe, Norman, county Meath, parcel of the possessions of Gerald, Earl of Kildare, attainted. To hold for 21 years, at a rent of £48 4s. 9d.—28 November, xxxvi.

442 (252). Lease to Henry Coweley; of the site of the castle or manor of Carbery, lands, Cassevanna, Clonkeyne, 20s. rent in Couleveaghe, lands, Carbre, Cowleneveagh, Clonmyne, Ballyhagan, Ballyvean, Kylmore, and Dirrygart, county Kildare, possessions of Walter Dalahyde, knt., attainted, and leased to said Coweley for 21 years, 9 March, xxix. To hold for 10 years from 1558, at a rent of £24 7s. 6d.—29 November, xxxvi.

443 (253). Lease to John Alee, of Ballyna, county Kildare, yeoman; the site of the castle of Ballyna alias Ballycadan alias Adamston, lands, Ballyna, Thomaston, Norne, Ballymone, county Kildare, possessions of Walter Dalahyde, knt., attainted, and leased to said Alee for 21 years, 8 March, xxix. To hold for 10 years from 1558, at a rent of £15 4s. 8d.—2 December, xxxvi.

444 (251). Lease to Richard Rove, of Kilcoke; of two parts of the alturages of Kilcoke, belonging to the rectory of the same, parcel of the possessions of the late hospital of St. John of Jerusalem, in Ireland. To hold for 21 years, at a rent of 40s.—2 December, xxxvi.

445 (249). Lease to Martin Pelles, of Athy, gent. ; of Kylmede, Ballenebarn and Ardescull, Inchecovcntre, and Yongeston, county Kildare, possessions of Gerald, Earl of Kildare, attainted. To hold for 21 years, at a rent of £8.—8 December, xxxvi.

(Extent attached.)

1544-5.

446 (471.) Grant, under King's Letter, 9 July, xxxv., to Murrogh, Earl of Tomond ; of the reversion of Culmyne and Ranvelston, county Dublin, parcel of the possessions of the abbey of the B.V.M., by Dublin, and leased to Walter Pipparde for 21 years, 20 July, xxxv. To hold in tail male, by the service of one knight's fee, paying yearly 40s. to the chief lords of the manor of Castleknocke, and 3s. 4d. to the heirs of Walter Hussey. In full satisfaction for all possessions claimed by him in Oynaghe or elsewhere, on this side the Shanon.—3 January, xxxvi. (See No. 400.)

447 (248). Lease to John Parker, of Dublin, gent. ; of the site of the priory of Holmpatrike, lands, Holmpatrike, Mylwardiston, Estau, Newgrang, Hacketiston, Longhbraghe, Lane, Barnegersghe, Baltrastin, Skerres, Mallahouyn, Sadilliston, Pierston, Kylnure, Dalabrune, Swerds, Hamonston, Hayeston, and Balrothery, and custom, poundage, wreck of the sea, tithe of fish, &c., of the port of Skerres. To hold for 10 years, at a rent of £57 4s. 4d.—5 January, xxxvi.

1544-5.   FIANTS.—HENRY VIII.

448 (492). Livery to Richard Nugent, baron of Delven, son and heir of Christopher, late baron, cousin and heir of Richard Nugent, knt., late baron. Fine £50.—5 February, xxxvi.
(Cal. P.R., p. 110, art. 47.)

449 (469). Grant, under King's Letter, 5 July, xxxvi., to Edward Basnet, dean of St. Patrick's, Dublin, in consideration of the sum of £57 ; of the reversion of the castle and lands of Kiltiernan, county Dublin, parcel of the possessions of the abbey of the B.V.M., by Dublin (leased 26 October, xxx., by William, late abbot, to Walter Golding, and 20 July, xxxv., by the Crown to Walter Pipparde, for 21 years.) To hold to him his heirs and assigns for ever, by the service of a twentieth part of a knight's fee, and a rent of 3s.—7 February, xxxvi.   (Cal. P.R., p. 110, art. 48).

450 (247). Lease to Henry Draicott, of Dublin, gent.; of Ballygowyn, parcel of the possessions of the abbey of Donbrody, county Wexford ; Clercston and Noreston, county Wexford, parcel of the possessions of the Earl of Shrewsbury ; the rectory of Roche, and the tithes of Ballylorgan and Jenkenston, county Louth, parcel of the possessions of the hospital of St. Leonard, by Dundalke. To hold for 21 years, at a rent of 40s. for premises in county Wexford, and 46s. 8d. for those in county Louth.—9 February, xxxvi.

451 (258). Lease to James Bathe, of Dromnaghe, gent.; of Grangende, grange of Travete, Halton, Shanraghe, county Meath, Kylnanyrron alias Archideaconston, county Kildare, 3 messuages in Thomastrete, by the house of Nicholas Lamken, 2 messuages and a garden, in the parish of St. James, occupied by Dermot, laborer, and a tenement and garden in said parish in the suburbs of Dublin, rectories of Crickiston, county Meath, Fennaxes, Dromine, Barraghe, Kylrosuarryn, Ballykelly, Dromphe, Castelmore, with the tithes of a carucate of land of the late priory of Tullaghfelym, in the counties Carlow and Kildare ; parcel of the possessions of the abbey of Thomas court, by Dublin. To hold for 21 years, at a rent of £18 14s.—12 February, xxxvi.

452 (250). Lease to Patrick White, of Clontarff, knight, second baron of the Exchequer, Walter Tyrrell and Rowland White, of Dublin, merchants; of the customs, cockett, poundage, and byllett of the port of Dublin. To hold for twenty-one years, at a rent of 220 marks and 10 shillings.—15 February, xxxvi.

453 (468). Grant to Thady M'Bryen, of Grane Ogonagho; of the manor or castle of Toghexgrene, with appurtenances, lately recovered from certain robbers called the "Uolde Children" in Ogonaghe, county Limerick. To hold in tail male, by the service of a twentieth part of a knight's fee, and a rent of 6s. 8d. sterling.—22 February, xxxvi.   (Cal. P.R., p. 111, art. 59.)

454 (493). Livery to Christopher, son and heir of Walter Chewer, late of Maston, knight.   Fine, £3 6s. 8d.—23 March, xxxvi.
(Cal. P.R., p. 111, art. 57.)

455 (256). Lease to James Buttler, Earl of Ormond and Ossory; of the rectory of Kyltcyham, and land in Kepdromyn and Sleboyne belonging thereto, parcel of the possessions of the late abbey of Osseney in England. To hold for twenty-one years, at a rent of £5.—[(sic.)], xxxvi.

456 (405). Lease to Humphrey Sexten, of Limerick ; of the site of the

1545. FIANTS.—HENRY VIII.

monastery of Franciscan friars by Limerick, with appurtenances. To hold for twenty-one years, at a rent of 43s. 2d. sterling.—[   ], xxxvi. (Torn.)

457 (269). Lease to Thomas Agarde, of Bectyff, gent.; of the site of the abbey of Bectyff, lands, Bectyff, Balbroy, Cloncoillen, Donlogh, Balgill, Balbraddogh, Reneghan, Monkton by Trym, Balson and Balaughe, in the counties Meath and Louth, and the tithes, &c., of the same, leased to him 8 Dec., xxix. To hold for ten years from 1558, at a rent of £80.—1 May, xxxvii.

458 (264). Grant to Edmund Power, bastard brother of the late Lord Power; of the site of the abbey of SS. Koan and Borgan alias Brogan, of Mothell, [county Waterford, lands, Mothell and Kylncnaghe alias Kylbreni, Rathcormyke, Molargy alias Monolargy, Ballylaughlyn alias Ballylany by Moghyn, Illanywryke alias Teamplewryke, and Templeny, county Waterford, and the grange of Moyclere, in the country of Compsy, alias Compshenagh, county Tipperary], leased for twenty-one years to Catherine Butler of Curraghmore, widow, and Peter, late Lord Power, 1 Aug., xxxiii. [To hold for his life, without account during the said term of twenty-one years] and 10s. subsequently.—2 May, xxxvii. (Much defaced). (Cal. P.R., p. 115, art. 7.)

459 (149). Grant to Thomas Clynton, yeoman of the chamber; of the place of a horseman, to serve in the wars. To hold for life, with a fee of 9d. sterling a day.—8 May. xxxvii.
(Cal. P.R., p. 116, art. 9.)

460 (495). Grant to John Traverse, esq., groom of the chamber; of the manor, castle, and mill of Rathmore alias Ramore in Leinster; lands, Rathnekyll alias Rathtorkyll, Mousfyne alias Monfyne, Bouestowne alias Boyestowne, Knokkenyng, Butler's Courte, Rathmore, Phillippestown, Eddestowne, Ballitas, Colenshill alias Clonshill, Ballycane alias Plowlande, Firhill, Skeyocks, Olde Ponchestowne, Russellstowne, Humfraystowne alias Umfreiston, and Tollaghoferrys, in Leinster, belonging to the manor of Rathmore, Hoynston, Agrett, and little Newton, Ratoole, Rasallagh and Balyodde alias Ballytyltas, the Three Castles by the mountain, Balore alias Balligore and Comenston, Holywood, Whytston in occupation of Christopher Eustace, in Leinster, possessions of James FitzGerald, attainted; Carbrynan alias Monkston, the grange and capital messuage there occupied by William Kellye, Newton occupied by John Moran, in Leinster, parcels of the possessions of the abbey of the B.V.M. by Dublin; Cornylly's Courte, county Dublin, parcel of the possessions of the late abbey of Lussemolen; Muche Grange, Lytell Grange, manor of Graungeforthe, tithes of Lyttelton, Ballygory, Glenocke, Rathveon, Clyncloghe, and lands of Gylton partly in the occupation of Alice Eustace, widow, in Leinster, possessions of the abbey of Balkyngglas; with full manorial and Admiralty rights. To hold in tail male, by the service of a twentieth part of a knight's fee, and a rent of 10 marks English.—20 June, xxxvii.
(Cal. P.R., p. 116, art. 18.)

461 (404). Lease to Dermot McCormoke oge, late preceptor of Morne alias Manynymon, county Cork; of the site of the preceptory of Morne; lands, Morne, Kilcavan, Tynekoraughe, and Garryuriallaghe; rectories of Ardesky, Kilcorne, Granaghe,

1545.   FIANTS.—HENRY VIII.

Garryclone, Kylmory, Templetaghe, Cloneneth, Kilmoghill, Mocrompne, Ballyburney, Inchegeulaghe, Agherys, Clondrohid, Moviddye, Carrygroughanbeg, Whitechurche alias Templegen, Kiltunny, Moally, le Navye, Kilvoyle, Kilnomney, Shangarry in Ymokell, Rostelane in Ymokell, the Graunge, and Clonmyne, county Cork. To hold for twenty-one years, at a rent of £9.— 9 July, xxxvii. Mem.—Void because granted to Earl of Desmond.

462 (148). Grant to William Walsche, late prior of Ballyndrohyd, county Cork; of a pension of £6 13s. 4d.—11 July, xxxvii.
(Cal. P.R., p. 117, art. 21.)

463 (150). Grant to John Goldsmyth, on surrender of a previous grant (No. 355); of the office of clerk of the Council. To hold for life, with the accustomed fees and a fee of £20 sterling.— 17 September, xxxvii.   Cal. P.R., p. 118, art. 30.)

464 (261). Lease to Walter Pepparde of Dublin, gent.; of the manor of Kylca, county Kildare; lands, Domahenocke, Hallohoyes, 'Bolton, Marshallston, Little Newton, Byrnston, Castelrow, Ballycullan, Becanston, Jordanston, Livitston, Crokot, Callan, Aylmarston, Corbally, Byrtonsland, Ballyndreny, Killerowe, Turbetas, Gurtenmoclaghe, Tancardeston, Dullardeston, grange of Rosnalvan,' and half Mygayn, possessions of Gerald, earl of Kildare, attainted, and leased to William Brabazon, Sub-treasurer, 26 February, xxix., for 21 years. To hold for ten years, from 155[ ], at a rent of £85.—12 November, xxxvii.

1545-6.

465 (474). Grant to Robert Sentleger, esq., in consideration of the sum of £261 2s. 6d.; of the manor of Kill, county Kildare; lands, Kyll, Artewoll, Arterstoune, Nicholstoune, Arteslande, Ballibrogg, Barronragh, Alestoune, county Kildare, possessions of the abbey of Thomas court. To hold for ever, by the service of a fortieth part of a knight's fee, and a rent of 13s. 9d. sterling.—5 January, xxxvii.

466 (262). Lease to James Bathe, Chief Baron of the Exchequer; of Blakerathe alias Canonrathe, and the rectory of Castelwarninge, county Kildare, parcel of the possessions of the abbey of Thomas court by Dublin. To hold for twenty-one years, at a rent of 43s. 4d. for Blakerath and £4 for the rectory.—28 January, xxxvii.

467 (265). Lease to John Pluncket of Donsoghly, gent.; of the hospital of St. John the Baptist of Neweton by Trym; lands, Newton and the Rathe, Longwodde alias Moderve, Balreyne, Warenston, Aghir, a cart shed in Trym, Saint Johniston, Litle Moreton, Corraghton, Richardiston, Nynche, Moyaghir by Kenlys, and Cloncguffin; rectories of Tollonoge and Fynnor, county Meath. To hold for twenty-one years, at a rent of £35 15s.— 28 January, xxxvii.

468 (267). Lease to John Brereton, of Dublin, esq.; of Agher, Ballyntoghyr, Trowbley, 4d. chief rent out of certain lands of Thomas Dyllon, 4d. out of lands of Walter Bathe there, 1d. out of lands of Christopher Barnewall of Crykeston, and 1d. out of lands of Thomas Cusake of Cousingeston, knight; and lands of Parysrathe, county Meath, late possessions of William Parys of

1545-6. FIANTS.—HENRY VIII.

Aghar. To hold for twenty-one years, at a rent of £17 2s. 10d.
—29 January, xxxvii.

469 (477). Grant to Patrick Barnewall of Gracedieu, serjeant-at-laws, for a fine of £20; of custody of the lands lately belonging to John Serle, son of Patrick Serle of [Shallon], and of the wardship and marriage of Marion, sister and heiress of the said John. Also license to said Marion to enter into possession without further process upon her attaining the age of sixteen years.—3 February, xxxvii. (Cal. P.R., p. 121, art. 59.)

470 (263). Lease to William Brabazon, sub-treasurer, and Elizabeth, his wife; of the site of the abbey of Mellifont, county Louth, with its appurtenances (as in No. 254). To hold for seventeen years, at a rent of £316 16s. 8d.—8 February, xxxvii.

471 License to John Parkar, gent., to alienate to John Blake, of Rosso, merchant; the site of the monastery of friars preachers of Rosbarcan, county Kilkenny, with appurtenances; also the site of the monastery of Augustin friars of Clonmene, and premises by St. Keran's pvll, and 2s. chief rent out of Collen's lands in Clonmene, county Wexford. To be held for ever. Fine, 15s.—19 February, xxxvii. See No. 370.
(Cal. P.R., p. 121, art. 64.)

472 (494). Grant to Gerald Aylmer, knight, Chief Justice, for a fine of £10; of the custody of the possessions of John Bathe, late of Colpe, and the wardship and marriage of Robert, his son and heir.—26 February, xxxvii. (Cal. P.R., p. 121, art. 65.)

473 (260). Lease to Robert Eustace, prebendary of Malahidret, and Thomas Flemyng, of Lutrelliston, chaplain; of the rectories or chapels of Kilclone, Balrodan, and Gallowe, county Meath, parcels of the rectory of Galtrym. To hold for twenty-one years, at a rent of £10. The premises had been leased by the prior of St. Peter's of Trym to Peter Lynche and others for 40 years, at a rent of £8 13s. 4d.—27 February, xxxvii.

474 (496). Livery to John Wssher, of Dublin, merchant, son and heir of Christopher Wssher, late of the same, merchant. Fine 20 marks.—1 March, xxxvii. (Cal. P.R., p. 122, art. 68.)

475 (497). Livery to Gerald, son and heir of David Sutton, late of Connall, gent. Fine £10.—20 March, xxxvii.
(Cal. P.R., p. 122, art. 70.)

476 (475). Grant to Robert Dyllon, of Newton, attorney-general, in consideration of the sum of £30 13s. 4d.; of the site of the monastery of Carmelite friars of Athnecrane, with appurtenances, county Westmeath. To hold for ever, by the service of a tenth part of a knight's fee, and a rent of 16d.—20 March, xxxvii.
(Cal. P.R. p. 122, art. 71.)

477 (368). Pardon to Thomas Cusake, of Gerardeston, county Meath, gent., Patrick, his son, Walter Michell, of the same, cottier, John O'Murnyghan, of the same, labourer, Thomas Gogourtie, of Folleston, husbandman, William M'Loys, of the same, husbandman, Philip Manchan, of Staffardeston, husbandman, and Hugh, his son.—20 March, xxxvii.
(Cal. P.R., p. 121, art. 61.)

478 (270). Lease to the Hon. John Alen, esq., chancellor; of the castle and manor of Lexlip alias Salmon-leap, lands, Lexlip, Aderge, Balmadure, Stacumny, Newton, Keladowan, Possewy-

1545-6.   FIANTS.—HENRY VIII.

kyston, Caresland, in the parish of Kyldrought, and Confye, county Kildare, possessions of James Fitzgeralde, attainted; Loghlenston, Potterston, Symondeston, Calbegeston, Meyeston, Colfyche, and land near the Rewe, by Prioriston meades, leased to said Alen for 21 years, 4 December, xxix. To hold for ten years from 1558, at a rent of £32 6s. 8d.—23 March, xxxvii.

479 (369). Pardon to Donogh O'Coyllone, alias Donogh ballough, of Kilmaynan, horse boy.—24 March, xxxvii.
(Cal. P.R., p. 121, art. 62.)

1546.

480 (259). Lease to James Bathe, chief baron of the Exchequer; of the tithes of Rathtouthe, county Meath, belonging to the late abbey of Thomascourt, by Dublin. To hold for twenty-one years, at a rent of £10 13s. 4d.—25 March, xxxvii.

481 (266). Lease to Edward Garnon; of Ballybalrycke, county Louth, parcel of the possessions of John Burnell, attainted. To hold for twenty-one years, at a rent of £4.—26 March, xxxvii.

482 License to William Wyse, of Waterford, knight, to alienate to Thomas Plunket, of Killester, gent., and Thomas Fyane, of Dublin, merchant; a watermill, land, and a salmon-weir, in Chapell Isoulde, county Dublin. To be held for ever.—26 March, xxxvii.   (Cal. P.R., p. 123, art. 78.)

483 (476). Grant to Edmund Felde, of Cousingeston, gent., Patrick Clynche, of Scryne, and Philip Pentney, of Taneraght, gent., in consideration of £80 to be paid; of the site of the monastery of friars preachers observants of Mountyfernant alias Multyfernan, county Westmeath, with appurtenances. To hold for ever, by the service of a twentieth part of a knight's fee, and a rent of 4s.—5 April, xxxvii.   (Cal. P.R., p. 123, art. 79.)

484 (268). Lease to John Brereton, esq.; of the manor of Kilco[wan], lands, [Kilcowan,] Rathton, Newton, [Rathawle,] great Colycayll, old Colycayll, [Shannoo,] Kylcowan-strete, Coilishill, [Clongadden,] Bastareston, Churcheston of Kylryan, land and a fishery in the barony of Slewcultier alias Whitchurche by Dunbrodye, Kilcowanmore, in Fassaghe Bentre by the Irish, Knockansawyn, Glas[coon alias Clonawolcum,] Fiddert, 8s. rent in Kylmenraghe, possessions of Nicholas Ketinge, of Kylcowan, attainted; the manor of Rosgarlan, county Wexford, land in Rosgarlan, 18s. chief rent out of Ballenan, 18d. out of Grenehill, 10s. out of Ballenan, 11s. out of Byenston and Sheweston, 18s. out of Cloneken, 5s. out of [Knocloght, 2s.] out of Knockeshill, 5s. out of Yongeston, 5s. out of Herweston, 12d. out of Faneston, 12d. out of [Gaynesland] by Cullen, 6d. out of Horeton, 3d. out of Clonefadd, 3s. out of Clonmakeran, 20s. out of the Graunge and Balenan, 20s. out of Rospoyll, lands, Montayneston, Leghton, Globbyston, Maudelenston, Ballysynnan, Balydondon, Ballydon, Balmahannoke, le Hoke, Saint Nymoke, 6d. chief rent out of Clomene, a mill in Ballanon, land in Rathton, county Wexford, possessions of David Nevell, esq., of Rosgarlon, attainted; the islands of the Salts, and the rectory of Kilmore, county Wexford, possessions of the abbey of Tynterne, county Wexford; land in the manor of Garge by Wexford, and the ferry of the water of Wexford, possessions of the late Earl of Shrewsbury. To hold for

F

1546.   FIANTS.—HENRY VIII.

twenty-one years, at a rent of £50 3s. 5d.—[2] April, xxxvii. (Torn and defaced).

See Auditor-General's Patents, Vol. ii., p. 39.

485 (375). Pardon to Thomas Dalton, of Ballyntample, county Westmeath, horseman; especially for the death of James Dalton, horseman.—28 May, xxxviii. (Cal. P.R., p. 129, art. 1.

486 (501). Livery to Nicholas Dewerous, of Balinagir, gent., grandson and heir of John Dewerous, late of Ballytege, gent. Fine £5.—30 May, xxxviii. (Cal. P.R., p. 129. art. 2.)

487 (381). Pardon to Patrick O'Conyne, tiler; especially for the death of Dermot Rathtor.—10 June, xxxviii.
(Cal. P.R., p. 129, art. 3.)

488 (382). Pardon to Gerald Forster, of Busserston, county Kilkenny, labourer; especially for the death of Richard Londay, of Folerston.—10 June, xxxviii. (Cal. P.R., p. 129, art. 4.)

489 (317). Presentation of Robert Johns, chaplain; to the vicarage of Tullaghefelyn, diocese of Leighlin, vacant by the death of Gerald M'Morertagha.—26 June, xxxviii.
(Cal. P.R., p. 129, art. 11.)

490 (316). Congé d'Elire, under King's Letter, 30 May, for Master Cornelius O'Dea, chaplain of the Earl of Tomond, to the bishopric of Killaloe, vacant by the resignation of James Curyn.—3 July, xxxviii. (Cal. P.R., p. 130, art. 20.)

491 (377). Pardon to Robert FitzWilliam Powire, of the county Waterford, gent.; especially for the death of Peirse FitzEdmund Poir.—6 July, xxxviii. (Cal. P.R., p. 129, art. 5.)

492 (318). Mandate for the investiture and consecration of Master Cornelius O'Deay, as bishop of Killaloe.—12 July, xxxviii.
(Cal. P.R., p. 130, art. 22.)

493 (376). Pardon to Walter oge Bermyngham, of Meylerston, county Kildare, gent.; especially for the robbery of four cows and fourteen pigs, of which he stands indicted.—20 July, xxxviii.
(Cal. P.R., p. 129, art. 8.)

494 (499). Livery to Maurice, son and heir of Thomas Fitzgeralde, late of Ballyfeighan, county Meath, gent. Fine, £26 13s. 4d.—12 August, xxxviii. (Cal. P.R., p. 131, art. 27.)

495 (315). Presentation of Richard Bermyngham, clerk; to the rectory of Ballemory, diocese of Meath, vacant by the death of John Coffy.—12 August, xxxviii.
(Cal. P.R., p. 130, art. 23.)

496 (319). Presentation of Thomas Flemyng, chaplain; to the vicarage of S. Michnel of Rathmolean, diocese of Meath, vacant by the death of Thomas Schell.—20 September, xxxviii.
(Cal. P.R., p. 130, art. 24.)

497 (384). Pardon to Elenor Fitzgerald, sister of Gerald, late earl of Kildare.—30 September, xxxviii.
(Cal. P.R., p. 131, art. 26.)

498 Grant of English liberty to Con [O'Mulmoy] of Dervack, clerk.
(Cal. P.R., p. 129, art. 12.)

Like grant to Thady O'Corryan of Dervack, scholar, and his issue.—23 September, xxxviii. (Cal. P.R., p. 130, art. 13.)

499 Grant of English liberty to Patrick O'Donylan alias Dongan, chaplain. Fine, 6s. 8d.—24 September, xxxviii.
(Cal. P.R., p. 130, art. 14.)

1546. FIANTS.—HENRY VIII.

500 (378). Pardon to Donald boy Onare of Kilheale, county Kildare, husbandman or kern, lately of Ofayley, idleman; especially for the murder of John Vale.—24 September, xxxviii.
(Cal. P.R., p. 129, art. 6.)

501 (379). Pardon to Peter Boyse of Calgughe, county Meath, gent.—25 September, xxxviii. (Cal. P.R., p. 130, art. 19.)

502 Grant of English liberty to William M'Carmyke, chaplain.—1 October, xxxviii. (Cal. P.R., p. 130, art. 15.)

503 Grant of English liberty to William Doyn alias O'Doyn, clerk.—4 October, xxxviii. (Cal. P.R., p. 130, art. 16.)

504 (386). Pardon to John Eustace, gent.—9 October, xxxviii.
(Cal. P.R., p. 129, art. 9.)

505 (380). Pardon to James Nugent of Multyfornan, gent., Nicholas Nugent of Loghegarmore, horseman, Patrick or Paden O'Morran of Dardeston, horseman, Patrick Brode, yeoman, Oliver Ledwiche, Edmund O'Roerk, Donald O'Trover, Patrick Holer, and Rory Oferall, kerns; especially for the death of Walter, son of Theobald Nugent.—22 October, xxxviii.

506 (320). Presentation of Donogh M'Gynd, clerk; to the rectory of S. Canice of Agheboo, diocese of Ossory, vacant because Donald M'Costygyn, the incumbent, is of the Irish nation.—3 November, xxxviii. (Cal. P.R., p. 131, art. 30.)

507 (371). Pardon to Walter FitzJamys FitzHabart Fitzgerrot of Artwell, gent., and Thomas Veldon of Stacallan, late of Cloncurry, yeoman.—8 November, xxxviii. (Cal. P.R., p. 129, art. 7.)

508 (374). Pardon to John Omelon of Taghdowe, husbandman.—8 November, xxxviii. (Cal. P.R., p. 129, art. 10.)

509 (383). Grant to Baptist Crean of Slegaugh; of a fee of 12d. sterling a day for life. Windesor, 28 September, xxxviii.—Delivered into Chancery, 17 November, xxxviii.

510 (25). License to George, archbishop of Dublin, to alienate (with consent of the chapters of the cathedrals of the Holy Trinity and S. Patrick) to Robert Eustace, prebendary of Malahiderte, and others, in trust for Patrick Barnewall of Gracediewe, esq., his heirs and assigns for ever; the constableship of the manor of Swerdes, upon the death or surrender of Thomas FitzSymon; also (in satisfaction of an annuity of £5 belonging to said office) the Broode Meade, Dalafeldes park in Clomethan, land in Swerds, upon the north of the bridge of Balhary, at the Holy banke, and in the Castelfelde, on the east of the high road from Swerds to Rckynhore, held by Robert Brocton and Maurice Serjaunt; in the Castelfelde, held by Philip Gastill; near the road from Swerds to Dreynan, held by John Tipper; Whitesparke in Swerds; Roganston, in the parish of Swerds, held by Philip Strong; Newhagarde and Curduffe alias the Busshop's lande, in the parish of Luske. . To be held for ever, at a rent of £6 19s. during the life of Thomas FitzSymon, and of 39s. thereafter.—18 November, xxxviii. (Cal. P.R., p. 131, art. 35.)

511 (500). Livery (reciting inquisition taken at Dublin, 7 November, xxxiiii.) to Thomas Delahide, son and heir of Jenet Hill of Drogheda, gentlewoman; of her lands in Ballygorne, county Kildare, valued at 20s. a year. Fine, 10s.—21 November, xxxviii.

512 (385). Grant to Nicholas Pigote; of the office of soldier or gunner in the castle of Dublin, upon the first vacancy. To hold for life.—8 December, xxxviii. (Cal. P.R., p. 131, art. 29.)

1546-7. FIANTS.—HENRY VIII.

513 (515). Lease to James Bathe of Dromnaghe, chief baron of the Exchequer ; of the tithes of the rectory of Testeldelane, county Kildare, parcel of the possessions of the abbey of Thomascourt by Dublin. To hold for twenty-one years, at a rent of £5 9s. 6d. —10 January, xxxviii. Extent attached.

514 (271). Lease to Robert Seyntleger, esq. ; of the preceptory or manor of Killerge, county Carlow ; lands, Frereton, Cort of Killargan, Russellston, Tollaghphell, Myganny, county Carlow ; rectories of Killarge and Kilmakayll, county Carlow, and Powerston, county Kilkenny. To hold for twenty-one years, at a rent of £22 16s. 11d.—27 January, xxxviii.

515 (24). Order of the Lord Deputy and council for a lease, for (English.) twenty-one years, at a rent of £8 5s. 1d. sterling, to Rayney Bell, soldier, one of the King's retinue in Ireland ; of Carten, in the parish of Maynothe.—*28 January, xxxviii.

516 (372). Pardon to James Walche, son of Oliver Walche of Moyvally, gent., and Richard Tyrrell, brother of Remond Tirrell of Nevcastell, gent.—4 February, xxxviii.
(Cal. P.R., p. 131, art. 33.)

517 (373) Pardon to Nicholas Felde of Mulafene, or of Lesmolen, gent. ; especially for the death of Charles Aspinall of Duleke, county Meath, yeoman.—4 February, xxxviii.
(Cal. P.R., p. 131, art. 31.)

518 (272). Lease to Con O'Mulloy, late prior of Dorrowe ; of the site of the priory, lands of Dorrowe, Newton, and Taghtillyn, rectories of Kylbryde, Ballygroder, Fryvenagho, Kilpallyse, and Dorrowe. To hold for twenty-one years, at a rent of 5 marks.— 5 February, xxxviii.

519 (273). Lease to Remund oge Fytzgaret of Rathangen, county Kildare, gent. ; of Calloughton, parcel of the possessions of the nunnery of Kildare. To hold for twenty-one years, at a rent of 36s 8d.—7 February, xxxviii.

520 (387). Grant to John Bathe, gent. ; of the office of principal or chief solicitor, vice Walter Cowley. (See No. 61.) To hold during pleasure, with a fee of £10.—7 February, xxxviii.
(Cal. P.R., p. 131, art. 20.)

521 (388). Pardon to William Richin of Glascarne, county Meath, husbandman, senr., and William Richin of Watton, same county, junr. ; also of John Parker of Holmpatricke, gent., constable of the castle of Dublin.—7 February, xxxviii.
(Cal. P.R., p. 131, art. 34.)

522 (498). Livery to Walter Whyttey, gent., uncle and heir male of Robert Whyttey, late of Ballytege, and son of Patrick Whyttey. Fine £10.—8 February, xxxviii.

WITHOUT DATES.

523 (152). Letters of protection for [   ] O'Donell, chief captain of his nation. (Torn.)

524 (168). Grant to Gabriel le Mayster, gent. ; of the office of chief serjeant of the county of Offale, Oregane, Kynnaleghe, and Ferkeall, parcel of O'Dempsey's country called Ferryn Clondermott.

---

* King Henry died on this date, so that the seven following fiants should correctly be of 1 Edward VI. I have left them, however, as they bear date, more especially as such of them as are enrolled are upon the Patent Roll xxxviii. Henry VIII.

FIANTS.—HENRY.VIII.

To hold during pleasure, with such fees as the serjeant of any other county has.

525 (169). Grant for John Rawson, knt., late prior of the hospital of St. John of Jerusalem, in Ireland; of a pension of £500, out of Drogges, by Kilmaynan, &c.

526 (510). Grant to Robert Talbott, esq.; of Corbali, Salesbane, Kilardan, Fyngowre, Birrawght, land by Balmalice, Ballymarge by Kilmannaght, and Kyng's Wood by Tassagarde, county Devilinia (Dublin). To hold for ever at a rent of 66s. 8d. for Ballimarge and Kyng's Wood, and 20s. for the remaining lands.

527 (480). Livery to Edmund Buttler, knt., baron of Dunboyn, son and heir of James, late baron. Fine £50.—(defaced).
(See No. 55.)

528 (321). Fragment of Congé d'Elire. By K.L., at Grenewyche.

529 (184). Lease to James Sherloke of Waterford, gent.; of the preceptory or manor of Kilclogan, county Wexford, lands, Kilclogan, the Hoke, Tampulton, the late hospital of St. John by the town of Wexford, Balligelaghe, Rocheston, Tamon, rectories of the Hoke, and Tempulton, tithes of Kilbryde, Ballysyllan, St. Brigitte's in Tamon, and Whytchurche, county Wexford. To hold for twenty-one years, at a rent of £26 13s. 4d. By commission under King's Letter, dated at Wyndesore, 20 August, xxxii. (See No. 546.)

530 (185). Lease to James Sherloke, of Waterford, gent.; of the site of the priory of St. Katherine, by Waterford, lands in Waterford, and Graunge of St. Katherine in the Newton, county Waterford; Prioreston, Clonmel, Blakrath, county Tipperary; Corraghanyeley, Bally-M'Ilian, Cosvynie, and Kilgarvan, county Cork; rectories of St. Nicholas in Waterford, Kyllon, tithes of Carricknygogh, rectories of Killowran and Clonemham, county Waterford; Carrickmagryffyn, Tampulenyme, Kilcloan, Kilgrant, Noddanys, Whytchurche, Sankenygh, Tempultownyghe, Killmyghlaisshe, Ballyharry in Fanynswod, county Tipperary; Dungarven, Kilbrede, Kilcollombe, Fitz Downe, county Kilkenny; Ballaghnymcloghir in Ordmond, Kilcomynytley, Kyarney, Kilcoan, Kilmaconoke, Kilcroghan, Teampulbrecan, Drommary, Dryssan, two rectories in the lordship of Dowalley, Dirreweala and Ballyloghyr, Kilvynye, Collyn, Sheanrehyn, Kyllassy, Teampult[   ], Ballymarscally, and Kildarirye, county Cork. To hold for twenty-one years, at a rent of £100. By commission under King's Letter, dated at Wyndesore, 20 August, xxxii.

531 (274). Lease to Nicholas Stanyhurst and John Ryan of Dublin, gent.; of Kilmakargyn alias Kilmakeregan, within the liberties of the city of Dublin, parcel of the possessions of the late hospital of St. John of Jerusalem, in Ireland. To hold for twenty-one years, at a rent of 10s.

532 (275). Lease to Nicholas Dowan of London, merchant; of the site of the hospital of the B.V.M. de Urso of Drogheda, lands, &c., in Drogheda, Mylfelde, Wyne myll felde, Kyllanayre, Carlyngforde, Dundalke, Glaspistle, county Louth, 2s. rent in Priortowne, rectory of Ennessmoght, and a chapel in Carlyngforde, county Louth. To hold for twenty-one years, at a rent of £19.

533 (276). Lease to Edward Galwey of Corke, merchant; of the site of the monastery of friars preachers by Corke, the Halfe Skeaghebege, and other land in Cork, Rathmyny and Galweyston

FIANTS.—HENRY VIII.

alias Killen. To hold for twenty-one years, at a rent of £6 14s. 2½d. sterling.

534 (277). Lease to George Byrckbecke, merchant; of the site of the monastery of St. Leonard by Dundalk; lands in Dundalk, the Raith, and Drumyaken; rectories of the Mawdelens, Dundalk, and Hagarde, county Louth. To hold for twenty-one years, at a rent of £28 2s. 11d.

535 (278). Lease to Terence M'Morho, of Arclowe, gent.; of the site of the monastery of friars preachers of Arclowe, county Wexford, with appurtenances. To hold for twenty-one years, at a rent of 26s. 8d.

536 (279). Lease to James Butler, earl of Ormond and Ossory, treasurer; of all possessions in Little Carricke, county Waterford, of the monastery of friars minor of Carricke aforesaid. To hold for twenty-one years, at a rent of 66s. 8d.

537 (280). Lease to Robert Apryce, soldier; of the Banno, county Wexford, with the ferry of the Banno; parcel of the possessions of the abbey of Tynterne, county Wexford. To hold for twenty-one years, at a rent of 4 marks.

538 (281). Lease to Walter Cowley of Browncston, gent.; of the rectory of Aghetinagh alias Aghenynagh, and lands of Ballybroke, Granan, and Aghtynan, county Kilkenny, or country of Ossory, parcel of the possessions of the abbey of Thomascourt by Dublin. To hold for twenty-one years, at a rent of 26s. 8d.

539 (282). Lease to James Bathe of Dromnaghe, gent.; of Newton in the march of Dublin, in the county Dublin, parcel of the possessions of the abbey of the B.V.M. by Dublin. To hold for twenty-one years, at a rent of £4 13s. 4d.

540 (283). Lease to Robert Flemyng, senior, John Casshell, Robert son of Thomas Flemyng, and Thomas Delahyde, of Drogheda, merchants; of the customs, cocket, poundage and billet of the port of Drogheda. To hold for ten years, at a rent of 207 marks.

541 (284). Lease to Leonard Gray, knight, lord Gray, viscount of Grane; of the site of the priory of Lowthe, lands, Loweth, Colcredane by Louth, Cordyr, Kylcrony, Carryknccanonaghe, Duudalke, Rosmakaa, Rathrolloo, Ruthbryste, Stagrennan, Cannantoun in the parish of Tarfoghen, Donyleston, Castelcowe, Lurnghmynche; tithes of Louth, Cordyrroghe, Rathcassan, Lowrathe Leys, and in the parish of Kylcrony, and of Rathbriste, Rathgarrona, Agneteston, and of the parishes of Dromyaken, Tarmonfeghan, Mayn, Kylcloghyr, Faghyrte, Ferney, Donaghmayn, Maghyrroshe, Aghnemullyn, Inneskyn, and Dromauye, Balbraghe of the parish of Donamayn Uryell, Clonkyn, Philpeston, Dromyn, Rosmakaa, Ayshe, and Tarmonfesohen. (See No. 196.) Also the site of the house of friars minor of grey friars of Waterford, with appurtenances. Also the site of the house of friars minor of grey friars of Trym, with appurtenances. To hold for twenty-one years, at a rent of £100.

542 (285). Lease to Edmund Hyffernan of Casshell, chaplain; of the site of the abbey of the B.V.M. of the Rock of Cashel, lands, Hore abbay, Casshell, a gallon of ale from each brew of ale for sale in Casshell, called the Mary gallons, lauds, Graungeery, little Graunge, rectories of Hore abbay, Graungeery, little Graunge, and Lasmalyn, and the vicarage of Railiston, county Tipperary. To hold for twenty-one years, at a rent of £15.

Fiants.—Henry VIII.

Abstracts of the following appear amongst the entries in the Auditor-General's Patent Books as fiants. The originals cannot now be found, nor do they appear in the Record Commissioners' Catalogue.

543 Lease to William Brabazon, esq., and Richard Delahyd; of the grange of Clare, diocese of Kildare, the tithes, &c., of Donarde, Kylbele, Cryhelpe, and Welchetown, diocese of Dublin; Cloughir, diocese of Cashel; Cordeugyn, Ballenecall, and Kylahane, diocese of Emly; Arbystyll, Ruskagh, Templemurrye, and Rathtough, diocese of Leighlin; demised by Thomas Everarde, late prior of S. John the Baptist without the Newgate of Dublin, to the earl of Kildare, at a grain of corn for the first 6 years and 13s. 4d. for the remainder of a term of 31 years. To hold for 21 years, at a rent of 3s. 4d. and paying the rent reserved by the prior.—3 April, xxix. (Vol. II., p. 43.)

544 Grant to Richard Newgent, heir of Richard, late baron of Dellvyn, and to Sir William Newgent, priest, his son; of the manors of Bellgard and Fower, county Meath, and the market of Fower and Templeton. To hold for thirty-eight years, at a rent of £10.—11 February, xxxii. (Vol. I., page 28.)

545 Grant to Nicholas Stanyhurst, gent.; of the site of the monastery of Carmelites or white friars of Dublin, with appurtenances. To hold for ever, by the service of a twentieth part of a knight's fee, and a rent of 2s. 6d.—10 July, xxxiiii. (p. 67.)

546 Lease to Katherine Lambarde of Waterford, widow, Bellflor Sherloke and Anne Sherloke, daughters of James Sherloke, late of Waterford, executrices of the said James; of the preceptory of Kilclogan, &c. (as in No. 529). To hold for 21 years, from 28 March, xxxii., at a rent of £27 13s. 4d.—16 March, xxxv.
(p. 122.)

547 Grant to William Brabazon, esq.; of the site of the monastery of St. Thomas Courte, near Dublin, the mallte myllne, the wood myllne, and the double myllnes, land called Denouer, and appurtenances near the said house. To hold for ever, by the service of a twentieth part of a knight's fee, and a rent of 18s. 5d. sterling.—31 March, xxxv. (p. 19.)

548 Grant to Terence O'Toole, gent.; of the manor and castle of Powerscourte, county Dublin, lands, Powerscourte, Kylpeter, Kylcolin, Beanaghhege, Beanaghmore, le Ouenaghe, Ballycortie, Templebegan, Killtagoran, Cookeston, Anecrew, Kyllmolinge, Ballinbrone, Killeger and Manyster in Fercollyn, county Dublin. To hold in tail male, by the service of one knight's fee, and a rent of five marks. Provided, that he keep the castle of Powerscourte in good repair; that he cause the inhabitants of all the lands to use the English habit and language as much as they can, and to till the tillage lands, he building houses for the husbandmen; that he shall not keep kern without permission of the deputy, or levy any black rent, coyn or livery; that he shall clear the way through the woods and mountains whenever directed by the deputy; that he shall answer the king's writs, and attend the deputy with his men on all hostings; and that he shall not support the king's enemies on pain of forfeiture.

The like patents to be made to Arthur (junior) O'Thole, of the castle and town of Castlekevin, and the Ferter, and for the like rents and services.—No date. See No. 283; and Cal: P.R., pp. 80-81. (pp. 45-47.)

INDEX TO FIANTS.—HENRY VIII

Abbayton, co. Meath (now Westm.), 79.
Ahington, co. Lim. *See* Wothonia.
Adamiston, co. Louth, 416.
Adams, Robert, 282.
Adamston, co. Kildare, 184, 443.
Adare (co. Lim.), 311.
Adenston, co. Meath, 127, 317.
Adarge, co. Kildare, 478.
Agarde, Thomas, 251, 318, 457.
Agarret—Agrett, co. Kildare, 184, 460.
Aghahoo rectory, diocese Ossory, 509.
Aghaminagh. *See* Aghetlungh.
Agher, co. Meath, 467, 468.
Agherya rectory, co. Cork, 461.
Aghetcart rectory, co. Kilk., 239.
Aghetinagh—Aghrinagh—Aghtynan—Aghenlnagh, co. Kilk., 249, 638.
Aghirbally rectory, co. Carlow, 304.
Aghnamallyn (co. Mon.) tithes, 541.
Aghtinagh—Aghtynan. *See* Aghetinagh.
Aguetaston (co. Louth) tithes, 541.
Agrett. *See* Agarret, 460.
Ash park, Dublin, 386.
Alasty, co. Kildare, rectory, 245.
Aldrenwodde, co. Kilk., 369.
Alee, John, 443.
Alen, John, 238, 313, 385, 478.
  „   „ grant of land, 57.
  „   „ Chancellor of the Exchequer, 4 L
  „   „ Constable of Maynoth, 109.
  „   Thomas, 77, 89, 118, 120, 245.
  „   „ Clerk of the Hanaper, 40.
  „   „ 2nd Chamberlain of Exchequer, 42.
  „   „ Constable of Maynoth, 160.
  „   Warin, 42.
Alcuston, co. Dublin, 243.
Alestonne, co. Kildare, 465.
Allarneston (co. Louth), 262.
All Saints, Dublin, Priory of, 79.
Almonston (co. Louth), 374.
Amerew, co. Dublin (now Wick.), 542.
Aneu—Aucy—Anye, Preceptory, co. Lim., 212, 218, 285, 311, 329.
  „   „ rectory and land, 311.
Angevileton, co. Meath, 252.
Aulifly—Auliffe (River Liffey), 367, 374.
Aukisters park, Dublin, 386.
Annall, the (a district in co. Longford), 189, 199.
Aunor, Newton of, co. Tip., 308, 308.
Aimors Bridge, 300, 308.
Anye. *See* Anee.
ApDavid, Rees, Controller of Customs, Drogheda, 4.
Apryce, Robert, 537.
Arboystyll. *See* Ardristell, 543.
Archer, Walker, 309.
Archidraconston, co. Kildare, 451.
Archldecrans rectory (co. Westm.), 128.
Arclowe, co. Wexford (now Wick.), Monastery of Friars Preachers, 163, 404, 535.
Ardagh (co. Lim.), 311.
Ardaghmegran, co. Kilk., 369.
Ardarro (co. Lim.) rectory, 311.
Arderly (co. Kerry), 311.
Ardbrackan—Ardbraccan, co. Meath, 220, 252.
Ardcathe, co. Meath, manor, &c., 393.
Ardcolme, co. Wexford, rectory, 343.
Ardcvaghe, co. Meath, 318.
Ardee. *See* Atrio Dei.
Ardekennels, co. Wex., 230.
Ardemulghan, *See* Ardmulghan.
Ardescull, co. Kildare, 443.
Ardesky, co. Cork, rectory, 461.

Ardfinnan. *See* Areffynan.
Ardgalf, co. Meath, 46.
Ardgossan (? co. Galway), 383.
Ardkewan—Arkewan (co. Wex.), 343.
Ardlowe, co. Kilkenny, 242.
Ardmulghan — Ardemulghan — Ardmulkan, co. Meath, manor, &c., 250, 252, 342, 393.
Ardmylowan (co. Galway), 283.
Ardnought—Ardnothe, co. Dublin, 469.
Ardrahon—Ardrnyne, rectory, diocese of Kilmacduagh, 208, 352.
Ardrio, co. Kildare, 590.
Ardristell—Arbystyll (co. Carlow) rectory, 874, 543.
Ardsallaghe, co. Meath, 266.
Ardvillegoghe (? co. Galway), 383.
Ardylley, co. Kilkenny, rectory, 242.
Ardynewe, co. Meath, 441.
Areffynan (Ardfinnan, co. Tip.) rectory, 311.
Arkewan. *See* Ardkewan.
Arlagh, co. Tipperary, 398.
Armagh, Archbishop of, 273.
  „   George Dowedall, Archbishop of, 389.
Armaughe bregaughe (co. Armagh), 427
Arnemallan (co. Meath), 178.
Artereston—Artercstoune. *See* Artzreston.
Arteslande, co. Kildare, 445.
Artewell. *See* Artwell.
Artureston — Arteraton — Arterstoune — Arterton, co. Kildare, 245, 445.
Artnreston, co. Louth, 227.
Artwell—Artewell, co. Kildare (*see* Hartwell), 465, 507.
Ash. *See* Ayshe.
Ashe, John, 75.
Askeyny (Askeaton, co. Lim.), 311.
Aspinall, Charles, 517.
Asshebolde, or Asbolde, Charles, pardon, 171.
Athboy, co. Meath, 317.
  „   priory of Carmelites, 127, 317.
Athcarue (co. Meath), 305.
Athenry friary, 216.
Athforthe—Athfathe (co. Tip.), 374.
Athlomney, co. Meath, 252.
Athnecrane, co. Westm., Monastery of Carmelites, 476.
Athy—Athie, 232, 399, 445.
  „   manor, 135.
  „   Monastery of Preachers, 126, 399.
Atrio dei, de (Ardee), co. Louth, Hospital of St. John the Baptist, 339.
Aylmer, Gerald, 2nd Justice Common Bench, 25, 30, 38.
  „   „ Chief Baron, Exchequer, 38.
  „   „ grants of land, 66, 359.
  „   „ Knt., 238, 472.
Aylmerston, co. Kildare, 464.
Ayshe (Ash, co. Louth) tithes, 541.
Ayshton (co. Dublin), 374.

Babutt, rectory, co. Meath, 320.
Bacbellaston, rectory, co. Cork, 804.
Baggotiston, co. Louth, 416.
Baggotrathe (co. Dublin), 81, 267, 365.
Bagote, Thomas, 77.
Baker, Thomas, lease, 248.
Balaughe (? co. Louth), 457.
Balbraddogh (co. Meath), 457.
Balbragho tithes (? Ballybarrnck, co. Louth), 541.
Balbroy, co. Meath, 467.
Baldonston, co. Wex., 371.
Baleman. *See* Ballanon.
Balenebonrich, co. Meath, 82.
Balgatheran, co. Louth, 254.
Balgethbe in parish of Arcath, co. Meath, 393.

INDEX TO FIANTS.—HENRY VIII.

Balgeth—Balgeythe, Grange of, co. Dublin, 65, 884.
Balgill (co. Meath), 457.
Balgryffyn, co. Dublin. 456.
Balhary, bridge of, at Swords, 510.
Ballbetagh, co. Dublin, 372.
Bulleff, or Bayly, David, 307, 434.
Ballnachorse, co. Dublin, 283.
Ballnagir (co. Wex.), 486.
Ballusbolot, co. Meath, 198.
Balkyngiss. *See* Baltinglas.
Ball, John, 77.
Ballscormyke, co. Meath (now Longford) rectory, 326.
Ballaghaha, co. Cork, rectory, 408.
Ballaghnymologhtir in Ormond, rectory, 530.
Ballaloghlowe, diocese Clonmacnoise, vicarage, 337.
Ballanon—Ballonan—Balenan, co. Wex., 72, 484.
Ballohoke, (co. Wick.), 211.
Ballelogluriaghe—Balleloghry. *See* Ballyloghreagh.
Ballcuiory, diocese Meath, rectory, 495.
Ballouan. *See* Ballanon.
Ballinebarn, co. Kild., 445.
Ballenecall, dio. Emly, tithes, 543.
Ballcnegallaghe,—Ballenegelaghe (*see* Ballynegallagie), (co. Lim.), 179, 367.
Ballenocerthy. *See* Ballyncoorthle.
Ballcorcley, co. Tip., (*see* Balliborteiye), 150.
Bulliboter, or Boteriston, co. Dub., 267.
Ballibrogg. *See* Ballybrolge.
Ballichelmor, grange of, co. Dub., 401.
Ballicutland. *See* Ballycotland.
Bulligelaghe, co. Wex., 529.
Balligore. *See* Ballygore.
Ballihacke, port of (co. Wex.), 297.
Ballibortclye, co. Tip. (*see* Ballcorcley), 339.
Ballikelocke, co. Wex., preceptory, 230.
Ballinbrone, co. Dub. (now Wick.), 545.
Ballinlug, (co. Kild.), 197.
Balliscanlan. *See* Ballyscaolan.
Ballistrowan, co. Dub., 914.
Ballltas. *See* Ballytas.
Ballnekyll. *See* Ballynekill.
Ballokestle, (co. Mea.), 197.
Ballore—Balore, co. Dub. (now Wick.), 184, 450.
Ballyandreyhett — Ballyndrohyd, co. Cork, 408.
" Monastery, 406, 462.
Rallybaghull—Ballybaghill, co. Dub., manor, &c., 196, 270, 320, 321.
Ballybulrycke, co. Louth, 681.
Ballybogan, co. Meath, 197.
" Monastery, 197.
Ballybonghte, co. Wex., 262.
Ballybrolge—Ballibrogg, co. Kild., 245, 465.
Ballybroke, co. Kilk., 349, 528.
Ballyburney, co. Cork, rectory, 401.
Ballycadan, co. Kild. castle, 443.
Ballycan—Ballycane (co. Kild.), 184, 460.
Ballyclowan (? co. Tip.), 397.
Ballycortio, co. Dub. (? co. Wick.), 548.
Ballycottlan. *See* Ballycutland.
Ballycrosse, co. Wex., 235.
Ballycullan (co. Kild.), 464.
Ballycutland—Ballicutland—Ballycutlane—Ballycottlan, co. Kild., 304, 458.
Ballydon, co. Wex., 72, 484.
Ballydon, Little, co. Wex., 72.
Ballydowde, co. Dub., 374, 414, 415.
Ballyedas, " 184.
Ballyegyn, (? co. Gal.), 383.
Ballyen, co. Wex., rectory, 242.
Ballyenaaghs, (co. Kild.), 197.
Ballyernan, co. Wex., rectory, 239.
Ballyfadoke, co. Meath, 254.
Ballyfelghan, " 494.

Ballygore—Balligore—Ballore—Balore, co. Dub. (now Wick.), 184, 460.
Ballygory (co. Car.) tithes, 460.
Ballygorne, co. Kild., 511.
Ballygowin, co. Kilk., 309.
Ballygowyn, (co. Wex.), 456.
Ballygroder, rectory, 513.
Ballygruvegge, (co. Kild.), 407.
Ballygyrdery, co. Kilk., 335.
Ballyhagan, co. Kild., 442.
Ballyhurry, co. Tip., rectory, 530.
Ballyhide, (? co. Gal.), 382.
Ballyhode, co. Kilk., 335.
Ballyhwe, (? co. Gal.), 383.
Ballykelly, rectory, 451.
Ballykilly, co. Waterf., rectory, 232.
Ballyla, Little (co. Wex.), 548.
Ballyhackyn—Ballylakan, (co. Tip.), rectory and land, 574.
Ballylnoy, co. Waterf., 458.
Ballylaughlyn, " 458.
Ballylenche, co. Kilk., 341.
Ballyleutlo, (co. Tip.,) 374.
Ballyloghreagh — Balleloghriaghe — Balleloghry, dio. of Clonfert, rect. and vic., 262, 283, 378.
Ballyloghyr, co. Cork, rect., 530.
Ballylorgan, co. Louth, tithes, 450.
Ballymabyn, co. Waterf., 72.
Ballym'llken, co. Cork, 530.
Ballymarge, co. Dub, 526.
Ballymarscally, co. Cork, rectory, 530.
Ballymen (? co. Wex.), rectory, 543.
Ballymolan, co. Meath, 91.
Ballymoignan, 304.
Ballymone, co. Kild., 443.
Ballymore, co. Dub., 439.
Ballyna, co. Kild., 443.
Ballynanlanaghu, co. Cork, rect., 406.
Ballyndrony (co. Kild.), 464.
Ballyndrohyd. *See* Ballyandreyhett.
Ballynecargotown, co. Meath (now Westm.), 79.
Ballyneclogblre, 211.
Ballynecortlds — Ballenocerthy (co. Gal.), vicarage, 262, 378.
Ballynegallaghe—Ballenegallaghe, by Loghgyre (co. Lim.) 179, 347.
Ballynegeraghs, co. Kilk., rectory, 242.
Ballynekill—Ballnekyll, co. Westm., 428.
Ballynere (co. Tip.), rectory, 374.
Ballynevan, co. Meath, 252.
Ballynllegan, co. Cork, rectory, 304.
Ballynolan, co. Kilk., 362.
Ballynra (co. Tip.), 374.
Ballyntample, co. Westm., 485.
Ballyntoghyr, co. Meath, 468.
Ballynuner, co. Louth, 254.
Ballynwillyn, co. Lim., monastery of Preachers, 405.
Ballynylarahlr, co. Lim. (*see* Loghger), 405.
Ballyorgan, 407.
Ballypatrik—Belpatrik, co. Louth, 254.
Ballyrelly—Ballyrelike (co. Wex.), manor, &c., 113, 343.
Ballyscaulan—Balliscanlan, co. Louth, manor, &c., 254, 312.
Rallyskeaghe, 395.
Ballysowko (co. Kild.), 407.
Ballysyllan, co. Wex., tithes, 529.
Ballysynnan—Ballynyuan, co. Wex., 72, 484.
Ballytas—Ballitas (? co. Kild.), 184, 460.
Ballytarmey (? co. Wex.), 271.
Ballytege (co. Wax.), 484, 622.
Ballytyltas, 450.
Ballyrean, co. Kild., 542.
Ballywalden (co. Wex.), rectory, 343.
Ballywodan, co. Kilk., 338.
Ballywrode (co. Kild.), 407.
Balmacarnane, co. Dub., 91.
Balmadon, " rectory, 235.

Index to Fiants.—Henry VIII.

Balmadure, co. Kild., 478.
Balmagarvey, (co. Meath), rectory, 123.
Balmahannoke, co. Wex., 484.
Balmalice, co. Dub., 528.
Balnocloighe, co. Meath, rectory, 312.
Balnecloy, co. Westm., 428.
Balnekyll (co. Meath), 197.
Balore. *See* Ballore.
Balranny, co. Meath, 254.
Balregan, „ rectory, 254.
Balreske, „ 252.
Balreyne, „ 467.
Balrodan, „ rectory, 473.
Balrothery—Balrothry, co. Dub., 79, 447.
Balsoon (co. Meath), 457.
Baltingias—Balkynggias, Abbey and land, 211, 460.
Baltingias, Thomas, Viscount, creation and grant of land, 211.
Balirastin (co. Dub.), 447.
Balwenston (co. Wex.), 348.
Balydondon, co. Wex., 434.
Balymany, co. Dublin, 283.
Balyodde, 460.
Banbrege, Oswald, pardon, 414.
Banno, the, co. Wex., land and ferry, 537.
Bareleston, co. Louth, rectory, 254.
Baren, James, 132.
Barleys, curacy (*see* Bardeston), 77.
Barnegeraghe (co. Dublin), 447.
Barneton (co. Wex.), 237.
Barnewall, Allenor, 410.
„ Andrew, 270.
„ „ presentation, 333.
„ Christopher, 408.
„ Edward, wardship, 81.
„ Geneta, 103.
„ Patrick, 235, 270, 469, 510.
„ „ grant of land, 335.
„ Robert, 81.
„ Thomas, 105.
„ *See* Trimileston, Baron of.
Baronston, (co. Wick.), 211.
Barrnghe, (co. Car.), rectory, 451.
Barret, James, 95.
„ John, 95.
Barronragh, co. Kildare, 405.
Barrowe, the river—island and weirs on, 393.
Barry, Philip FitzDavid, Abbot de Choro Benedicti, 410.
Bartholomew, Clement, 77.
Basnet, Edward (Dean of St. Patrick's), leases, 339, 413; grant of land, 449.
Basnetic, Finian, 66.
Bastardeston—Bastareston, co. Wex., 73, 444.
Bath, William, 66.
Bathe, James (Chief Baron), leases, 451, 456, 480, 512, 539.
Bathe, John, 267, 473.
„ „ Chief Solicitor, 520.
„ Robert, wardship, 473.
„ Thomas, 417.
„ „ appointed Chamberlain of Exchequer, 21.
„ Walter, 1, 453.
Bawne, co. Kilk., 241.
Bayly. *See* Balleff.
Beallaghe, co. Kilk., rectory, 242.
Beanaghbege, co. Dublin (now Wick.), 548.
Besmaghmore, „ „ 548.
Bearnanely, co. Tip., rectory, 242.
Behecko, co. Drogheda, 360.
Becansion, (co. Kildare), 464.
Becke, Edward, grant of land, 331.
„ lease, 243.
Bectyff (co. Meath), 313, 457.
„ abbey, 457.

Bedlowe, Christopher, 377.
„ George, 305.
„ John, livery, 377.
„ Walter, Knt., 377.
Bedloweston, co. Meath, 381.
Behe (Beagh, co. Galway), 333.
Belaghtobyn, diocese Ossory, vicarage, 257.
Belegarde. *See* Bellgard.
Belgrawe, co. Dublin, 91.
Belingiston, „ 270.
Bell, Rayney, 513.
Bellantre, co. Dublin, 91.
Bellewe or Bedlewe, George, 305.
Bellgard—Belegarde, co. Meath (now West.), manor, 13, 544.
Bellings, John, 267.
Belpatrik. *See* Ballypatrik.
Bennet, Patrick, 95.
Bentre, Fassough of, co. Wex., 73, 434.
Bermyngham, or Bremyngham, Patrick, 1, 41.
„ Richard, presentation, 495.
„ Walter Oge, 493.
„ William, Knt., lease, 191.
„ „ created Baron of Corbrie, and grant of land, 197.
Bernarde, Thomas, presentation, 269.
Bertrameston, in parish of Ardcath, co. Meath, 393.
Betaghe, John, 76.
Betaghton, co. Meath, 91.
Betogheston (? co. Meath), 128.
Bieton, James, 137.
Birrawgbt, co. Dublin, 523.
Bishops' Land. *See* Busshops.
Blake, John, 471.
„ Philip, 143.
„ Walter, 143.
Blakerathe, co. Kildare, 466.
Blakbull, co. Meath, 186.
Blakrath, co. Tip., 530.
Blakrathe, co. Kilk., 241.
Blanchevillestou — Blaunchfeldestowne, co. Kilk., rectory, 151, 241.
Blechington, William, 260.
Blondeston, co. Meath, 81.
Bloyke, co. Dublin, 283.
Bodnamiston, co. Meath, 183.
Bohirnybrynee—Borhrune (co. Dublin), 315, 324.
Boleston. *See* Boyestowne.
Bolaghe, co. Kilk., 239.
Bolike (co. Tip.), 374.
Bolton (co. Kildare), 464.
Boneston, co. Meath, 272.
Borhrune. *See* Bohirnybrynee.
Bosserston, co. Kilk., 488.
Bossher, David, 131.
Boteriston, alias Bollboter, co. Dublin, 267.
Boureman, William, grant of land, 369.
Bourke, Theobald, 298.
Boyestowne — Boucstowne — Boleston (co. Wick.), 134, 466.
Boynardiston, parish of Ardcath, co. Meath, 393.
Boyne, mills on, 250, 392.
„ watercourse and soil, 392.
„ weirs and fishing, 254, 325, 392.
Boyratho, co. Louth, 254.
Boyse, Peter, pardon, 301.
Brabazon, Elizabeth, 470.
„ William, 404, 470, 543.
„ „ grant of land, 547.
Brace, John, 83.
Brackenbury, Ninyan, appointed Gauger of Waterford, 299.
Braolyn (co. Westm.), 167.
Bramarghton, (co. Wick.), 211.
Brandon, James, 357.
Branganston, co. Meath, 156.
Brannaxe's park (Dundalk), 357.

INDEX TO FIANTS.—HENRY VIII.

Bravyn Ibryn, co. Meath (the Barony of Brawny, co. Westm.), 326.
Bray, Edmund, 166.
„ See Brey.
Braye, co. Kildare, 364.
Brayston, co. Meath, 66.
Bremyngham. See Bermynghame.
Brenagbe, Edmund, pardon, 121.
Brenane, Patrick, 185.
Brene, Donogh, annuity, 170.
Breny, the; rectories in, 128.
Brereton, John, 468, 484.
„ Ranulph, 440, 441.
Brwyn. See Bruna.
Brey, co. Dublin (now Wick.), rectory, 304.
Brocton, Robert, 510.
Brode, Patrick, pardon, 505.
Brodeston, co. Carlow (now Kildare), 504, 407.
Brokes, John, lease, 232.
Browe (Bruff, co. Lim.), rectory, 311.
Browns, John, 398, 419.
„ Robert, 406, 419.
„ „ grant of land, 405.
„ Thomas, 255.
Browneston, co. Dublin, 270.
Browneston—Brownestowne, co. Kilk., 151, 155, 176, 349, 553.
Brownestonwaring—Brownistonwaring, co. Kilk., 369.
Brownslsland, co. Meath, 325.
Brows Weir, on the Boyne, 254.
Brune—Brewyn (co. Dublin), 315, 324.
Bryane, Katherine, 204.
„ Richard, 204.
Brystow (Bristol), export of wool to, 37.
Bcyta, John, 144.
Bulganringhe, co. Wex., 162.
Bullock, co. Dublin. See Bloyke.
Burgo, Roland de, Bishop of Clonfert, 260, 278.
Burnell, John, 156, 481.
Busshe—Bushe, Lewis, appointed Serjeant-at-Arms, 7.
„ Lewis, 15.
„ William, appointed Chamberlain of the Exchequer, 21.
Busshops lande, parish of Luske, 510.
Butler—Buttler—le Butler;—
„ Catherine, 458.
„ Edmund (Archbishop of Cashel), grant of a monastery, 357.
„ Edmund, created Baron of Dunboyne, 194.
„ Elicia, 116.
„ James, 20.
„ James (Abbot of Inyiawnaghe) pension, 140.
„ John, 83.
„ Richard, 239, 393.
„ Robert, 336.
„ Thomas, Knt., 165, 172.
„ „ „ created Baron of Chaler, 338.
„ See Ormond, Earl of; Ossory, Earl of; Danboyne, Baron of.
Butlerscourte, (Oldcourt, co. Wick.), 154, 469.
Bwurysehaston, co. Meath, 82.
Byenstowa, co. Wexford, 484.
Byrckbocke, George, 534.
Byrlye, Laurence, 32.
Byrnston. (co. Kildare), 444.
Byrroll, John, 77.
Byrt (Brett) William, 365.
Byrtas, co. Westmeath, 428.
Byrtonsland, (co. Kildare), 464.

Cabraght, co. Meath, 32.
Caddell, Robert, 270.
„ Walter, 75.
Cahill, Edmund, 111.

Cabill, Mathew, 111.
„ Thomas, 76.
„ William, 111.
Cahir, Baron of. See Chaler.
Cahir—Cahyr—Chaier, co. Tip., 165.
„ curate of, 124.
„ Priory of the B.V.M., 110, 124, 165, 338.
Cahirdoneiske—Chaierdowneyske(Cabir), 165, 333.
Cahirleyak, co. Kilk., rectory, 242
Cahir—, See Kayr—, Kar—, Car—.
Cairge. See Carge.
Caisshill. See Cashel.
Calgaghe, co. Meath, 501.
Callan (co. Kildare), 464.
Callan, co. Kilk., Monastery of Augustin Friars, 243.
Callan, co. Louth, 77, 254, 418.
Calloughton, 519.
Canonrathe, co. Kildare, 466.
Canons of the order of St. Augustin, Ynystooke, 17.
Canons of the order of St. Augustin, Clonefert, 876.
Canonton—Cannantoun (co. Louth), 196, 541.
Canon.—See Chanon—.
Cantwell, Anastacia, 116.
„ Richard, prior of St. John, Kilkenny, 136.
Cappagh—, See Kep—.
"Captain of his Nation," O'Conor of Othfaly, 23.
„ „ O'Donell, 523.
„ „ O'Grada, 391.
„ „ O'Meare, 306.
„ „ O'Shaughlyn, 363.
„ of Ely Ikeroyll, 411.
„ Offaly, 259.
Captains in the Marches, 411.
Carbery—Carbre, co. Kildare, manor, &c., 168, 442.
Carbrie, William, Baron of, creation and grant of land, 197.
Cardonstoo (co. Meath), 197.
Caresland, co. Kild., 478.
Carge—Cairge—Carge, co. Wex., manor, &c., 73, 343, 434.
Cargestown — Kargistou, co. Mea. (now Westm.), 79, 105.
Cargyn (co. Wick.), 311.
Carikeshinaghe, co. Louth, 416.
Carlingford — Curlyngforda, co. Louth, 54, 532.
„ Constable of Castle, 54.
„ Monastery of Preachers, 231.
Carns, co. Wex., rectory, 304.
Carnoway (? co. Lim.), rectory, 311.
Carnulls, co. Mea., 250.
Carpinderestowne (co. Westm.), 128.
Carragbewryn (co. Cork). 394.
Carrickbrenan—Carybrynan, co. Dub., 310, 460.
Carricks, rectory (see Carrickmagryffyn), 123.
„ See Carryke, Karricke.
Carricke, Little, co. Waterf., Mon. of Friars, Minor, 536.
Carrickellir, co. Kilk., 369.
Carrickmagryffyn, co. Tip., rectory, 520.
Carrickmayne (co. Dub.), 246.
Carrickmygogh, co. Water., tithes, 530.
Carrintobbyr, rectory, 311.
Carroll, John, Abbot of Cnocke, 92.
Carrygroughanbeg, co. Cork, Rectory, 461.
Carryke, 511.
Carrykncoanonaghe (see Chanowaroke), 541.
Carybrynan. See Carrickbrenan.
Caryck, Katherine, 204.
Carycklom Le Heyler, co. Cork, rectory, 404.
Carten, parish of Maynothe, 515.

INDEX TO FIANTS.—HENRY VIII.

Casey—Casye—Casy:—
" Nicholas, 256.
" Robert, Controller of Customs, Dublin, 89.
" " Gauger of Dublin, 56.
" " 180, 278.
" Thomas, 127.
" " grant of land, 317.
Cashel—Cashell—Caisshell, co. Tip., 178, 311, 361, 542.
" Abbey of the B. V. M. of the Rock, 109, 542.
" Monastery of Friars Minor, 157, 387.
" " of Preachers, 361.
" Edmund Butler, Archbishop of, 157, 387.
Cassevanna, co. Kild., 442.
Cashell, John, lease of Customs, 540.
Castelcromer, co. Kilk., rectory (see Comfr.), 175.
Castelcowe (co. Louth), 196, 541.
Casteletowne, co. Wex., 238.
Cnstelfelde, Swords, 510.
Castelkevin. See Castlekevin.
Castell Dermot (see Triateldermot), 290.
Castelmero (co. Car.) rectory, 451.
Castelring (co. Louth) rectory, 282.
Castelrow (co. Kild.), 464.
Castelton, co. Cork, rectory, 406.
Castelton of Moylagh, co. Meath, manor, &c., 440, 441.
Casteltoun upper (co. Louth), 318.
Casteltown of Delvyn (co. Westm.), 333.
" See Casteletowne.
Castelwarulage, co. Kild. rectory, 486.
Castlekevin—Castelkewln (co. Wick.) castle and land, 319, 548.
Castelknocke (co. Dub.) manor, 446.
Castles, the three. See Three Castles.
Casy. See Casey.
Cayledowie, co. Cork, 406.
Chaler or Chalerdowneyske, Thomas Butler, baron of, creation, 388.
" See Cahir.
Chamerlayne, Jenico, 222.
Chancery, Clerk of the Crown, 50.
" " Hanaper, 40.
" Keeper of the Rolls, 3.
" Master of the Rolls, 41, 66, 312.
Chanons Growe, co. Kilk., 175.
Canonsroke—Carryknecanonagbe—Petra Canonicorum (co. Louth), 198, 541.
Chanonton, co. Meath, 318.
Chapel Isoulde, co. Dub., 247, 482.
Chapelmydway (co. Dub.), 270.
Chaple Robyn, co. Cork, rectory, 406.
Chester. See Weschester.
" county, 190.
Chaver—Chewer:—
" Christopher, livery, 454.
" Philip, 195.
" Walter, knt., 454.
Chief Place (King's Bench) Clerk of Crown and Pleas, 373.
" Second Justice, 34, 44.
Choro Benedicti, de, co. Cork, Abbey, 410.
Churcheston, co. Meath, manor, &c., 365.
Churcheton—Churcheston of Kylryan, co. Wex., 72, 484.
Churchton by Wicklowe, 374.
Cistercians—Abbey of Newry, 366.
" Abbey of Wothonia, 149.
Claghan, co. Meath, 91.
Clamadiffe, co. Meath, rectory, 252.
Clancarwill, 293.
Clane, co. Kild., Mon. of Friars Minor, 174, 313.
" Newton of, 318.
Claragbe—Claraght, co. Kilk., rectory, 137, 175.

Clare. See Grangeclare.
Claterston, co. Meath, 91.
Clere, Anne, 118.
Clereston, co. Wex., 450.
Clerke, John, 365.
Cleyngiays, co. Lim., 242.
Clogher—Cloughir (co. Tip.), 374, 543.
Clogbfada, co. Tip., 322.
Cloghran Swerdes, (co. Dub.) rectory, 10.
Clomene—Clomyn. See Clonmene.
Clomethan (co. Dub.), 510.
Clonard—Cloynard, co. Meath, Abbey, 191, 197.
" manor, &c., 197, 318, 393.
Clonawolcam, co. (Wex.), 484.
Cloncoillen (co. Meath), 457.
Cloncurry—Clonecurry, co. Kild., 507.
" Mon. of Carmelites, 395.
Cloncurrye, co. Meath, 441.
Clondalye, (co. Meath) rectory, 191.
Cloudolkan—Clondolcan, co. Dub., 181, 324.
Clondrohid, co. Cork, rectory, 461.
Clonefadd, co. Wex., 484.
Clonefert. See Clonfert.
Cloneguffin, co. Meath, 487.
Clonehagh (? co Gal.), 383.
Clonoken, co. Wex., 484.
Cloneliffe, Grange of, co. Dub., 386.
Clonem'gfflomant, co. Meath, 408.
Cloncmliam, co. Water., rectory, 530.
Cloneneth, co. Cork, rectory, 461.
Clonepetb, (co. Tip.) rectory, 374.
Clonetarf. See Clontarff.
Clonfert—Clonefert, Bishopric and Deanery, 263, 378.
" Monastery de Portu Pura, 378.
" Roland de Burgo, Bishop of, 260, 263, 378.
Clongadden (co. Wex.), 484.
Clongyme—Clonkyshe, (co. Long.), rectory, 189, 326.
Clonkayne, co. Kild., 442.
Clonkyn, (co. Louth) tithes, 541.
Clonmacnoise, Florence, Bishop of, confirmation, 262.
Clonmakaran, co. Wex., 484.
Clonmell, 166, 236, 306, 338, 530.
" Monastery of Friars Minor, 306, 308.
" grant to Sovereign, &c., 306.
Clonmene—Clomeue—Clomyn, co. Wex., 72, 471, 484.
" Monastery of Aug. Friars, 142, 370, 471.
Clonmyne, co. Cork, rectory, 461.
Clonmyne, co. Kild., 442.
Clonshill, 460.
Clontarff—Clonetarf (co. Dub.), 452.
" John Rawsou, Viscount of, creation, 201.
Clony, (co. Clare), 391.
Clony, co. Meath, 393.
Clonyng—Clonyngs, (co. Tip.), 374.
Clorane, Grange of, co. Kilk., 241.
Cloughir. See Clogher.
Clowanston, co. Tip., 168.
Cloyuard, see Clonard, 318.
Cloyneboynaghe, co. Meath, 156.
Clynche, Patrick, grant of Monastery, 483.
" Thomas, presentation, 328.
Clyncher, Patrick, 83, 84.
Clyncloghe, (co. Car.) tithes, 460.
Clynton, Thomas, 459.
Cnocke. See Knocke.
Cnock in Prechayn, (co. Clare), 391.
Cnockmahan. See Knockamoghan.
Cnocknerbury, 223.
Cnograffyn (Knockgraffon, co. Tip.) [rectory, 311.
Cnokdromyn, co. Dub., 68.
Cockes, William, 393.

INDEX TO FIANTS.—HENRY VIII.

Coffe, Onorius, presentation, 337.
Coffy, John, 495.
Collshill, (co. Wex.), 484.
Cokeston. *See* Cookeston.
Cokmyll, (Tuckmill, co. Wick.), 211.
Colaghe—Coleghs (co. Tip.), 374.
Colbugo, co. Louth, 254.
Colcredane—Coleryedan, by Louth, 196, 541.
Coldreynold, co. Louth, 254.
Colenshill, (*see* Cullenshill), 469.
Colenston, co. Kild., 384.
Colfyche, (co. Kild.), 478.
Colle, (*see* Colycayll), 73.
Collen's lands in Clonmene, co. Wex., 370, 471.
Colloy, Patrick, appointed a soldier, 64.
Colloghton, co. Meath (now Westm.), 336.
Collyeriande, co. Kild., 345.
Collyn, co. Cork, rectory, 430.
Colman, co. Tip, 155, 374.
Colodan, John (*see* Colton), 143.
Cologhe. *See* Colaghs.
Colpe, (co. Meath), 472.
Colton, John (*see* Colodan), 144.
Columkille—Columkyll, co. Kilk, rectory, 181, 239.
Colycayll—Collo, Great (co. Wex.), 73, 484.
 " " Old (co. Wex.), 73, 484.
Comanston—Comyngston (co. Wick.), 184, 460.
Common Bench, Chief Justice, 29.
 " Second Justice, 28, 30, 35, 45.
 " Prothonotary and Chirographer, 34.
Comoylestowns (Rallycomoyle, co. Westm.), 128.
Compsy, country of, co. Tip., 458.
Comyr in Odoghe (Castlecomer, co. Kilk.) vicarage, 412.
Confye, co. Kild., 478.
Connall—Conall, co. Kild., 475.
 " Priory of the B. V. M., 147, 148.
Conor, Tyriagh, pardon, 364.
Constables of Castles. *See* Cartingford, Dublin, Maynoth, Trym, and Wykeloo.
 " of Manor of Swerdes, 510.
Contowrs, Patrick (*see* Connator), 77.
Controller of Customs, Drogheda, 4.
 " Dublin, 59, 378.
Cookeston—Cokeston, co. Dub. (now Wick.), 67, 283, 548.
Copo, Thomas, 248.
Copland, William, presentation, 353.
Copynger, Adam, 218.
Corball, co. Dub., 528.
Corbally, (co. Kild.), 464.
Corbally, co. Meath, 223, 441.
Corbally, Nicholas, Prior, B. V. M. de Urso, Drogheda, 98.
Cordasgen—Cordangyn—Cordagen, (co. Tip.), 374, 543.
Corder—Cordyr—Cordyrroghe, (Corderry, co. Louth), 194, 541.
Corfanton, co. Meath, 91.
Cork—Corke, 176, 374.
 " Archdeacon of, 422, 429.
 " fishery at, 176.
 " the Halfe Skeaghebege, &c., 388, 533.
 " Monastery of Friars Minor, 176.
 " " Preachers, 388, 533.
 " possessions of S. John's, Waterford, in city and county, 72.
 " county, dissolution of religious houses in, 251.
Corneliscourte—Corayllys Courte, co. Dub., 91, 459.
Corraghanyeley, co. Cork, 530.
Corraghston, co. Meath, 467.
Corregan, Thomas, 73.
Corriston, co. Meath, 392.
Corroke, co. Tip., rectory, 165.

Corthrekke (co. Lim.), 362.
Coserowe, Margaret, 102.
Cosyngeston. *See* Cousingeston.
Cosvynie, co. Cork, 530.
Cottrall, James, Abbot of Thomascourt, 83.
 " William, 88, 329.
Cottrelliston (co Dub.), 374.
Cottresboly, co. Kilk., 175.
Coule (co. Louth), 316.
Coulere, co. Meath, 441.
Coulevenghe. *See* Cowlonevesghs.
Couly, Denis, 396.
Council, Clerk of the, 355, 463.
Countor, Richard, Abbot of Melyfount, 77.
Courcy, James, 396.
Courtt of Killergie—Cort of Killargau, co. Car., 222, 514.
Cousingeston—Cosyngeston, co. Meath, 309, 312, 330, 393, 468, 483.
Cowls (7 co. Gal.), 383.
Cowleneveagho—Coaleveaghs, co. Kild., 442.
Cowley—Cowcley:—
 " Henry, 442.
 " Nicholas, 219.
 " Robert, 313; Ganger of Ireland, 11; Clerk of the Crown of Chancery, 50; Customer of Dublin, 52; Master of the Rolls, 68.
 " Walter, 151, 155, 175, 349, 520, 538; Clerk of the Crown of Chancery, 50; Customer of Drogheda,51; of Dublin, 52; Chief Solicitor, 61.
 " [ ] licence to trade with Gascony, 8.
Cowllshill—Cowlyshill, co. Kilk., 369.
Cowlneskreaghe (co. Wick.), 67.
Cowteshale, Norfolk, 57.
Cracamothan. *See* Knockamaghan.
Crean, Baptist, annuity, 509.
Cref, Thomas, 237, 240.
Crege, 383.
Creroke, co. Meath, 318.
Crowodd, co. Meath, 254.
Crickiston—Cryksston, co. Meath, 451, 458.
Crogho (co. Lim.), 311.
Croke, John, 234.
 " Richard, 135.
 " Thomas, 135.
Croket (co. Kild.), 464.
Crokwrrke, (Knockarigg, co. Wick.), 211.
Cromeston—Cromston, (co. Tip.), 374.
Cromlyn, co. Dub., manor, 16, 21, 22, 24, 48, 235.
Crosardo, (co. Tip.), 397.
Crossan, Fergall, 99.
Crossetooke, co. Kilk., 241.
Croten, co. Dub., 272.
Crucerathe, co. Meath, rectory, 254.
Cryhalpo (co. Wick.), tithes, 513.
Crykeston (*see* Crickiston), 488.
Cullen, co. Wex., 484.
Cullenshill—Colenshill (7 co. Kild.), 184, 469.
Cullydraghe, co. Meath, 441.
Cullyn, co. Meath, 254.
Culmyne, co. Dub., 400, 446.
Curduffe, co. Dub., 510.
Curraghmore (co. Water.), 458.
Curyn, James, 490.
Cusake, James, 373.
 " John, livery, 204.
 " Patrick, 477.
 " Richard, 204.
 " Thomas, 45, 91, 330, 466; grant of land, 309; Justice of the Common Bench, 35; Master of the Rolls, 312.
 " Thomas, pardon, 477.
Customer and Collector of Drogheda, 51.
 " of Dublin, 52.
 " of Dublin and Drogheda, 366.
Customs, leases of, 452, 540.

INDEX TO FIANTS.—HENRY VIII.

Dalabrune (Dallabrown, co. Dub.), 447.
Dalnfeldesparke, in Clomotban (co. Dub.), 510.
Dalshide. *See* Delahide.
Dale, Hugh, 344.
Dalltonston, co. Meath, 156.
Dalton, James, 485.
   „   Thomas, 485.
Darcy—Darcye:—
   „   James, 406.
   „   Robert, livery, 408.
   „   Thomas, Keeper of the Rolls, 3.
Dardes, Geffre, Abbot of Trym, 75.
Dardeston (co. Westm.), 505.
Dardiestown (co. Dub.), 374.
Dardieston, co. Meath, 235.
Daveston—Davieston, Little, co. Carl. (now Kild.), 304, 407.
Daveston, co. Wex., 152.
Davy, Thomas, Prior of S. John, Drogheda, 97.
De Burgo, Roland, Bishop of Clonfort, 260, 263, 378.
Dece, Walter, 132.
Delahide—de la Hyde—Dalahide—Dalahyde:—
   „   Christopher, Justice of Chief Place, 94.
   „   George, livery, 272.
   „   Richard, 61; Justice of Common Bench, 29.
   „   „   272, 543.
   „   Thomas, 511, 540.
   „   Walter, knt. 442, 443.
Dellyncallen (Derrycallan, co. Gal.), 363.
Delman, or Yans, Robert, 51, 70.
Delven—Dellvyn—Delwyn:—
   „   Christopher, Baron of, 448.
   „   Richard, knt., Baron of, 13, 14, 448, 544.
   „   Richard, Baron of. 448, 544.
Delvyn, Castletown of (co. Westm.), 833.
Denanston, co. Meath, 393.
Denerayhe, co. Louth, 254.
Dengille (Dingle, co. Kerry), 311.
Dengyn in Offaly, 65, 259.
Denouer (Donore, near Dublin), 547.
Deputy, Lord, casements reserved to, in Kilkenny, 309.
Deranston, co. Meath, 252.
Dercoouer (co. Meath), 176.
Darnor, William, 266.
Dermyn, Thomasine, 102.
Dervack (*see* Darvaghe), 408.
Derver, co. Louth, manor, &c., 416.
Derver, co. Meath, manor, 20.
Desert (? co. Kilk.), 161.
Desmond, Earl of, 251, 461.
   „   James, Earl of, 210; grants of land, 362, 388.
   „   Mora Ene Karwell, Countess of, 202.
   „   John, grant of land, 398.
   „   Maurice, 207.
   „   County, dissolution of religious houses in, 251.
Dessardkeran—Tristelkeran, co. Meath, rectory, 78, 365.
Dewerouse, James, grant of land, 409.
   „   John, 486.
   „   Nicholas, livery, 486.
Dickson, William, grant of land, 295.
Dillon. *See* Dyllon.
Dirreweala, co. Cork, rectory, 530.
Dirrygart, co. Kild., 442.
Disert, 171.
Dobyn, David, 132.
Dologht, co. Dub., 235.
Domahenocke (co. Kild.), 464.
Donabate, co. Dub., 272, 304.
Donaghmayn (co. Mon.), 541.
Donaghmore (co. Meath), 84.
Donamayn, 541.
Donameston, co. Meath, 91.

Donamore, co. Meath, 252.
Donarde (co. Wick.), rectory, 374, 543.
Donatl. John, 110.
Donawda, co. Kild., 439.
Donboyn. *See* Dunboyne.
Donbrody. *See* Dunbrodyo.
Dondalke. *See* Dundalk.
Dondrom, co. Dub., manor, &c., 267.
Donelston—Donyleston (co. Louth), 196, 541.
Dongan, Patrick, 490.
Donganston, co. Dub., 270.
Donkytt. *See* Dunkilt.
Donlogh (co. Meath), 467.
Donlwrne. *See* Dnulwyre.
Donmoghan, co. Louth, 416.
Donmowe, co. Meath, 272.
Donnore, or Troeswodd, co. Kilk., 369.
Donohill, co. Tip., rectory, 165.
Donore. *See* Denouer.
Donore—Donowro—Donnowre, co. Meath, 77, 254.
Donshaghlen—Donsbaghlyn—Donsoghly, co. Meath, 5, 272, 467.
Dungan, Patrick, 74.
Donyleston—Donelaton (co. Louth), 196, 541.
Doo, co. Meath, 254.
Dorchan—Durran, Roger, Rector of Ardmulkan, 342, 303.
Dormereston, 396.
Dorniskyll (Kilpatrick, co. Westm.), rectory, 128.
Dorrowe (King's co.), 513.
   „   Priory, 513.
Douro, Diocess of Killaloe, rectory, 203.
Dowalley, rectories in Lordship of, co. Cork, 530.
Dowan, Nicholas, 532.
Dowding, John, 365.
Dowodall—Dowdall—Dowedale:—
   „   Christopher, 322.
   „   George, Prior of Ardee, 339; Archbishop of Armagh, 380.
   „   James, knt., 316.
   „   Laurence, 329.
   „   Robert, 20.
   „   Walter, 249; grant of land, 381.
Downecaunan, part of (co. Wex.), 297.
Downegarven, diocess of Lismore, vicarage, 295.
Downemore (Dunmore, co. Gal.), house of Augustin Friars, 217.
Downfert, co. Kilk., 175.
Doyne—Doyn:—
   „   Hugh, 148.
   „   Nicholas, 148.
   „   Snwo Ny., 188.
   „   William, 503.
Drakeland, co. Kilk., 175.
Draycott—Draicott, Henry, 450; Treasurer of Wexford, 439; Remembrancer of the Exchequer, 437.
Dreynan—Dreynan, 280, 510.
Drime M'Veyran, co. Kilk., rectory, 242.
Drishoke—Dryeshoke, near Dublin, 93, 401.
Drishoke, co. Dub., 270.
Drogges, by Kilmaynam, 201, 525.
Drogheda, 15, 95, 222, 235, 264, 264, 358, 359, 374, 393, 402, 511, 533.
   „   Charter of, 55.
   „   Customer of, 51, 263.
   „   Customs of, 4, 34, 51, 512, 540.
   „   grant of land to town of, 26.
   „   Port of, 15, 54, 278, 540.
   „   Bebocke, &c., 250.
   „   Bowestreet, 381.
   „   Colverhouse park, 381.
   „   Dweleke-street, 381.
   „   the Fayre-street, 381.
   „   Hospital of the B.V.M. de Urso, 95, 532.
   „   Hospital of S. John, 97.

INDEX TO FIANTS.—HENRY VIII.

Drogheda, Hospital of, S. Laurence, 358, 359.
" Irish-street, 381.
" Monastery of Augustin Friars, 248.
" " " Friars Minor, 350.
" " " " Preachers, 249, 381, 402.
" Myllmoteor Windmyllmote, 28.
" S. Laurence-street, 381.
" S. Peter's, Vicar of, 276.
Dromange (co. Louth ?), tithes, 541.
Dromedalgen, co. Kilk., 389.
Dromine, rectory, 451.
Dromiskin — Dromysgen — Drommyskyn — Dramyskan, co. Louth, 106, 289, 296, 384, 541.
Dromle (co. Gal.), 883.
Drommary, co. Cork, rectory, 530.
Dromnaghe (co. Dub.), 81, 451, 513, 589.
Dromneyll (? co. Gal.), 383.
Dromphe (co. Car.) rectory, 451.
Dromyn (co. Louth) tithes, 541.
Dromynhaull, co. Meath, 254.
Droneskenan (co. Gal.), 383.
Drongan (co. Tip.), 374.
Drumawry (co. Westm.), 128.
Drumyskan, see Dromiskin.
Dryssan, co. Cork, rectory, 530.
Dryshoke, see Drishoke, 93.
Dublin, 18, 264, 283, 374, 420, 474.
" George, Archbishop of, 168, 357, licenses to alienate, 417, 510.
" Controller of Customs of, 89, 278.
" Customer of, 52, 208.
" Customs of, 39, 47, 52, 278, 312, 452.
" Fee-farm of, 20, 70.
" grant of land, and remission of fee-farm to, 70.
" Port of, 15, 56, 452.
" Abbey of the B. V. M. (S. Mary's Abbey), 310, 418, 530; pensions to monks, 88, 93, 94, 95, 100, 320, 321; grants of its possessions, 380, 400, 401, 440, 449, 480.
" Abbey of S. Thomas the Martyr (Thomas-court), 245, 349, 451, 466, 460, 513, 538; pensions to monks, 83, 84, 755, 756; grant of the site, 547; grant of possessions, 465.
" Aleh park, 386.
" Ankletere park, 386.
" Bridge, 309.
" Castle, Constable of, 47, 521.
" " gunners in, 60, 62, 164, 324, 512.
" " soldiers in, 64, 512.
" Cathedral of S. Patrick, 389, 417, 432, 510.
" Fyrris of S. Mary's Abbey, 386.
" Helen Hores Meade, alias Gybbetes Mead, 238.
" Hoggen-green, 823, 374.
" Hospital of S. John the Baptist without the Newgate, 85, 155, 272, 367, 374, 548; grant of the site, 400.
" Hospital of St. Stephen, &
" Kilmakargyn in the liberties, 53 L
" Mary's Abbey demesne lands, 386.
" Monastery of All Saints, 70.
" " " Aug. Friars, 180, 313, 323.
" " " Carm. Friars, 545.
" " " Friars Minor, 181, 315, 324.
" " " Preachers, by the bridge, 208, 309.
" Nowe-street, 238.
" Newgate, see Hospital of S. John the Baptist.
" S. Andrew's parish, 323.
" S. Francis-street, 181, 324.
" S. James's parish, 83, 451.
" S. Katherine's Church, 88.

Dublin, S. Michan—Mighans, parish, 234, 323.
" S. Patrick-street, 238, 323.
" Suburbs, 374, 386, 451.
" Thomas-court, 417.
" " (see Abbey of S. Thomas).
" Thomastrete, 451.
" County, chief serjeant of, 53.
" " issues of, 20.
" " marshes of, 389, 539.
Duff, Cornell, Prior of S. John Koulis, 72.
" Henry, Abbot of Thomas-court, 83.
Duffe, Edmund, 163.
Duleke—Dweleke, co. Meath, 377, 517.
Dullard, John, 7.
Dullardeston (co. Kild.), 464.
Dullardeston, co. Meath, manor, &c., 66.
Dunbilly, co. Kilk., 241.
Dunboyne (co. Meath), 106.
Dunboyne—Donboyn, Edmund Butler, Baron of, wardship, 55; livery, 527; creation, 194; grant of Monastery 397.
" James, Baron of, 55, 527.
Dunbrodye—Donbrody, co. Wex., 454.
" Abbey, 450.
Dundalk—Dondalke, 198, 231, 281, 357, 532, 534, 541.
" Charter of, 18.
" Port of, 15, 58, 278.
" Hospital of S. Leonard, 450, 534.
" Monastery of Friars Minor, 357.
Danfert (co. Kild.), 191.
Dungarvan—Dungarwan, co. Kilk., rectory, 101, 530.
Dungennyn, Mathew O'Nelle, Baron of, 436.
Dunkenay, co. Meath, 158.
Dunkit—Dunkitte—Dunkyt—Donkytt, co. Kilk., rectory, 131, 132, 134, 239.
" pyll, or pyle of, 109, 434.
Duulekor, co. Car., rectory, 304.
Dunlwyr—Donlwrus, co. Meath, 52.
Dunsany, Robert Plunket, Lord of, pardon, 12.
Dunsluke, co. Dub., 81.
Dun—, see Don—, Dowu—
Durran. See Dorehan.
Durvagise, co. Meath, rectory (see Dervaak), 205.
Dwcleke, see Duleke, 377.
Dyamore, co. Meath, manor, 20.
Dylion, Bartholomew, knt., 34.
" James, Prior of Kilkenny West, 468.
" Robert, grants of land, 156, 476.
" Thomas, 468.

Echingham, Osborn, knt., 394.
Egypt, little, 264.
Egyptians, 258, 284.
Egyr, John, alias Pety John, 52.
Elenstonred, co. Meath, 250.
Ely Ikeroyll, country of (in King's co.), 411.
Emlagbe—Emlebogan—Emlobegan (co. Mea.), 87, 223.
Emly, Bishopric of, 829.
" Dean of, 339.
Emper. See Impere.
Enaglidune, Diocese of (Annaghdown, co. Gal.), 262.
Enescortie, co. Wex., manor, &c., 402.
" Monastery of Observants, 404.
Eneskawnaghe—Enislawnaght. See Inyslawnaghe.
Eusstioke—Enistiok—Enystioke—Ynystsoke, co. Kilk., 107, 108.
" rectory, 108, 280.
" Priory of S. Columbe, 17, 107, 108, 131, 132, 239.
English, the, war made upon, 171.
Ennessmogut (co. Meath) rectory, 532.
Snocko in precbayn (Knochaphreaghans, co Clare), 391.

INDEX TO FIANTS.—HENRY VIII.

Erliston, co. Kilk., rectory, 242.
Ernestowne, co. Wex., rectory. 175.
Esker—Eskyr, co. Dub., manor, 3, 22, 418.
Esmond, Walter, 98.
Estun, 447.
Ethelton, co. Meath, 91.
Etlea, William Roche, 287.
Eustace—Ewstace—Wstace—Ewsace:—
" Alice, 460.
" Alison, 103.
" Christopher, 156, 439, 460.
" John, 504.
" Katherine, 102.
" Robert, 270, 313, 335, 473, 510.
" Thomas, Lord of Kilcollen, 305; created Viscount Baltinglas, and grant of land, 211.
Eworarde, Thomas, Prior of S. John Baptist, Dublin, 273, 543.
Ewstace. *See* Eustace.
Exchequer—Chief Baron, 39.
" Second Baron, 31.
" Chancellor, 41.
" Chief Chamberlain, 21.
" Second " 42.
" Chief Engrosser, 177.
" Second " 42.
" Remembrancer, 437.
" Second Remembrancer, 183.
" Summonister, 49.

Faganston, co. Meath, 68.
Faghlyn, (co. Westm.) rectory, 128.
Faghyrte, (co. Louth) tithes, 541.
Faneston, co. Wex., 464.
Fannyng, Nicholas, 216, 311.
Fanynawod, co. Tip., 530.
Faran, Robert, 270.
Fasaghe Roo, co. Duh. (now Wick), manor, 67.
Fassough—Fassaghe of Bentre, co. Wex., 73, 484.
Fayoff, Powyll, Egyptian, 264.
Fayron (co. Westm.), 128.
Foddamore, co. Lim., rectory, 165.
Felde, Edmund, 393 ; grant of land, 483.
" Nicholas 517.
Feldiston—Feldeston, co. Dub., manor, &c., 235, 270, 535.
Fennaxes (Fennagh, co. Car.) rectory, 451.
Feraghes, 196.
Ferall, Richard, Bishop of Ardagh, 215, 227.
" *See* O'Ferall.
Fercolyn—Fercollyn, co. Dub. (a district in co. Wick., comprising the parish of Powerscourt and neighbouring mountains), 87, 283, 548.
Ferkeall (a district in the west of King's co.), 524.
Fernes, 239.
Ferney (co. Mon.) tithes, 541.
Ferns, co. Wex., Archdeacon of, 279.
Ferryn Clondermott, part of O'Dampeey's country, 524.
Ferrynnemanoaghe, co. Water., 150.
Ferter, tho (a district in co. Wicklow, comprising the northern part of the barony of Ballinacor, and including the upper basin of the river Vartry), 548.
Fertnokeragbe, co. Kilk , Priory of S. Kevin, 158, 219.
Farynbroke, co. Kilk., 369.
Festame, John, 95.
Fetherde—Fothirde—Fyddert, co. Tip., 374.
" Monastery of Aug. friars, 166, 897.
Fiddert (co. Wex.), 484.
Finkanston, co. Meath, 365.
Firhlll—Firrohill (co. Kild.), 184, 480.
First Fruits, Clerk of, 435.
Fitz Downe. *See* Fydowne.

Fitz Gerald—Fitzgeraldo—Fitzgerrot—Fytzgarot:—
" Bartholomew, 53.
" Eleanor, sister of the Earl of Kildare, pardon, 497.
" James, knt., 184, 460, 478.
" John, knt , 20.
" Maurice, livery, 494.
" Remund oge, 512.
" Richard, 67.
" Thomas, presentation, 285.
" Thomas, 404.
" Walter fitz Jamys fitz Habart, 507.
" *See* Desmond, Earl of ; Kildare, Earl of, Geralds.
Fitz Incroghe, David, 302.
" *See* Incrogho.
Fitz John, Egidia, 116.
Fitz Patrick. *See* Upper Ossory, Baron of.
Fitz Symon, Alison, 102.
" Thomas, 510.
Fitz Tyrrelagh, Alexander, 171.
Fitz William, Richard, 81, 267 ; Seneschal of Newcastell Lyonya, 22.
" Stephen, gunner, 144.
" Thomas, 365 ; wardship, 81; livery, 287.
" William, 40.
Flemyng, Ellenor, license to marry, 291.
" Gerald, knt., 291 ; grant of land, 323.
" Katherine, 377.
" John, 113.
" Robert, 540.
" Robert, son of Thomas, 540.
" Thomas, 475, 496, 540.
" Walter, grant of land, 261.
" *See* Slane, Baron of.
Flemyngton, co. Meath, 272.
Flen, Moryarder, 217.
Flesheston, co. Kild., 313.
Floyde, David, 129.
Flyngiston (co. Gal.), 383.
Foghanhill, co. Meath, 252.
Folanc, Thomas, 76.
Folerston, 463.
Folleston (co. Meath), 477.
Fonte vivo, de, Abbey, co. Cork (see Mayo), 394.
Foroughmore, co. Kilk., 241.
Forster, Gerald, 488.
" Richard, trading license, 50.
Forsterston, co. Meath, 325.
Foster, Robert, 355.
Fostneston, 426.
Foteman, William, 261.
Fower—Fowre—Fovyr, co. Meath (now Westm.), manor, &c., 13, 544.
" Priory of SS. Taurin and Feghin, 122, 128, 413.
" rectory of the B. V. M., 128.
" of S. Feghin, 128.
Freffanc, co. Meath, 318.
Frereton, co. Car., 514.
Friars. *See* under Monasteries.
Friars mead in Adenston, co. Meath, 317.
Fryvenaghe (co. Westm.) Rectory, 518.
Furlonge, Henry, 162.
" James, 162.
" John, 162.
" John, son of William, 162.
" Mayne, 162.
" Nicholas, 162.
" Patrick, 162.
" Philip, 162.
" Thomas, 162.
" Thomas, son of Patrick, 162.
" William, 162.
Fyane, Thomas, 482.
Fyddert. *See* Fetherde.

INDEX TO FIANTS.—HENRY VIII.

Fydowne—Fitzdowne, co. Kilk., 386, 530.
Fymoayn, eo. Tip., rectory, 242.
Fynglas, Patrick, 58, 75.
„ Thomas, 81, 267; prothonotary of the Common Bench, 36.
Fyngowre, eo. Dub., 536.
Fynnaghe (co. Clare), 391.
Fynne, Nicholas, 185.
Fynnor, co. Meath, rectory, 74, 467.
Fynokeston, co. Meath, 252.
Fytzgaret, Remund oge (see FitzGerald), 319.

Gaal, Elicia, 116.
Galbally, eo. Tip. (now co. Lim.), see Mowre, 398.
Galbegeston, 478.
Gallanestou, co. Dub., 272.
Gallowe, eo. Meath, rectory, 478.
Galrygiston, eo. Cnri., 304.
Galtrym, co. Meath, rectory, 478.
Galway—Galwey, 33.
„ fees of, 11.
„ fishing of the water of, 33.
„ port of, 274.
Galwey, Edward, lease, 533.
Galweyston—Galveiston, eo. Cork, 888, 538.
Garge. See Carge.
Garnon. See Gernon.
Garran, 286.
Garrangibbon, co. Kilk., rectory, 242.
Garran O'Dowgeade, eo. Kilk., 335.
Garryclone, co. Cork, reetory, 461.
Garrynriallago, co. Cork, 461.
Gascony, trade with, 6.
Gauger of Ireland, 11.
„ and Searcher of Dublin, Drogheda, and Dundalk, 36, 278.
„ „ Limerick, 277.
„ „ Rosse, Ballihaoke, and Downeoaunan, 297.
„ „ Waterford, 299.
Gawran, eo. Kilk., 287, 240, 241.
Gaydon, Anne, 146.
Gayneslaud, eo. Wex., 484.
Geffray, Simon, presentation, 295.
Genynga, Silvester, 417.
Gerald, Thomas (Rector of Cloghran Swordes), licence of absence, 10.
Gerardcstou, eo. Meath, 477.
Gerawan, Florence, Bishop of Clonmacuoise, 262.
Gerbardo, William, lease, 225.
Gernon—Gernoon—Garnon:—
„ Edward, 481.
„ James, 203, 341.
„. John, 86.
„ Patrick, knt., 202, 341.
Gernonston—Garnoonstowne, co. Louth, 303, 341.
Gessell—Gessell in Offaly, rectory, 185, 288.
Gestill, Philip, 510.
Gibbiston, co. Louth (see Gyhbeston), 410.
Gibbons, John, 56.
Gibbousshepehouse, eo. Kilk., 241.
Gillanauewe, Con, 99.
Gilton, eo. Meath (see Gylton), 254.
Glanmunder, co. Dub., 283.
Glanwidan—Glanwedan, co. Waterf., 150, 838.
Glascarne, co. Meath, 531.
Glascon, 484.
Glashalyn, eo. Meath, 254.
Glasuymycky—Glasobymcky (co. Dub.), 315, 324.
Glaspistle, eo. Louth, 582.
Glassanaghe, co. Kilk., 300.
Glenocke (eo. Car.) tithes, 460.
Globbeston—Globhyston, co. Wex., 73, 484.
Gogourtie, Thomas, pardon, 477.
Golding—Goldynge, Walter, 267, 365, 440; Second Engrosser of the Exchequer, 43.

Goldsmith—Goldsmyth, John, Searcher of Galway, 274; Clerk of the Council, 335, 482.
Gouaght, co. Lim. (see O'Gonaghe), 405.
Goodyn, Richard, gunner, 60.
Gormaneston, Jenico Preston, knt., Baron of, grant of land, 402.
Gortonchegory (? Gort, eo. Gal.), 383.
Gowle, Patrick, leases, 216, 311.
Grace, James, 184.
„ Olivor (Abhot of Joripount), pension, 133.
Graoedien—Graoediowe, eo. Dub., 96, 102, 235, 469, 510.
„ manor, &c., 270.
„ Priory of the B. V. M., 96, 102, 235.
Gradge (eo. Cork), 394.
Gragyn, co. Kilk., 335.
Grallaghe (eo. Dub.), 374.
Granaghe, eo. Cork, rectory, 461.
Granarde, Abhey (co. Longf.), 99, 200, 218.
Grane—Granno—Grayn, eo. Carl. (now Kild.) Abhey, 60, 71, 304, 407.
„ manor, &c., 304, 407.
„ Leonard, Viscount of. See Gray.
Grano, litle, alias Granovegge, 407.
Grang, eo. Kilk., 335.
Grang, the, co. Meath (now Westm.), 79.
Grangelaro—Grange of Clare (co. Kild.), 374, 543.
Grangeon (eo. Wick.), 211.
Grange, tho (eo. Kilk.), 161.
Grange, the, alias West Grange, co. Meath (? Westm.), rectory, 318.
Grange—Graungo, eo. Tip., 150, 166.
Grange, the great, 171.
Grango, great, eo. Tip., 838.
Grange, litle, eo. Louth, 254.
Grange, lytell (Grango Beg, eo. Kild.), 460.
Grange, muche (Grango Moro, co. Klld.), 460.
Grange by Allardestou, rectory, 282.
Grange by Foghanhill, eo. Meath, 252.
Grange by Mylton, 282.
Grangehirweye—Graungharvey, co. Tip., 150 336.
Grangeithe—Graungeithe, eo. Meath, 77, 254
Grangende, co. Meath, 451.
Grangeston, 228.
Granggodley (co. Wiek.), 211.
Grangliegan, co. Kilk., 241.
Graunge (co. Westm.), 145.
Graunge, the, co. Cork, rectory, 461.
Graunge, eo. Tip. (see Grange), 150.
Graunge, the, eo. Wex., 484.
Graunge, litle, co. Tip., 165, 542.
Graunge, the long, co. Wex., 72.
Graunge, mouche, co, Tip., 165.
Graungeery, co. Tip., 542.
Graungeforthe (co. Car.) manor, 460.
Graungefoura, eo. Kild., 354.
Graunge in the Marche, eo. Dub., 384.
Graungeithe. See Grangeithe.
Groungharvey. See Grangehirwaye.
Gray—Grey, Leonard, knt., Lord Gray, Viscount Grane (Lord Deputy), 150, 171, 541; grant of land, 71.
Gray, Richard, 393.
Grayn. See Grano.
Gronan, co. Kilk., manor, &c., 849, 538.
Grene, Owin, see O'Doyn, 290.
Groneeasteli, castle of, 54.
Greneblll, co. Wex., 484.
Grene Ogonaghe (Pallas Grean, co. Lim.), 453.
Grenoke, co. Meath, 235.
„ (co. Meath), 374.
„ parsonage, 53.
Greseton, co. Wex., 162.
Gret, Christopher, livery, 204.
Grey. See Gray.
Griffith, John, Searcher of Dublin, &c., 15,
Griffyn, John, see M'Morehowe, 108.

G

INDEX TO FIANTS.—HENRY VIII.

Growe, le (Grovebeg, co. Kilk.), 161.
Gunner. *See* Dublin Castle.
Gurtcamoclaghe (co. Kild.), 404.
Guynam, Margaret, 382.
Gyanston, 228.
Gyhheston (*see* Gihbiston), 426.
Gybbutes monde, Dublin, 238.
Gyfrynston (Griffinstown, co. Wick.), 211.
Gylbertestowne (co. Westm.), 128.
Gylton (co. Kild.), 460.
Gypsies. *See* Egyptians.
Gyrly (Girley, co. Meath) rectory, 374.

Habarde, Margaret (Prioress of Tarmafeghen), pension, 146.
Hacket, co. Car., rectory, 304.
Hacketiston (co. Dub.), 447.
Hagarde, co. Louth, rectory, 534.
Hakete, Thomas, 43.
Hallohayve (co. Kild.), 484.
Halton, co. Meath, 451.
Hamlen, William, 270.
Hamond, Laurence, Controller of Customs, Dublin, 278.
Hamonston (co. Meath), 447.
Hamper, Clerk of. *See* Chancery.
Hancoke, Matilda, 80.
Hande—Hand, William (gunner), 62, 181, 261, 334.
Hansard, Richard, 46.
Harbbart, Francis, grant of land, 430.
Hariston, vicarage in dio. of Kildare, 354.
Harrold's Graunge, co. Dub., 384.
Harte, William, 75.
Hartwell—Artwell—Artewell, co. Kild., 345, 405, 507.
Hayeston (co. Dub.) (*see* Heyeston), 447.
Hayneston—Heynston, co. Kild., 184, 460.
Henricston (co. Meath), 107.
Henryestan, co. Meath, 91.
Harhertston, co. Kild., 120.
Herford—Herford, Richard, 122, 224.
Hernan, Eneas. *See* O'Hernan.
Herweston, co. Wex., 484.
Hey, Edmund, pardon, 195.
,, Gerald, ,, 195.
,, John, ,, 195.
,, Mathew, ,, 195.
,, Patrick, ,, 195.
Heyeston (*see* Hayeston) co. Meath, 250.
Heynston. *See* Hayneston.
Higham, William, Serjeant of co. Kildare, 150.
Hill—Hyll:—
,, Galfrid, 105.
,, Jenet, 511.
Hillstonstono (co. Wick.), 211.
Hoke, the, co. Wex., 73, 484, 520.
Hokiston (co. Wick.), 211.
Holer, Patrick, pardon, 505.
Holgrave, Hugh, Summonister of the Exchequer, 49.
Hollyvodraliho, co. Dub., 91.
Holmpatriks—Holmpatricke, 447, 521.
,, Priory, 447.
Holybanke, the, Swerds, 510.
Holywood, 450.
Hopper, Edmund, 396.
Horo Abbay, co. Tip., 542.
Horeton, co. Wex., 484.
Horganston—Horeganuston, co. Car., 304, 407.
Horicstone (co. Louth), 76.
Horseman, appointment of a, 459.
Houth (co. Dub.) rector of, 8.
Howelliston, co. Kilk., rectory, 342.
Howth—Houth—Howeth:—
,, Robert, 40.
,, Thomas, 437; Second Justice of Chief Place, 44.
Huhiston, co. Louth, 416.

Humfraystowne (co. Wick.) (*see* Umfrelston, 460.
Huntesland, co. Meath, 156.
Hursto, Richard, pardon, 190.
Hussey, Allenor, 416.
,, Meiler, 416.
,, Walter, Chief Engrosser of the Exchequer, 177.
,, ,, 400, 446.
Huyston, co. Kild., 364.
Hyfferman, Edmund, lease, 543.
Hyll. *See* Hill.
Hyltowne (co. Westm.), 128.

Ibrackane, Don. O'Breane, Baron of, grant of land, 401.
Icoyne, co. Meath, 326.
Ilande Ilely, co. Wex., rectory, 175.
Illunywryke, co. Waterf., 458.
Imokilly. *See* Ymokell.
Impere (Emper co. Westm.) church, 105.
Inchecoventre, co. Kild., 445.
Inchegenlaghe, co. Cork, rectory, 461.
Incroghe—FitzIncroghe:—
,, David, english liberty, 302.
,, Katherine, ,, 302.
Iniskyne—Inneskyn (co. Mon. and Louth), 196, 541.
Inyslawnaghe—Inislawnaghe—Inyslawnaght
—Eneslawnaghe—Enislawnaght
—Enyalswnaghe, co. Tip., 111, 149, 150, 338.
,, Abbey of the B. V. M., 111 140, 150, 164, 179, 338.
Irish—the Irishry, 171, 208, 215, 316, 328, 504.
Irishton, co. Dub., 91, 270.
Irishton—Iryshton, parish of Palmariston, co. Dub., 367, 374.
Irishton—Iryshton, by Kilkenny, 360.
Irishton, parish of Ardcath, co. Meath, 303.
Iryshton, 427.
Iryshton, co. Dub., 272.
Isermon, co. Wex., 343.
Isottiston, co. Meath, 441.

Jackestowne, co. Kilk., 341.
Jenkenston, co. Louth, tithes, 450.
Jenkynstowne, co. Kilk., 175.
Jennings. *See* Genynge.
Jeripount—Jerypoante—Jerepount, co. Kilk., Abbey of the B. V. M., 133, 134, 135, 151, 241.
,, Newtown of, 175, 241.
Johneston, co. Meath, 441.
Johns, Robert, presentations, 204, 489.
Johnston, co. Kild., 80, 120.
Johnston—Johniston, co. Meath, 155, 374.
Jopeston (Jobstown, co. Dub.), 164.
Jordanston (co. Dub.), 374.
Jordanston (co. Kild.), 464.

Kahekan, William, presentation, 279.
Kardoragh, co. Meath, 354.
Kargiston. *See* Cargeston.
Karlane—Kerulan, Edmund, english liberty, 192.
,, ,, presentation, 424.
Karricke (Carrick, co. Wex.), rectory, 343.
Karry, George, 356.
Karryngs (co. Gal.), 382.
Karwell, Mora Enc, 202.
Kayrcoorney (Cahercorney, co. Lim.), rectory, 311.
Kayrfussoke, rectory, 311.
Kastyng. *See* Keting.
Keladowan, co. Kild., 478.
Kellaghtonn—Kellaghton, 229.
Kelleeston, vicarage, dio. of Leighlin (*see* Kelliston), 304.
Kelleeston—Kelleston, co. Dub., 91, 314.

INDEX TO FIANTS.—HENRY VIII

Kelliston, co. Car., rectory (see Kelloosion), 342.
Kelliston, co. Meath, 254.
Kells—Kellos—Kellys—Kenles—Keulis—
   Kenlys, co. Meath, 126, 253, 467.
  „ Archdeaconry, 0, 585, 430.
  „ Abbey of the B. V. M. 87, 223.
  „ Hospital of S. John the Baptist, 78, 205.
  „ rectory of S. John, 265.
Kelly—Kellye—Kelle—Kelli:—
  „ John, 108, 281, 421.
  „ Patrick, english liberty, 284.
  „ William, 460.
Kellys—Kenles—Kealis, co. Kilk., Priory of the B. V. M., 117, 118, 139, 101, 242, 257.
  „ rectory, 139, 101.
Kentystown, co. Meath, 12.
Kopdromyn (Cappadrummin, co. Tip.), 455.
Keppaghe, co. Kilk., 362.
Kepparell (co. Gal. ?), 383.
Kerdiff, Walter, Second Justice, Common Bench, 45.
Keres, Robert, 381.
Kern, Captain of the, 290.
Kerry county, dissolved houses in, 251.
Kerulan. See Karlane.
Keting—Ketyng—Ketin—Kotinge—Kotynge
   —Keatyng:—
  „ David M'Newhittey, pardon, 287.
  „ Gerald, 258.
  „ James, 73, 195.
  „ „ livery, 371.
  „ John, 371.
  „ Nicholas, 484.
  „ Philip, 287, 371.
  „ Richard, lease, 283.
  „ Walter, pardon, 195.
  „ William (Preceptor of Kilclogan), pension, 230.
  „ „ 290, 364.
Ketingeston, co. Kilk., 369.
Kotyngeston by Dromedelgen, co. Kilk., 369.
Keyrry, Maurice, 111.
Kilardan, co. Dub., 528.
Kilartre (co. Louth), 97.
Kilbarran, vicarage, dio. of Killaloe, 293.
Kilbecoke, co. Kilk., rectory, 239.
Kilbegan, co. Westm., Abbey of S. Becan, 376.
Kilbrode, co. Kilk., 530.
Kilbride, co. Dub., castle and land, 66.
Kilbryde, co. Wex., tithes, 529.
Kilbycksy—Kilbysky, co. Meath (now Westm.) rectory, 79, 105.
Kilea—Kilcan—Kilka—Kylea—Kyleas, co. Kild., manor, &c., 364, 384, 388, 400, 401, 464.
Kilcashell, co. Car., rectory, 304.
Kileavan, co. Cork, 461.
Kilclom, co. Tip., rectory, 530.
Kilclogan, co. Wex., 530.
  „ Preceptory, 230, 529, 546.
Kilclone, co. Meath, rectory, 473.
Kilcoan, co. Cork, rectory, 530.
Kilcoghan, co. Kilk., rectory, 239.
Kilcoke, rectory, 444.
Kilcollombe—Kilcolme, co. Kilk., rectory, 123, 530.
Kilcomynytlley, co. Cork, rectory, 530.
Kilcorbre, Rectory, 403.
Kilcorne, co. Cork, rectory, 461.
Kilcorny, co. Car. (?now Wick.), rectory, 304.
Kilcoule—Kilcowle, co. Tip., parish church, &c., 144.
  „ Abbey of the B. V. M., 115, 143, 144.
Kilcowan—Kilkowan, co. Wex., manor, &c., 78, 484.
Kilcowanmore, co. Wex., 78, 484.
Kilcroghan, co. Cork, 530.
Kilcronie—Kylcrony (co. Louth), 196, 541.
Kilcrosse, co. Kilk., 239.

Kilcullen—Kilkolen, Thos. Eustace, lord of (See Baltingias, Viscount of), 211, 305.
Kildalke, co. Meath, rectory, 318.
Kildare, Monastery of Friars Carmelites, 345.
  „ „ Friars Minors, 345.
  „ Nunnery, 519.
  „ Bishopric of, 187.
  „ County, serjeant of, 150.
  „ Gerald, Earl of, 125, 156, 184, 282, 250, 440, 441, 445, 484, 497, 543.
Kildarirye, co. Cork, rectory, 530.
Kildreynaghe, co. Kilk., rectory, 175.
Kilemlaghe, co. Tip., 165.
Kilferaghe, co. Kilk., 369.
Kilgarvan, co. Cork, 530.
Kilgiasse, co. Meath (now Long.), rectory, 326.
Kilgrant, co. Tip., rectory, 530.
Kilbeale, co. Kild., 500.
Kilka. See Kilca.
Kilkaishe (co. Tip.), rectory, 374.
Kilkalyn—Kilkollyn, co. Kilk., 112.
  „ Abbey of S. Kilkin, 112, 116.
Kilkenny, 219, 241.
  „ Cathedral of S. Kanice, 240.
  „ Hospital of S. John the Evangelist, 136, 137, 138, 175.
  „ mayor, burgesses, and commonalty of, grant to, 309.
  „ Monastery of Franciscans, 360.
  „ Preachers, 369.
  „ Church of S. John the Baptist, 136.
  „ the King's Chambre, 360.
  „ the Magdelen Strete, 175.
  „ See Irishton.
Kilkeny—Kilkenny, co. Westm., 423.
  „ Hospital of S. John the Baptist, 423, 438.
Kilkolon. See Kilcullen.
Kilkowan. See Kilcowan.
Kill—Kyll, co. Kild., manor, &c., 245, 465.
Killaghe, 118.
Killaghe, co. Kilk., rectory, 239.
Killaloe, Archdeacon of, 292.
  „ Cornelius, bishop of, 490, 492.
Killamalrve—Kytlarmair, vicarage, diocese of Clonfert, 263, 678.
Killoneyr—Kyllanayre, co. Louth, 93, 532.
Killarge—Killargan. See Killergie.
Killeaghe—Kyllaghe, co. Meath, rectory, 87, 233.
Killeme manor, &c., 393.
Killegryo—Kyllogryo—Killeger, co. Dub. (now Killegar, co. Wick.), 67, 282, 548.
Killen, 533.
Killeneoth (co. Kilk.), 161.
Killensaghne, co. Westm., 478.
Killooke (co. Wex.), 73.
Killergie—Killerge—Killarge, co. Car., Rectory, 222, 514.
  „ Preceptory, 221, 222, 514.
Killergie, Courtt of,—Cort of Killargan, 222, 514.
Killerowe (co. Kild.), 484.
Killester, 482.
Kilmyghlaizshe, co. Tip., rectory, 530.
Killoglue, co. Meath (now Long.), rect. and advowson, 79.
Killowran, co. Water., rectory, 123, 158, 530.
Kiltagoran, co. Dub. (see Kyigarran), 548.
Kiflyn, co. Kilk., rectory, 239.
Killyncrosse, Castle against the O'Conors, 32.
Kilmack—Kilm^e, co. Water., 150. 838.
Kilmacodriko, co. Dub., 401.
Kilmaconoke, co. Cork, rectory, 530.
Kilmadoc, co. Kilk., rectory, 175.
Kilmahancoke, co. Wex., 73.
Kilmakaiill—Kilmakayil, co. Car., rectory, 222, 514.
Kilmakurgyn—Kilmakerogan, in the Liberties of Dublin, 531.

G 2

Index to Fiants.—Henry VIII.

Kilmalasbe. *See* Kilmolasche.
Kilmalloke—Kylmalloke—Kyllmalloke, 218, 311.
" Monastery of Preachers, 310.
Kilmannagbt, co. Dub., 526.
Kilmatalway (co. Dub.) prebend, 6.
Kilmaviaghe—Kilmawcaghe, co. Tip., 150, 338.
Kilmaynan—Kylmaynam—Kilmoynam, 126, 201, 359, 479, 525.
Kilmaynanbege, co. Dub., 283.
Kilmaynan Wodde, co. Meath, 252.
Kilmenynenan (? Kilvemnon, co. Tip.), rectory, 118.
Kilmoare (co. Wex.), 343.
Kilmoghill, co. Cork, rectory, 461.
Kilmolasbe—Kilmalasha, co. Tip. (compare Killmyghlaisbe), 150, 338.
Kilmore, co. Meath, 255.
Kilmore, co. Wex., rectory, 73, 484.
Kilmore, Grange of, co. Wex., 225.
Kilmore, Edmund, bishop of, 104.
Kilmoynam, *see* Kilmaynam.
Kilncsaghne, co. Westm., rectory, 428.
Kilnomney, co. Cork, rectory, 461.
Kilpallyne, rectory, 518.
Kilpatrick. *See* Dorniskyll.
Kilpatrike, co. Meath, rectory, 91.
Kilpoter—Kylpoter, in O'Byrnes' country, co. Dub., 245, 546.
Kilpype, co. Car. (now Wick.), rectory, 304.
Kilreney—Kylreyny (co. Kild.), 191, 197.
Kilrogan, co. Cork, rectory, 304.
Kilshynne, co. Meath, rectory, 252.
Kiltalaght, co. Louth, 223.
Kiltaleyn (co. Meath or Kild.), 197.
Kiltenny, co. Cork, rectory, 461.
Kiltegan, co. Car. (now Wick.), rectory, 304.
Kiltiernan, co. Dub., castle and land, 449.
Kiltula (co. Clare), 391.
Kilvoyle, co. Cork, rectory, 461.
Kilvyaye, co. Cork, rectory, 530.
Kilwanlon, co. Cork, rectory, 304.
Kil—. *See* Kyl—.
Klugeston, co. Meath, 255.
King's Bench. *See* Chief Place.
Knockamoghan—Knocamohan—Cnockmahan—Cracamothan, co. Meath, 77, 254.
Knockamore, co. Meath, 252.
Knockangowie (co. Meath), 197.
Knockansawyn (co. Wex.), 484.
Knockapbreaghaun. *See* Knock in prechayn.
Knockarigg. *See* Crokwrrke.
Knocko—Cnocke, co. Louth, 282.
" Abbey of S Peter, 92, 262.
Knocke, co. Meath, 325.
Knockeshill, co. Wex., 484.
Knockbeleya, co. Tip., 338.
Knocklong. *See* Loynga.
Knockmelan, 121.
Knockamyll Rectory, 252.
Knocktoffer—Knocktoffer, co. Kilk., rectory, 242.
" Monastery of Carmelites, 835.
Knockynym—Knokkenyng (co. Wick.), 154, 460.
Knock—, for other names commencing with, *see* Cnock.
Knoologht, co. Wex., 484.
Knoytbe, co. Meath, 254.
Konowe, John, 114.
Krydan, co. Water., 72.
Kyarney, co. Cork, rectory, 550.
Kylbary, co. Water., 152.
Kylbelod—Kylbelo (co. Dub.), 374, 543.
Kylborde (co. Meath), 393.
Kylbrede (co. Meath), 223.
Kylbrenl, co. Water., 152.
Kylbryde (King's Co.) rectory, 516.
Kylbysky, *see* Kilbyckey.
Kylica—Kylcaa, *see* Kilca.

Kycalano, rectory, 311.
Kylchomvrayn (co. Clare), 391.
Kylelashe (Kilglass, co. Kild.), 197.
Kyelene, 171.
Kyicloghyr (Clogher, co. Louth), 220, 541.
Kylclone, co. Meath, rectory, 478.
Kylcolln, co. Dub (? co. Wick.), 545.
Kylconyll (co. Tip.), 374.
Kylcowan-strete (co. Wex.), 484.
Kylerony, *see* Kilcronie, 541.
Kyleury (Kilturin, co. Wex.), 343.
Kyldroght (co. Kild.) manor, 57.
Kyldrum, 222.
Kyldyr, co. Kilk., 349.
Kylfrusso (Kilfrush, co. Lim.), rectory, 311.
Kylgarran—Killtagoran (co. Wick.), 67, 283, 545.
Kylgrellan, co. Kilk., 241.
Kylkenny, *see* Kilkenny.
Kylkneddy, co. Kilk., rectory, 242.
Kyll, *see* Kill.
Kyllaghe, *see* Killenghe.
Kyllaghan, rectory, 191.
Kyllallan, co. Wex., rectory, 304.
Kyllally—Kyllalie, co. Tip., Monastery of Franciscans, 173, 879.
Kyllame, rectory, 311.
Kyllanayre, *see* Killaneyr.
Kyllarmair, *see* Killamairvo.
Kyllassey, co. Carl., rectory, 242.
Kyllassy, co. Cork, rectory, 530.
Kyllean (Killiane, co. Wex.), 343.
Kyllelinghe, co. Tip., 166.
Kylleny (? Killebenny, co. Kerry), rectory, 311.
Kyllegrye, *see* Killegrye.
Kyllimalloke, *see* Kilmalloke, 311.
Kyllmolings, co. Dub (now Wick.), 546.
Kyllocammoke, co. Meath (now Long.), rectory, 336.
Kyllokendy (co. Clare), 391.
Kyllon, co. Water., rectory, 560.
Kylloskilling (co. Meath), 197.
Kyllthombe, co. Meath, 156.
Kyllnchulybegg (co. Clare), 391.
Kyllachulymore (co. Clare), 391.
Kyllurin (co. Wex.) rectory, 343.
Kyllusky (co. Wex.), 343.
Kyllyllin (co. Wex.), 343.
Kyllyue Rectory, 311.
Kylmabloke (co. Dub.), 67.
Kylmahod, co. Dub., rectory, 304.
Kylmalloke, *see* Kilmalloke.
Kylmaynam, *see* Kilmaynan.
Kylmode, co. Kild., 445.
Kylmclagh, co. Tip., 338.
Kylmenraghe (co. Wex.), 484.
Kylmeenan (co. Meath), 365.
Kylmollogo—Kylmolege (co. Wex.), 343.
Kylmore, co. Car., rectory, 304.
" co. Kild., 445.
Kylmoreth (Kilmurry, co. Wick.), 211.
Kylmary, co. Cork, rectory, 461.
Kylmoyesnny, co. Kilk., rectory, 242.
Kylnanyrron, co. Kild., 451.
Kylnaylaghe, 128.
Kylnedoboragbe (co. Meath), 197.
Kylnenaghe, co. Water., 458.
Kylnnre, co. Meath, 447.
Kylpatrike. *See* Kilpatrike.
Kylpoter (co. Wick.), *see* Kilpoter.
Kylroyny, *see* Kilreney.
Kylromarryn, rectory, 461.
Kylry, co. Kilk., rectory, 242.
Kylryan, co. Wex., 484.
Kylrye, Grange of, co. Kilk., 241.
Kylsblano (co. Tip.) rectory, 374.
Kylskyrr, co. Meath, 19.
Kyltayne (co. Tip.), 874.
Kylteyhara (co. Tip.) rectory, 455.
Kyltome ? Kiltomy, (co. Kerry), rectory, 311.

Index to Fiants.—Henry VIII.

Kylville (co. Kerry), rectory, 311.
Kyng, Mathew, 128.
" Thomas, *alias* M'Ynry, pardon, 186.
Kyngswood by Tassagardo, co. Dub., 526.
Kynnaleghe (a district in Westm. on the borders of King's Co.), 524.
Kynton, Jenet, 416.
" Patrick, 416.
Kyryhill, co. Kilk., rectory, 242.
Kyulle, co. Meath (Killashoo, co. Long.), rectory, 326.

Laborer, Dermot, 451.
Ladio Castell, co. Kild., 184.
Ladyrathe, co. Meath, 318.
Laginan, Edmund. 117.
Laby, Nicholas, 117.
Lalulotter, co. Dub., 272.
Lambarde, Katherine, 546.
Lambaye, co. Dub., rectory, 235.
Lamken, Nicholas, 451.
Lane (co. Dub.), 447.
Langton, co. Kild., 313.
Laraghmynche—Laraghmynse (co. Louth), 196, 541.
Largwy—Largay, co. Meath, 393.
Lasmalyn, co. Tip., rectory, 542.
Lasmullen—Lasmullyng—Lassomolen—Lasmollyn—Lesmolen, co. Meath, 91, 105, 517.
" Priory of the Holy Trinity, 91, 105, 314, 460.
Laspopel, co. Dub., 416.
Lattywe, 282.
Launderton, co. Dub., 1.
Launcey—Launde, William (Abbot of St. Mary's Abbey), pension, 100, 321.
Laurenco, Robert, 75.
Lawles, Patrick, 77.
" Richard, 113.
Lawleston, co. Louth, 416.
Ledwiche, Oliver, pardon, 505.
Ledwitche, John, 106.
Leghlynbridge, co. Car., Monastery of Carmelites, 244.
Leghton, *see* Loughton.
Leliscananaghe, co. Kilk., 239.
Le Maystor, Gabriel, app. Chief Serjeant of Offale, 524
Lense, *see* Leynce.
Lesmollyn—Lesmolen, *see* Lasmullon.
Letercorr, co. Meath, 255.
Lewed, co. Westm., 428.
Lowes, Robert, Controller of Customs, Dublin, 278.
Lex—Loxin, 171, 200.
Lexlip—Lexlyp, co. Kild., manor, &c., 255, 478.
Ley, William, 94.
Laymybanan, 214.
Leynaghe (co. Cork), 394.
Leynce—Lensa, Edward (Serjeant-at-arms), 16, 24.
Licmolassie—Lycmolassy, vicarage in dio. of Clonfert, 263, 378.
Lide, Robert, 94.
Lifey. *See* Anlyffy.
Lighbla—Lyckblaye, dio. of Meath, 128, 224.
Limerick—Lymeryke—Lymerick, 179, 216, 311, 347.
" fee farm of, 327.
" port of, 277.
" house of S. Peter, 179, 347.
" Monastery of Franciscans, 346, 368, 456.
" Preachers, 362.
" school-house in Franciscan Friary, 346.
" county, dissolved houses in, 251.
Lis—, *See* Lys—.
Livitston (co. Kild.), 464.

Loghan, William, 94.
Loghbran, co. Dub., 272.
Loghchynney, co. Dub., 272.
Loghegarmore, co. Westm., 505.
Loghger—Loghgyre—Loughyr, co. Lim., 179, 347, 465.
" Monastery of Friars Minors, 465.
Loghkoraghe—Loghekyraghe, co. Tip., 160, 338.
Loghlenston (co. Kild.), 478.
Loghlwyr, co. Tip., rectory, 163.
Loghsewde. *See* Loughsewdy.
Loghshallaghe, co. Meath, 236.
Loghton, co. Meath, 91.
Londay, Richard (*see* Laundey), 483.
Londreston, co. Meath, 309.
Longe, Dominick, 75.
Long Graunge, the, co. Wex., 73.
Lougwodde, co. Meath, 467.
Louorgane, Edmund (Prior of Cahyr), pension, 124.
Loneth. *See* Louth.
Loughbraghe (co. Dub.), 447.
Loughsewdy—Loghsewds—Lowghsewdie, co. Meath (now Westm.), 824.
" Priory of the B. V. M., 189, 320, 344.
Loughton—Leghton, co. Wex., 73, 484.
Longhyr. *See* Loghger.
Louth—Loueth—Lowthe, 86, 196, 282, 541.
" Priory of the B. V. M., 86, 196, 541.
" county, to pay £10 for building a castle, 316.
" " issues of, 29.
" Oliver, Baron of, creation and grant of land, 196.
Lowes Wodde, co. Kilk., 175.
Lowghsewdle. *See* Loughsewdy.
Lowraibe luyes (co. Louth) tithes, 541.
Lowtho. *See* Louth.
Loynge (Knocklong, co. Lim.), rectory, 311.
Lucan, co. Dub., 84, 374.
Lncoke, Henry, 92.
Lnske, co. Dub., 66, 235, 374, 510.
Lutrell, Thomas, knt. (Chief Justice, Common Bench), 274, 400.
" " grants, 313, 314, 315.
Lutrellston—Lutreleston, co. Dub., 313, 314, 374, 409, 421, 473.
Lyckbla. *See* Lighbla.
Lycknegaish, 383.
Lycmolassy. *See* Licmolassic.
Lyerkyll, 128.
Lymanaghan (King's co.), vicarage, 262.
Lyme, 196.
Lymerick—Lymeryke. *See* Limerick.
Lyname, James, 365.
Lynce's Park, co. Meath, 325.
Lynche—Lynces:—
" Anthony, 33.
" Dominick, 11.
" Jonet, 33.
" Peter, 325, 473.
" Stephan, 11, 33.
" *See* Leynce.
Lynnam, Newtown of, co. Kilk., rectory, 239.
Lyrpolo (Liverpool), export of wool to, 37.
Lysart, John FitzEdmund, presentation, 257.
Lysle (co. Cork), rectory, 394.
Lysyvan (co. Cork), 394.
Lynefunchin, 369.
Lyssent, co. Water., 72.
Lyttelton, tithes, 460.

MacBrien—MacBriain—M'Bryen—M'Brene:
" Cornalius, 303.
" Richard, 332.
" Thady, grant of land, 452.
" Thady M'Kennedy, 271.
" *See* Brene.
M'Carmyke, William, 502.

INDEX TO FIANTS.—HENRY VIII.

M'Cormoke, Dermot, Preceptor of Morne, 461.
M'Costygyn, Donald, 504.
M'Coyn, Schan, 171.
M'Donel roaghe, Thady, 354.
M'Gillepatricke, Bernard, created Baron of Upper Ossory, 103.
M'Gillernowe, Thady, 99.
M'Gyllananowe, Eugene, 99.
  " See Gillananewn.
M'Gynd, Donogh, presentation, 596.
M'Gynnos, Donald, 423.
  " Ferdlorghe, 423.
  " Prior, 428.
M'Loye, William, 477.
M'Morchowe—M'Morho:—
  " John, 108.
  " Terence, 535.
  " See Morchow.
M'Morartaghe, Gerald, 489.
M'Morho. See M'Morchowe.
M'My, Richard, presentation, 296.
M'ne Whitty. See Keting, David; Roche, Patrick.
M'Raynyldo—Raynolde, Thady, 187, 276.
M'Ynry, or Kyng, Thomas, 180.
Madanston, co. Kilk., 335.
Madokestowne, co. Kilk, 241.
Magdelen street, by Kilkenny, 175.
Maghlendane, 223.
Maghyn, co. Water., 458.
Maghyrroshe (co. Mon.), tithes, 541.
Nagray, James, presentation, 412.
Mahon, John, 266.
Malafone (co. Meath), 517.
Malahidret (co. Dub.), prebendary of, 473.
Mallahonyn (co. Dub.), 447.
Malraakne (co. Wex.), 419.
Malynntaghe, co. Meath, 441.
Manohan, Hugh, 477.
  " Philip, 477.
Mangertoriaght (co. Wick.), 211.
Manister ne Cahir, co. Tip., 165.
Mann, Patrick, 345.
Mannan, Maurice, 109.
Manynymon, or Morne, co. Cork, 461.
Manyster in Fercollyn, co. Dub. (now Wick.), 548.
Manyster in Harry (Abbeystrowry, co. Cork), 394.
Mapo, Margery, 90.
Marches of Dublin, 384, 389, 539.
  " of the Irish, 316.
  " of the county Kildare, 232.
  " of the Kingdom, 411.
Margetta, John, Clerk of First Fruits, 435.
Marnevin, prebend in diocese of Ferns, 279.
Marshall, Thomas, 138.
Marshallston (co. Kild.), 464.
Mary's Abbey. See Dublin—Abbey of the B. V. M.
Mason, Patrick, 113.
Maston (Macetown, co. Meath), 454.
Maudelenston—Maudelenton, co. Wex., 78, 484.
Mawdelena, the, co. Louth, rectory, 534.
Mawdlen chapel and church yard, Trym, 325.
Mayn (co. Louth) tithes, 541.
Maynothe (co. Kild.) manor, &c., 160, 171, 515.
  " Constable of Castle, &c., 160.
Maynothesley (co. Kild.), manor, 160.
Mayo, co. Cork, 394.
  " Abbey (probably Abbeymahon, but said to be in the parish of Myross), co. Cork, 394.
Mayster. See Le Mayster.
Meath, Archdeacon of, 228.
  " Bishop of, 223, 325.
  " Edward, Bishop of, 27, 220, 335; license to alienate, 303.
  " bishopric, union of benefices to, 335, 430.
Meath, county, issues of, 29.
Meganaar (co. Tip.), 374.
Mellifont—Mellifunt—Melyfount, co. Louth, manor, &c., 354.
  " Abbey of the B. V. M., 77, 254, 470.
Meniscorte, Litle, co. Dub., 270.
Meniscorte, Mych, co. Dub., 270.
Merrynerton, co. Meath, 351.
Meyeston, 478.
Meylerston, co. Kild., 493.
Michell, Walter, 477.
Midleton, co. Cork, 410.
Millerston (co. Wick.), 211.
Milno Townfforan, co. Meath (now Westm.), 79.
Moally, co. Cork, rectory, 461.
Moerompne, co. Cork, rectory, 461.
Mockally, co. Kilk., rectory, 175.
Moderve, co. Meath, 467.
Mogowre—Mogare, co. Tip., rectory, 155, 374.
Mokhowmne, Grange of, co. Kilk., 241.
Molargy, co. Water., 459.
Moldony, Edmund, 114.
Molo, Patrick, Second Remembrancer of the Exchequer, 183.
Mollaghcurre, co. Louth, 91.
Mollaro, co. Louth, 359.
Molle, co. Louth, 254.
Mollingar (co. Westm.), priory of the B.V.M., 106, 145.
Mollonsgrange, co. Kild., 899.
Moltyfernan. See Multyfernan.
Monamore, co. Drogheda, rectory, 254.
Monasteries, Abbeys, Hospitals, &c.—
Aney, co. Lim. (preceptory), 212, 216, 285, 311, 329.
Arclowo, co. Wick. (Monastory of Prenshers), 152, 404, 535.
Ardee, "de Atrio Dei," co. Louth, 339.
Athboy (co. Meath (Carmelite Friars), 127, 317.
Athenry, co. Gal., 218.
Athnecrann, co. Westm. (Carmelites), 470.
Balliketocke, co. Wex. (preceptory), 230.
Ballyandreyhett, co. Cork, 406, 462.
Ballybogan, co. Meath, 167.
Ballyawillyn, co. Lim. (Preachers), 405.
Baldingas, co. Wick., 211, 460.
Cahir, co. Tip., 110, 124, 165, 388.
Callan, co. Kilk. (Augustin Friars), 243.
Carlingford, co. Louth (Preachers), 231.
Carrick, Little, co. Water. (Friars Minor), 530.
Casbel, co. Tip., Abbey of the B. V. M., 100, 542.
  " Friars Minor, 157, 387.
  " Preachers, 861
Clane, co. Kild. (Friars Minor), 174, 313.
Clonard, co. Meath, 191, 197.
Cloncurry, co. Kild. (Carmelites), 305.
Clonfert "de Portu Puro," co. Gal., 378.
Clonmell, co. Tip. (Friars Minor), 300, 308.
Clonmano, co. Wex. (Augustin Friars), 142, 270, 471.
Conuall, co. Kild., 147, 148.
Cork, Friars Minor, 170.
  " Preachers, 388, 523.
Dorrowe, King's co., 518.
Downemore, co. Gal. (Augustin Friars), 217.
Drogheda Hosp., B. V. M., de Urso, 98, 532.
  " " S. John, 97.
  " " S. Laurence, 358, 350.
  " " Augustin Friars, 248.
  " " Friars Minor, 350.
  " " Preachers, 249, 321, 402.
Dublin Abbey, B. V. M., 88, 93, 94, 95, 100, 310, 320, 321, 380, 400, 401, 412, 446, 449, 460, 539.
  " " S. Thomas the Martyr (Thomas Court), 83, 44, 345, 355, 356, 340, 451, 455, 406, 480, 513, 538, 547.

Index to Fiants.—Henry VIII.

Monasteries, &c.
Dublin Hosp., S. John Baptist, 85, 155, 272, 367, 374, 400, 543.
" " S. Stephen, O.
" Mon., All Saints, 70.
" " Aug. Friars, 180, 312, 323.
" " Carmelite Friars, 545.
" " Friars Minor, 151, 315, 324.
" " Preachers, 238, 309.
Dunbrody, co. Wex., 450.
Dundalk Hosp., S. Leonard, 450, 534.
" Friars Minor, 357.
Enescortic (observants), 404
Eusatloke, co. Kilk., 17, 107, 108, 131, 132, 239.
Fertnekeraghe, co. Kilk., 158, 219.
Fetherde, co. Tip. (Aug. Friars), 168, 307.
Fowre, co. Westm., 122, 123, 413.
Gracodieu, co. Dub., 96, 192, 235.
Granardo, co. Long., 92, 200, 215.
Grane, co. Kild., 69, 71, 304, 407.
Holmpatrike, co. Dub., 447.
Luyslawnaghe, co. Tip., 111, 140, 150, 166, 172, 338.
Jeripount, co. Kilk., 133, 134, 135, 151, 241.
Kells, co. Meath, Abbey B. V. M., 87, 223.
" Hosp., S. John Baptist, 78, 255.
Kellys, co. Kilk., 117, 118, 139, 161, 242, 257.
Kilbegun, co. Westm., 376.
Kilclogan, co. Wex. (preceptory), 230, 529, 546.
Kilcoule, co. Tip., 115, 143, 144.
Kildare Nunnery, 519.
" Carmelite Friars, 345.
" Friars Minor, 345.
Kilkollyn, co. Kilk., 119, 116.
Kilkenny Hosp. S. John the Evangelist, 136, 137, 138, 175.
" Friars Minor, 369.
" Preachers, 369.
Kilkenny, co. Westm., 426, 438.
Killergie, co. Car. (preceptory), 221, 222, 514.
Kilonalloke, co. Lim. (Preachers), 210.
Knooke, co. Louth, 92, 282.
Knoctoffer, co. Kilk. (Carmelites), 335.
Kyllaliy, co. Tip. (Friars Minor), 173, 879.
Lasmullen, co. Meath, 91, 103, 314, 460.
Leglilynbridge, co. Car. (Carmelites), 264.
Limerick, House of S. Peter, 179, 347.
" Friars Minor, 346, 352, 456.
" Preachers, 362.
Logher, co. Lim. (Friars Minor), 405.
Loughsewdy, co. Westm., 189, 326, 344.
Louth, 86, 186, 541.
Manyster in Feroollyn, co. Wick. 549.
Manyster In Horry (Abbeystrowry), co. Cork, 394.
Mayo, "de Fonte Vivo" (Abbeymahon ?), co. Cork, 594.
Mellifont, co. Louth, 77, 254, 470.
Midleton, "de Choro Benedicti," co. Cork, 410.
Mollingar, co. Westm., 166, 145.
Morne or Manynymon, co. Cork (preceptory), 401.
Mothall, co. Water., 458.
Mowre or Galbally, co. Lim. (Friars Minor), 398.
Moylaghe, co. Tip., 238, 300.
Multyfernan, co. Westm. (Preachers), 483.
Naas, co. Kild., Hosp. S. John Baptist, 80, 82, 120.
" " Preachers, 119, 313.
Novan, co. Meath, 76, 150, 252.
Nyvoric, the, (Newry), (Cistercians), 300.
Odder, co. Meath, 89, 90.
Ossency (Osney at Oxford), 455.
Rosbarcan, co. Kilk. (Preachers), 370, 471.
Rosse, co. Wex. (Aug. Friars), 247, 396.

Monasteries, &c.
S. John of Jerusalem, Hospital of, in Ireland (grand preceptory at Kilmaynham), 201, 226, 246, 253, 390, 444, 525, 531.
S. Wulstan's, co. Kild., 57.
Soryne, co. Meath (Aug. Friars), 309.
Selskyr, co. Wex., 113, 343.
Slane, co. Meath (Friars Minor), 375.
Strowill (Abboyshrule, co. Long.), 130.
Termonfeghan, co. Louth, 146, 229.
Thurles, co. Tip. (Carmelites), 243.
Tipperary (Aug. Friars), 322.
Tome in Ormond, 205.
Tristeldermot (Castledermot, co. Kild.), 304.
Tristirnaghe, co. Westm., 79, 104, 105.
Trym, Abbey of the B. V. M., 19, 75, 318, 340, 392.
" Hosp. of S. John the Baptist, by the Newton, 74, 156, 467.
" Monastery of Friars Minor, 9, 325 541.
" " of Preachers, 129, 309.
" " of S. Peter of the Newton, 156, 473.
Tullaghfelym, co. Car. (Aug. Friars), 244, 451.
Tullie, co. Kild. (preceptory), 226.
Tynterne in England, 73.
Tyntarne, co. Wex., 225, 233, 464, 537.
Waterford Monastery of Friars Minor, 162, 307, 431, 434, 541.
" " of Preachers, 152, 351.
" " of S. John, 72.
" " of S. Katherine, 101, 114, 123, 530.
Wexford Hosp. of S. John, 539.
" Mon. of Friars Minor, 409.
Wothonia (Abington, co. Lim.) (Cistercians), 149.
Yoghull, co. Cork (Preachers), 382.

Moncken Weir, on the Boyne, 254.
Mondassell (Modesbil, co. Tip.) rectory, 118.
Monefyne—Monfynn (co. Wick.), 184, 460.
Moukcton—Monckenton, co. Dub., 310, 400.
Mouknewton, co. Meath, 77, 254.
Monkton, by Trym, 457.
Monkwod (co. Wick.), 211.
Monolargy, co. Water., 458.
Montayneston. See Mountayntowne.
Monynenn (? co. Gal.), 383.
Moraghe, co. Louth, 254.
Moran, John, 460.
" Philip, 101.
Morchow, Thomas, 237.
More, Bartholomew, 365.
" Kedagbe, 206. (See O'Moro.)
" Patrick, 148.
" Richard, 365.
More, near Athy, 399.
Morechurch (co. Meath) Vicar of, 270.
Morehouselande, co. Kilk., 241.
Moreton, co. Meath (see Morton), 393.
Moreton, Litlo, co. Meath, 467.
Morno or Manynymou, co. Cork, 461.
" preceptory, 461.
Morraghau, 94.
Mortelstou (co. Tip.) rectory, 311.
Morton, John. Gauger of Rosse, 297.
Mortoo, co. Meath, 91.
Morton (Ballynamooa, co. Lim.) rectory, 311.
Motbell—Mothill, co. Water., 458.
" Abbey of SS. Koan and Borgan, 458.
Mothing, Katherine, Abbess of Kilkelyn, 112.
Mountown, co. Meath (now Westm.), 79.
Mountayntowne—Montayneston, co. Wex., 72, 484.
Monntyfernant, alias Multyfernan, co. Westm., 483.
Moviddye, co. Cork, rectory, 461.

Index to Fiants.—Henry VIII.

Mowre, alias Galbally, in Arlagh, co. Tip. (now Lim.), Monastery of Friars Minor, 398.
Moyagluz, co. Meath, rectory, 326.
Moyaghr, by Kenlys, co. Meath, 467.
Moyclere, Grange of, co. Tip., 458.
Moygano—Myganny—Mygayn (Maganoy, co. Kild.), 222, 404, 514.
Moygar, 154.
Moygowre, co. Meath (now Long.) rectory, 326.
Moylaghe, co. Meath, 265, 440, 441.
Moylaghe, co. Tip., rectory, 236.
" " Priory of S. Brigid, 238, 300.
Moylisse, co. Meath, 416.
Moymore, co. Meath, rectory (see Mymor), 326.
Moyvally, 510.
Muchrath, co. Kild., 513.
Mulryan, Egidia ny, 207.
Multyfernan—Moltyfernan, co. Westm., 14, 213, 360, 376, 505.
" Monastery of Preachers, 482.
Mygnnny (see Moygano), 514.
Mygayn (co. Kild.), 464.
Mylcastell (co. Westm.), 128, 213.
Mylfidde, co. Louth, 532.
Myllmote in Drogheda, 26.
Mylton (co. Louth), 292.
Mylton (co. Tip.), 374.
Myiwardiston (Milverton, co. Dub.), 447.
Mymor in the Aunall, rectory, 189.

Naas—Nase, co. Kild., 80.
" Hospital of S. John the Baptist, 80, 82, 120.
" Monastery of Preachers, 119, 313.
" Rectory of S. John, 80.
" Vicar of S. David, 320.
Nanger, co. Dub., 66.
Nangle, Richard, 40, 208, 352.
" Robert, 77.
Nariaghe, rectory, 511.
Naune, John (from Egypt), safe conduct, 258.
Navan. See Novan.
Navye, the, co. Cork, rectory, 481.
Nedilanya, co. Tip., rectory, 530.
Neghwnn, co. Cork, rectory, 504.
Nelliston, co. Louth, rectory, 254.
Newcastell, 516.
Nevell—Newell—Nevyle:—
" David, 73, 484.
" Laurence, 142.
" Patrick, 148.
Newabey (co. Wex.), 342.
Newcastell near Lyons (co. Dub.), manor, 32, 53.
Newcastell M'Kingan—M'Gyngane, co. Dub. (now Wick.), 235, 369.
Neweralh, by Kellys, 128.
Newgate. See Dublin, Hosp. of S. John.
Newgent. See Nugent; Delven, Baron of.
Newgraag (co. Dub.), 447.
Newgraug (co. Wick.), 211.
Newgrange, co. Dub., 401.
Newgrange, co. Meath, 254.
Newgrange, co. Tip., 334.
Newliagarde, parish of Luske (co. Dub.), 510.
Newhaghard Mill, on the Boyne, 392.
Newhouse (Ballynure, co. Wick.), 211.
Newry. See Nyvorie.
Newton, co. Dub., 270.
Newton (Newtown Blackrock, co. Dub.), 460.
Newton, in the parish of Luske (co. Dub.), 374.
Newton, co. Kild., 478.
Newton, King's co., 511.
Newton, co. Meath, 154, 467, 476.
Newton, co. Meath, Curacy (see Monknewton), 77.
Newton, co. Meath, manor, &c., 302.
Newton, co. Water, 530.
Newton, co Wex., 73, 484.

Newton (co. Wick.), 211.
Newton by Ardarre, rectory, 311.
Newton in the March of Dublin, 539.
Newton, Little (co. Dub.), 374.
Newton, Little, co. Kild., 184, 460, 464.
Newton of Annor, co. Tip., 306, 308.
Newton of Clane, co. Kild., 313.
Newton—Newtown, of Jeriponnte, co. Kilk., 175, 241.
Newton—Newetowne, of Trym. See Trym.
Newtown of Lynnam, co. Kilk., 239.
Nicholstowne, co. Kild., 465.
Nobbar, co. Meath, rectory, 345, 430.
Noreston, co. Wex., 450.
Norfolk, Thomas, Duke of, 269.
Norman, co. Meath, 441.
Norne, co. Kild., 443.
Norreys, William, 77.
Note, Cornelius, 105.
" Patrick, 105.
Novan—Nawan—Navan, co. Meath, 150, 252, 363, 374.
" Abbey of the B. V. M., 76, 150, 152.
" Rectory, 76, 252.
Nugent—Newgent—Neugent:—
" Christopher, 167.
" Edmund, Bishop of Kilmore, 104.
" Edmund, 213, 360.
" Edward, 213.
" Elienor, 201.
" James, 360, 505.
" Lavalin, 167.
" Nicholas, 505.
" Theobald, 505.
" Thomas, wardship, 14.
" Thomas, 130.
" Thomas, livery, 167.
" Walter, 14, 199, 505.
" William, Prior of Fower, 413.
" William, 544.
" See Delven, Baron of.
Nyche, co. Meath, 128, 467.
Nyvorie, the, (Newry) Abbey and College of the B. V. M. and S. Patrick, 366.

O'Breane, Donogh, Knt., Baron of Ibrackane, grant of land, 401.
O'Byrne's Country, 246, 389.
O'Cahan, Edmund, English liberty, 333.
O'Carroll. See O'Karvell.
O'Coughor. See O'Connor.
O'Conliske, Dermot, presentation, 202.
O'Connor—O'Conghor—O'Conor:—
" Bernard or Brene (Captain of Offaly), pardons, 28, 65, 259.
" Leshaglie Loy, pardon, 301.
" Tyrlagh. See Conor.
O'Conors, the, 32.
O'Conyne, Patrick, pardon, 487.
O'Corryan, Thady, English liberty, 498.
O'Coylione, Donogh ballough, pardon, 479.
Odder, co. Meath, 88, 90.
" Abbey of S. Brigid, 89, 90.
O'Deay—O'Dea, Cornelius, Bishop of Killaloe, 490, 492.
O'Dempsey's Country (in King's and Queen's cos.), 394.
O'Digenagh, Dubtag, presentation, 185.
Odogue, Dio. of Ossory, 412.
O'Donnell, 250, 523.
O'Donylan or Dongan, Patrick, English liberty, 499.
O'Donle, Thady, 195.
O'Doyn, Owen, 390.
" Sawe, English liberty, 188.
" William, " 503.
" See Doyn.
O'Duyn, country of (in the north of Queen's co.), 300.

INDEX TO FIANTS.—HENRY VIII.

O'Ferall—O'Ferrall—Ferall:—
,, Richard (Abbot of Granarde), English liberty, 200; Bishop of Ardagh, 215, 227.
,, Rory, pardon, 505.
,, Thady, English liberty, 199.
,, Thomas, 99.
Offaly—Ofuyley—Offale—Othfally (a district in King's co. and Kildare), 23, 253, 238, 500, 524.
Ogonaghe, co. Lim. (see Gonaght), 453.
O'Grada, Denis (Captain of his nation), grant of land, 391.
O'Harnan, Thomas, presentation, 252.
O'Hawrde, Odo, presentation, 293.
O'Hefermaen. See O'Hernan; Hyffernan.
O'Hegan, Uriel, presentation, 354.
O'Hernan—Hernan—O'Hefernaen:—
,, Eneas (Preceptor of Anee), pension, 212.
,, ,, Commission, 251.
,, ,, English liberty, 286.
,, ,, custody of Bishoprick of Emly, 329.
O'Hurnley, William, 332.
O'Hyffernan. See Hyffernan, O'Hernan.
O'Hyrraghti, Maurus, 99.
O'Karwell—O'Keroyll—Enekarwell:—
,, Ferganauym, 411.
,, More, wife of Earl of Dessmond, 202.
,, Thady, 214.
,, ,, app. Captain of Ely Iserojll, 411.
O'Konowan, Moriartaghe More, pardon, 287.
Oldbrige—Oldbrigge, co. Meath, 254.
Oldragh, co. Kild., 232.
Oldrosse, rectory in dio. of Ferns, 269.
O'Lyallorde, Neyll, 171.
O'Meare, Donald, 203.
,, John, English liberty, 209.
O'Melou, John, pardon, 503.
O'More—More, Kedagh or Keadaghe, 171, 205, 206.
,, See More.
O'Moro, Dorothy, English liberty, 505.
O'Morran, Owen, lease, 370.
,, Patrick, pardon, 505.
O'Mulloy—O'Mulmoy, Con, English liberty, 498.
,, Con (Prior of Durrowe), 518.
O'Mulryan, Dionysius, 110.
,, Egidia, wife of Manrice Desmond, 207.
O'Murnyghan, John, pardon, 477.
O'Nare, Donald boy, ,, 500.
O'Neile, 230.
,, Mathew, Baron of Dungennyn, 438.
O'Neyll, Felym, 77.
"Oolde Children," Robbers in Ogonaghe (Coonagh), 453.
Ooldotowne, co. Meath, 250.
Ophane, co. Kilk., 335.
Oranmore. See Uranmore.
Orche, William, 76.
Oregan in country of O'Duya (the north of Queen's co.), 390, 524.
O'Reyly, Charles Moddar, 12.
Organston, 407.
Ormond, Earl of, 203.
,, Anne, daughter of Thomas, Earl of, 23.
,, and Ossory, James, Earl of, grants of land, 151, 308.
,, and Ossory, James, Earl of, 149, 241, 242, 243, 244, 455, 536.
,, and Ossory, Peter, Earl of, 171.
,, See Ossory, Earl of.
Ormounde—Ordmoud, 203, 630.
O'Roerk, Edmund, pardon, 505.
O'Ryan, Donogh, pardon, 331.

O'Sheaghyn, Dermot (Captain of his nation), grant of land, 333.
Ossoney (Osney at Oxford) Abbey, 455.
Ossory, country of, 349, 528.
,, Milo, Bishop of, 17, 107.
,, Peter, Earl of 35, 171.
,, See Upper Ossory, Baron of.
Othfally. See Offaly.
O'Toole—O'Thole:—
,, Arthur (junior), 319, grant of land, 543.
,, Terence, grant of land, 543.
O'Trover, Donald, pardon, 505.
Ouldecastell (co. Meath) rectory, 128.
Ovenaghe, le, co. Dub. (now co. Wick.), 543.
Oveniston, co. Dub., 237.
Owen, William, 256.
Owlys (? Oola, co. Lim.) rectory, 311.
Owney. See Wothonia.
Oynaghe (Owney), 400, 401, 445.

Pale, the English, 11.
Palmereston—Palmeriston, co. Dublin, rectory, 367, 374.
Palmereston — Palmeriston, by Anllytly Manor, &c., 367, 374.
Palmereston, by Grenoke (co. Dub.), 374.
Panrise (in Galway), 33.
Parke, the, in Manor of Carge, co. Wex., 73.
Parker—Parkar, John, 343, 447, 471, 521.
,, grant of monasteries, 370.
Parliament, Clerk of the, 132.
Parysarathe, co. Meath, 465.
Payneston, co. Louth, 91.
Pecoke, Seth, 95.
Pelles—Pellis, Martin, 125, 126, 232, 445.
,, grant of land, 399.
Pentney, Phillip, 393.
,, grant of monastery, 483.
,, William, 270.
Peperton (co. Tip.), 374.
,, co. Meath, 35.
Peppard — Pepparde—Peparde — Pipperde—Pipperte—Pyppard, Walter, 334, 380, 490, 401, 446, 449, 464.
Percyvalston, co. Kild., 232.
Petit, John (Prior of Mollingar), pension, 145.
Petra Canonicorum (see Chanonsroke), 196.
Pety John. See Egyr, John.
Pherpoweston, co. Dub., 272.
Phillpiston, co. Louth, 416.
Philippiston, co. Drogheda, 240, 331.
Phillippiston—Phillippeston (co. Kild.), 184, 480.
Philpeston (co. Louth), tithes, 541.
Phulpotiston, co. Meath, 156.
Pierston (co. Duh.), 447.
Pigote, Nicholas, 612.
Pipparde—Pipperte. See Peppard.
Platen, co. Meath, 91.
Plonkiston—Plaukeston, co. Car. (now Kild.), 304, 407.
Plowlande, 400.
Plunket—Plunkett:—
,, Alexander, pardon, 426.
,, Edward, livery, 343.
,, John, lease, 467.
,, Nicholas (preceptor of Killerge), pension, 221.
,, Nicholas, pardon, 421.
,, Oliver, Knt., created Baron of Louth and grant of land, 196.
,, Patrick, pardon, 426.
,, Richard (Abbot of Kells), pension, 87.
,, Robert boye, pardon, 427.
,, Thomas, Knt., 348.

INDEX TO FIANTS.—HENRY VIII.

Plunket—Pinnoket:—
    Thomas, 437, 462.
    " See Dunsany, Baron of.
Polberton, co. Wex., 212.
Polr. See Power.
Polloxphil, co. Wex., 247, 396.
Poncheston, co. Kild., 91.
Ponchestowns, Old — Oolde Poinshston (co. Kild.), 184, 440.
Porchefeldes (Trym), 340.
Porteresplace (Galway), 33.
Porterston, co. Meath, 292.
Portmarnoke—Portmarnoke, co. Dub., manor, &c., 53, 100, 270, 365.
Portraine, co. Dub., rectory, 236.
Portu Pura, de, Abbey, Clonfert, 372.
Possike, Thomas (Prior of St. John the Baptist, Nass), pension, 32.
Posserwykyston, co. Kild., 478.
Potterston, 478.
Pouderloghe, co. Meath, 91.
Powers—Powere—Powire—Poir:—
    " Edmund (Prior of St. Katherines, Waterford), pension, 123.
    " Edmund, 458.
    " Johanna (Prioress of Moyinghe), pension, 300.
    " Peirce FitzEdmund, 421.
    " Peter, Lord, 458.
    " Robert Fitzwilliam, pardon, 491.
Powerscourte, co. Dub. (now Wick.), Manor, &c., 67, 283, 543.
Powerstowne—Powerston, co. Kilk., Rectory, 222, 514.
Poynton, co. Chester, 196.
Prensparks, co. Meath, 298.
Preston, co. Meath, 393.
Preston. See Gormanoston.
Priorstown, co. Tip., 530.
Priorstown Meades, 478.
Priorton (co. Louth), 97.
Priortowne, co. Louth, 572.
Prowse, John, 54.
Prowte, John, 17.
    " (Abbot of Nawry), 308.
Purcell—Pursell:—
    " Galfrid, pardon, 286.
    " James, pardon, 290.
    " Robert, 138.
    " William, pardon, 286.
Pypparde. See Peppard.

Qayne, John, 286.

Rabrest. See Rathbriste.
Racorbally, co. Meath (now Westm.), 79.
Radronoghe, co. Meath, 264.
Ragarff (co. Westm.), rectory, 128.
Raguwie (co. Tip.), rectory, 374.
Raman, co. Cork, rectory, 406.
Rahowla. See Rathawle.
Raloston, co. Meath, 66.
Ralliston—Rayliston, co. Tip., Rect., 374, 542.
Raith, the, co. Louth, 584.
Ramore. See Rathmore.
Ranvalston—Ranvalleston, co. Dub., 400, 446.
Rasynkyn, co. Meath, 264.
Rasallagh. See Rathesallaghe.
Rathangen, co. Kild., 519.
Ratharia (co. Wex.) rectory, 348.
Rathaspike (co. Westm.), Church, 195.
Rathawls—Rahowle, co. Wex., 72, 454.
Rathbrane (Rathbran, co. Wick.), 311.
Rathbriste—Rathbryde—Rabrest (co. Louth), 196, 541.
Rathcausun (co. Louth), tithes, 241.
Rathcarayke, co. Water., rectory, 468.
Rathcawitho (co. Tip.), 374.
Rathdowne, 267.
Rathdowne, co. Dub. (now Wick.), manor, &c., 67.

Railes (co. Gal.?) 342.
Raths, the, co. Meath, 467.
Rathernan (co. Kild.), rectory, 147.
Rathesallaghe—Rasallaghe, co. Dub. (now Wick.), 184, 460.
Rathfyske, co. Meath, 441.
Rathgarrons (co. Louth), tithes, 541.
Rathkenny—Rathkeny, co. Meath, 270, 518.
Rathkilly (Rathkeale, co. Lim.), 211.
Rathland, near Thomascourt Wodde (co. Dub.), 417.
Rathloghe, co. Meath, 252.
Rathlyn, co. Kilk., 241.
Rathmolian—Rathmolans, co. Meath, 234, 441, 490.
Rathmore—Ramore (co. Kild.) manor, &c., 184, 460.
Rathmore (co. Meath), 548.
Rathmyghell, prebend (co. Dub.), 270.
Rathnayny, co. Cork, 368, 533.
Rathnally, co. Meath, 156, 512.
Rathnekili—Rathnekyll (co. Wick.), 184, 460.
Rathnemanagha, 234.
Ratsowla, co. Dub. (now Wick.), see Batoola, 184.
Rathrolloo (co. Louth), 541.
Rathronas (co. Tip.), rectory, 311.
Rathtall, co. Dub., 270.
Rathtor, Dermot, 457.
Rathtorkyll (co. Wick.), 460.
Rathtowth—Rathtouthe, co. Meath, manor, &c., 201, 450.
Rathtowns—Eashton, co. Wex., 75, 454.
Rathtowthe—Rathtough (co. Car.), 374, 542.
Rathvean (co. Car.), tithes, 460.
Rathvilledown (co. Gal.), 383.
Rathwere (co. Wcstm.), Rector of, 393.
Rathynayoluge, co. Dub., 218.
Ratoole—Rathowle (co. Wick.), 184, 460.
Rawson, John, Knt (Prior of St. John of Jerusalem) pension, 525; created Viscount Clonetarf, 291.
Rayhen (Rahsen, co. Wick.), 311.
Rayliston. See Ralliston.
Raynolds, alias M'Baynylde, Thady, pardon, 187, 276.
Redman, Edmund, 84, 409.
Rekysboro, 510.
Relling, Thomas, 106.
Rely, the Ilande, co. Wex., rectory, 175.
Reneghan (co. Westm.), 457.
Rewe, the (co. Kild.), 478.
Rewe, Peter, 77.
Riaghestan, 196.
Richardeston, 355.
Richardiston—Richardeston, co. Meath, 318, 467.
Richin, William, senior, pardon, 521.
    " junior, pardon, 521.
Rispoylle. See Rospoyll.
Robenrath (Navan), 166.
Robockswalls—Robbockiswalls, co. Dub., 88, 270.
Roche, co. Louth, 460.
Roche, George (Archdeacon of Cork), 422, 428.
    " Gerald, pardon, 287.
    " Nicholas, " 287.
    " Patrick, 287.
    " Patrick M'Ne Whitley, 287.
    " Philip, pardon, 287.
    " Stephen (Prior of St. Laurence's, Drogheda) pension, 358.
    " Walter, pardon, 287.
    " William, alias Edew, pardon, 287.
Rocheford—Rochrdorde, John, 2, 255.
    " Walter, 145.
Rocherton, co. Wex., 530.
Rocheton, co. Meath, 318.
Rochiston, rectory, 311.
Rodton (co. Wick.), 311.

Index to Fiants.—Henry VIII.

Roganston, parish of Swords, 510.
Rogers, John, app. Constable of the Castle of Wykeloe, 46.
Rolanston, co. Meath, 66.
Rolls, Master and Keeper of. *See* Chancery.
Rome, Bishop of, 332.
Rome, John, 97.
Rosbarcan, co. Kilk., Monastery of Preachers, 370, 471.
Rosgarlau—Rosgarlon, co. Wex., Manor, &c., 75, 434.
Rosmagha—Rosmakan (co. Louth), 196, 541.
Rosnalvan, Grange of, 464.
Rospont, co. Wex., rectory, 175.
Rospoyll—Rispoylle, co. Wex., 73, 434.
Rosse, co. Wex., 241, 296, 471.
„ Port of, 297.
„ Monastery of Augustin Friars, 247, 394.
Rosse, New — Rospont — Rossinerowne, co. Wex., rectory, 175. ¦
Rosses, Old. *See* Oldrosse rectory.
Rossesbynnan, co. Kilk., rectory and land, 239.
Rosynry—Rosynry, co. Mea., rectory and land, 354.
Rostelane, co. Cork, rectory, 401.
Roths, Robert, 138.
Rove, Richard, 444.
Rowiston, co. Meath, 393.
Rowre, co. Kilk., rectory, 241.
Rudleche, Thomas, presentation, 415.
Ruskagh, Dio. Leighlin, tithes, 543.
Russell, Bartholomew, app. Clerk of the Crown, Chief Place, 373.
„ Patrick, 361.
„ Richard, 264, 381.
Russellstowne—Russelleiston (co. Wick.), 184, 460.
Russiston—Russelaston, co. Car., 322, 514.
Russonall in country of O'Duyn, 390.
Ryan—Ryane, Dermot, 173; grants of Monasteries, 322, 379.
„ Donogh (Dean of Emly), 337.
„ „ *See* O'Ryan.
„ John, Chief Engrosser of the Excheq., 177.
„ 367, 531.
„ John (Abbot of Wothonia), 149.
Ryngelston, co. Meath, 311.
Rynny, co. Cork, rectory, 364.

Sadilliston (co. Meath), 447.
S. Columbe, co. Kilk., Curate of, 131.
S. Ewers (S. Iberius, Wexford), rectory, 342.
S. Glanokes (co. Dublin), 93.
S. John, co. Kilk., rectory, 136, 175.
S. John of Jerusalem, Hospital of, in Ireland, 201, 226, 240, 252, 390, 444, 525, 531.
S. Johniston, co. Meath, 467.
S. John's, by Enescorrie, 403.
S. John's Raths, co. Meath, 265.
S. Johnys leyes (in Teranure, co. Dub.), 374.
S. Katherine in the Newton, Grange of, co. Watrr., 530.
S. Katherine's, co. Dub., 93, 245.
S. Karan's pyll, co. Wex., 370, 471.
S. Lawrence, de. *See* Howth, Thomas.
S. Leger. *See* Sentleger.
S. Loo. *See* Soyntloo.
S. Margaret (co. Wex.) rectory, 342.
S. Margaretstown (co. Wex.), 343.
S. Michael, Babutt, co. Mea. (now Long.), rectory, 376.
S. Michael's in country of Compsy, rectory, 239.
S. Movinoge, Vicar of, dio. of Cashel, 326.
S. Nicholas, co. Wex., 343.
S. Nymoke, co. Wex., 484.
S. Patrick's, Dean of. *See* Basnet, Edward.

S. Patrick's, Dean and Chapter of, licence of non-residence in their cures, 432.
S. Patrick's steps, co. Kilk., 175.
S. Patryk's, 352.
S. Peter the less by Wexford, rectory, 342.
S. Thomas's park and land, co. Mea., 325.
S. Tullogs (co. Wex.) rectory, 343.
S. Wulstan's, co. Kilk., priory, 87.
Saleparke, the, co. Meath, 325.
Salesbane, co. Dub., 526.
Salmon leap, co. Kild., manor, 478.
Saltchouse—Shalthouses, co. Louth, 77, 226, 354.
Saltcys—Salts, islands, co. Wex., 73, 484.
Saukenygh, co. Tip., rectory, 530.
Sarswell, Thomas, 254.
Saundrs, John, 96.
Savage, Richard, Chief Sergeant of co. Dublin, 53.
„ 347.
Sayrs, co. Mea., 326.
Scarleko, co. Kilk., rectory, 175.
Schell, Thomas, 496.
Scotland, 259.
Scryne—Skreene, Martin, 231, 260.
Scryne (co. Wex.) rectory, 343.
Scryne, co. Mea., 463.
„ Monastery of Aug. friars, 309.
Scurlocks, Roland, pardon, 378.
Scurlokiston, co. Mea., manor, &c., 393.
Scanboycronayn (co. Clare), 391.
Searcher of Dublin, Drogheda & Dundalk, 15.
„ Galway, 274.
„ *See* Ganger.
Secton, co. Dub., 373.
Sellerstowns, co. Kilk., 175.
Selskyr—Shelsker, co. Wex., 343.
„ priory of SS. Peter and Paul, 113, 343.
Seneschal of the manor of Maynoth, 100.
„ manors of Newcastell by Lyonys, Eskyr, Tassagart, and Crumlyn, 22.
Sentleger—Seyntleger ¦
„ Anthony, Knt. Lord deputy, grants of land, 304, 325, 340, 392.
„ „ to Lord Chancellor, 352.
„ George, knt. and Anne, his wife, 23.
„ Robert, 514; grant of land, 465.
Serjaunt, Maurice, 510.
Serjeant-at-Arms, 7, 10, 24, 48.
Serjeant or bailiff of co. Kildare, 159.
„ chief of the baronies of co. Dublin, and of the central of Newcastell by Lyons, 53.
„ „ of the county of Offale, Oregane, &c., 524.
Serle, John, 489.
„ Marion, wardship, 469.
„ Patrick, 469.
Sexten—Sexton, Edmund, 179, 216, 251, 311, 327, 346, 347; grant of monastery, 303.
„ Humphrey, lease, 458.
Seyntleger. *See* Sentleger.
Seyntloe, William, grant of land, 73.
Shalton, 469.
Shalthouses. *See* Saltehouse.
Shandonaghe, co. Meath (now Westm.), rectory, 79.
Shangarry, co. Cork, rectory, 401.
Shankill, co. Kilk., rectory, 239.
Shannon—Shanon, the, 391, 460, 401, 446.
Shannoe—Shanne, co. Wex., 73, 484.
Shamraghe, co. Meath, 451.
Sheanruhyn, co. Cork, 480.
Sheffold, James (Prebendary of Wyklo), 5.
Sheghan, David, lease, 176.
Shelskyr. *See* Selskyr.
Shensyaleston, co. Meath, 86.
Shephouse, co. Meath, 254.

INDEX TO FIANTS.—HENRY VIII.

Shopgrang, co. Louth, 254.
Shurloko, Ballfior and Anne, 546.
" James, app. treasurer of Wexford, 63.
" " 433, 529, 530, 546,
Sheweston, co. Wex., 464.
Shirlockston, co. Meath, 156.
Shortall, Robert (Prior of Fertnekeraghe), pension, 156.
" Thomas (Abbot of Kilcoule), pension, 115.
Shrewsbury, Earl of, 450, 484.
" George, Earl of, 63, 78.
Shrowliswodd, co. Kilk., 241.
Sigouus, Thomas, pardon, 193.
Siggenston—Syggenston, co. Kild., 30, 439.
Skadeston (co. Tip.), 374.
Skeaghbegge — Skeagbebege, co. Cork, 333, 533.
Skerres (co. Dub.), 447.
" customs, &c., of port of, 447.
Skeyocks (co. Kild. ?), 184, 460.
Skreene. *See* Scryne.
Skybbreston, co. Dub., 91.
Slane, James Flemyng, Baron of, grant, 375.
Slane, co. Mea., 252.
" Monastery of Friars minor, 375.
Slans (Ballynaslaney, co. Wex.), 343.
Sleboyne (co. Tip.), 455.
Slecoulter. *See* Slewoultier.
Slegangh, 509.
Sleurath (co. Wick. [? Slievereagh]), 211.
Slevin (co. Westm.), 145.
Slowcultier—Slecoulter, co. Wex., land and fishing, 73, 484.
Smarte, Patrick, 75.
Smermor (co. Louth), 73.
Smytbestowne, co. Kilk., 241.
Soldiers appointed. *See* Dublin Castle.
Solicitor, principal or chief, 61, 520.
Sonnaghe, co. Meath (now Westm.), rectory, 78, 105.
Srure, co. Meath (now Long.), rectory, 330.
Stabnaan, co. Louth, 416.
Stacallan (co. Meath), 507.
Stachmay, co. Kild., 476.
Staffardeston (co. Meath), 477.
Stafford, Robert, pardon, 195.
Staffordeston, co. Dub., 08.
Stagreunsn—Stakerenan (co. Meath), 196, 541.
Stahalmoke, co. Meath, 265.
Stakboll. *See* Staple.
Stakpoll, Patrick (Abbot of the Rock of Cashel), pension, 109.
Staleban—Stalsbone, co. Louth, 254.
Stallug, co. Mea., land and weir, 254.
Stanley, Richard, 268.
Stanyburst—Stanyburste, Nicholas, 50, 531; clerk of hanaper, 40; clerk of Parliament, 182; grant of monastery, 545.
Stanyslande, co. Kilk., 241.
Staple, *alias* Stakboll, Edward. *See* Meath, Bishop of.
Starensaghe, co. Mea., 254.
Stephens. *See* Stephins.
Stephenson, Richard, pardon, 425.
Stephins—Stephens—Stewns, Thomas, 3, 266, 303, 420; grant of land, 394.
Stonchall, 213.
Stonehall, co. Meath, 318.
Stonehall, co. Meath (now Westm.), rectory, 78, 265.
Stradballi in Lex (Queen's co.), 171.
Stradbally, co. Water., rectory, 239.
Strade Innyhrocray (Struct, co. Westm. and Long.), rectory, 90.
Struffan (co. Kild.), rectory, 374.
Stranewe, co. Mea., 441.
Stridebe, John, 396.

Stroug, Philip, 510.
Strongintbarme, Robert, 190.
Strowill, abbey of the B. V. M. (Abbey Shrule, co. Long.), 130.
Sutton, David, 174, 345, 407, 475.
" Edward, 365.
" Gerald, livery, 475.
" John, 267.
Swerds—Swerdes, co. Dub., 235, 264, 350, 447.
" manor, 510.
" the bridge of Balhary, the Holybanke, the Castelfelds, and Whitsspark, 510.
Swir river, 307.
Syddan, co. Meath, Vicar of, 192, 424.
Syffyn, co. Meath (now Westm.), 79.
Syggenston, co. Kild. (*see* Siggenston), 439.
Sylke, Margaret (Abbess of Odder), pension, 90.
Symondeston—co. Kild.), 475.

Taghanschurohe, co. Kilk., rectory, 230.
Taghdowe, 509.
Taghnewran (Tinoran, co. Wick.), 211.
Tagbtillyn (King's co.), 516.
Talbot—Talbote—Telbott:—
" Peter, grants of land, 67, 263.
" Robert, grant of land, 526.
Tamon, co. Wex., 529.
" S. Brigittes in, tithes, 529.
Tampulenyme, co. Tip., rectory, 530.
Tancardeston (co. Kild.), 464.
Tancardeston, co. Meath, 00.
Tanckardiston, co. Dub., 272.
Tancy, Johanna, 90.
Tarmonfeghen — Tarmonfeschen — Tarmafeghan—Tarfeghen. *See* Termonfeghen.
Tassagard—Tassagart, co. Dub., manor, &c., 23, 201, 536.
Tauraghe—Taueraght (Tara, co. Meath), 393, 483.
Taykillin (Tikillin, co. Wex.), rectory, 343.
Tcample Cargyo (Templecurrig, co. Wick.), 67.
Teamplewryko, co. Water., rectory, 458.
Teampulbreean, co. Cork, rectory, 530.
Tsampult [ ], co. Cork, rectory, 530.
Tegchroan, co. Meath, 372.
Taghbrodan, co. Dub., 283.
Telinge, Henry, 424.
Tempelmymrath, 176.
Templebagan, co. Dub. (? Wick.), 548.
Templeforan—Templefferen, co. Meath (now Westm.), 79, 104.
Templegon, co. Cork, rectory, 461.
Templenegallogbe (co. Lim.), 179, 347.
Templeny, co. Water., rectory, 453.
Temple Rowan, co. Cork, rectory, 406.
Templstagbe, co. Cork, rectory, 461.
Templeton Market, 544.
Tempulmorre—Templemarrye, dio. Leighlin, rectory, 374, 543.
Tempaltewnyghe, co. Tip., rectory, 530.
Tempulton, co. Wex., 529.
For other names beginning with Temple, see Tampul, Teample.
Termonfeghen — Tarmonfeschen — Tarmafeghen—Tarfeghen, co. Louth, 91, 198, 416, 541.
" Priory of the B. V. M., 148, 220.
Tessynert, co. Meath (Taghsheenod, co. Long.), rectory, 326.
Tessynnye, co. Meath (Taghshinny, co. Longford), rectory, 326.
Testeldelano, co. Kild., rectory, 513.
Theacneaghe—Theacneso, vic., dio. of Clonfert, 263, 373.
Thomas Court (abbey). *See* Dublin.
Thomas-courte Wodde (co. Dub.), 417.
Thomaston, co. Dub., 272.
Thomaston, co. Kild., 443.
Thomaston—Thomastowne, co. Kilk., 232, 241.
Thorncastell, co. Dub., manor, &c., 267.

INDEX TO FIANTS.—HENRY VIII.

Thoymcreny (Tomgraney, co. Clare), 391.
Three Castles by the mountain side, co. Dub., (now Wick.), 184, 460.
Thurles, co. Tip., monastery of Carmelites, 243.
Thurstonston, co. Meath, 66.
Tidder. *See* Tudyr.
Timoran. *See* Taghnewran.
Tipper, John, 510.
Tipper, co. Kildare, 267.
Tipperary—Tipperare, 322, 379.
   ,, priory of Augustin Friars, 632.
Tirrell. *See* Tyrroll.
Tobbyr, co. Dub. (? Wick), rectory, 235.
Tohon, William, 257.
Toboyne, 191, 107.
Tobyn, Nicholas (prior of Kellys, co. Kilk.), pension, 139.
   ,, Thomas, 118.
Toghexgrene, co. Lim., manor, 453.
Tolaghalen. *See* Tullaghalen.
Tolaghuoge—Tollonoge, co. Meath, rectory, 74, 467.
Tollaghferrys. *See* Tullaghferrels.
Tollaghphell. *See* Tullaghfelym.
Tolloghmorre, co. Kild., 399.
Tolonegan (co. Gal.), 363.
Tome, in Ormound, abbey, 206.
Tonenston, co. Kild., 304.
Tonigraney. *See* Thoymcreny.
Tomond, Earl of, 490.
   ,, Murrogh, Earl of, grants of land, 400, 446.
Tornor, Paul, grant of monastery, 409.
Toollgharde (Tullyard, co. Meath), 129.
Towniey, Lawrence, 254, 417.
Travers—Traverse:—
   ,, James, 306.
   ,, John, licence to export wool, 37; leases, 310, 403; grants of land, 404, 460.
Travete, grange of, co. Meath, 451.
Treasurer and bailiff of the lordship of Wexford, 63, 433.
Trigaran, John, 6.
Trim. *See* Trym.
Trimlleston, John Barnewell, Baron of, 82.
Tristeldermot—Tresteldermot—Castell Dermot, co. Kild., 80, 120, 290, 304, 804.
   ,, Hospital of St. John the Baptist, 364.
Tristelkeran (*see* Dessardkeran), 78.
Tristbrnaghe—Trysternaghe, co. Meath (now Westm.) rectory and land, 70, 195.
   ,, priory of the B.V.M., 79, 104, 195.
Troeswodd, co. Kilk., 369.
Troman, co. Meath, 441.
Trott, Walter, lease, 184.
Trowbloy, co. Meath, 468.
Trym, 164, 318, 457, 467.
   ,, constable of castle of, &c., 2, 268, 420.
   ,, gaol of, 268, 420.
   ,, abbey of the B.V.M., 18, 75, 318, 340, 392.
   ,, hosp. of S. John the Baptist by the Newton, 74, 156, 467.
   ,, monastery of Friars minor, 0, 325, 541.
   ,, priory of S. Peter of the Newton, 156, 473.
   ,, ,, of Preachers, 179, 209.
   ,, rectory of the B.V.M., 218.
   ,, bridge of S. Peter's near Newton, 392.
   ,, grange of, 318.
   ,, King's park, or park of Trym, 9, 325.
   ,, mills on Boyne, 392.
   ,, Newton—Nowtowne of, 74, 156, 392, 467, 470.
   ,, church of S. Patrick, 858.
   ,, Porchefeldes, 340.
   ,, Portchgate, 325.

Trymlettston (co. Meath), 416.
Tudyr—Tidder, Lewis, 289, 296, 325.
Tullaghalen—Tallaghallon—Tolaghalen, co. Louth, 77, 254.
Tullaghe in the Annall, 199.
Tullaghfelym — Tollaghphell — Tulleofelme, co. Carlow, 221, 514.
   ,, monastery of Augustin Friars, 244, 451.
   ,, vicar of, 469.
Tullaghferrels—Tollaghferrys (co. Wick.), 184, 460.
Tullaghmore, co. Westm., 428.
Tullagimccard, co. Westm., 428.
For names beginning with Tullogh, *see* Tolagh.
Tullio, co. Kildare, preceptory, 326.
Tulloke (co. Meath), 363.
Tully—Tullie, 845, 407.
Tullyhaght, co. Kilk., rectory, 242.
Tullyleyee, co. Cork (or Lim.) rectory and land, 242.
Tulmacarre, co. Kild., 126.
Tupertymain, co. Meath, 441.
Turhetas (co. Kild.), 464.
Tute, Thomas (prior of Loughsewdy), pension, 189.
   ,, *See* Twit.
Tutesland, co. Meath, 81.
Tweydall, Gregory, pardon 414.
Twit, Walter, 105.
Twrvay (co. Dub.), 270.
Tybberboyne, co. Dub., 180, 323.
Tybbride, co. Kilk., rectory, 175.
Tycnane, Rectory, 191.
Tynckuraughe, co. Cork, 461.
Tyntorne in England, Abbey, 73.
Tynterno, co. Wex., Ahbey, 235, 253, 484, 537.
Tyrone, Con, Earl of, grant of land, 430.
Tyrrelaghe (co. Gal.), 383.
Tyrrell—Tirroll:—
   ,, John, 94, 270.
   ,, Remond, 516.
   ,, Richard, pardon, 510.
   ,, Walter, 326, 452, grant of land, 323.
Tyscoffyn, prebend, co. Kilk., 240.

Unafraiston (Humphrystown, co. Wick.), 184, 460
Unane, 178.
Unshoke—Unchooke, co. Louth, 77, 254.
Upper Ossory, Bernard, Baron of, creation 193; grant of land, 384.
Uranmore—Uronmore, (Oranmore, co. Gal.), rectory, 263, 378.
Urier, 223.
Uryell—Uriel, 11, 541.
Usher, *see* Washer.

Vale, John (*see* Wale), 500.
Vastina (Castletown Kindelan, co. Westm.), rectory, 145.
Valsen, Henry, 95.
Veldon, *see* Weldon.
Verdon—Werdon:—
   ,, Oliver, 322.
   ,, Thomas, 86.
Vicombe, *see* Wycombe.

Wackley, John, 425.
Wafre, Thomas (Abbot of Navan), pension, 78.
Wafyr, Nicholas, 355.
Waloha, *see* Walsha.
Wale, Egidia (Abbess of Grane), pension, 69.
Walop, John, knt., Constable of Trym, 2.
Walshe—Walsh—Walecho—Walcho:—
   ,, Gerald, 185, 288.
   ,, Henry, 431, 434.
   ,, James, pardon, 516.
   ,, Oliver, 510.
   ,, Patrick, 431, 434.

Index to Fiants.—Henry VIII.

Walshe—Walsh—Walsche—Walehe:—
" Potet, pardon, 178.
" Robert, pardon, 372.
" Thomas, 94.
" Walter, 178.
" William, 94, 246, 363, 372.
" William (Prior of Ballyandreyhait), 402, 402.
Walcreston, co. Kild., 69, 120.
Waltoriston, co. Westm., rectory and land, 428.
Walyngton, John (Preceptor of Tallio), pension, 226.
Warenston, co. Meath, 407.
Waring, Thomas, 365.
Waterford, 114, 152, 153, 154, 482, 529, 530, 544.
" lease to city, 169.
" port of, 209.
" Hospital of the Holy Ghost, 431, 434.
" Monastery of Friars Minor, 180, 207, 431, 434, 543.
" " of Preachers, 152, 351.
" Priory of S. John, 72.
" " of S. Katherine, 101, 114, 122, 550.
" Great garden of the Friars Minor, 307, 434.
" Quay outside the walls, 307.
" S. Nicholas rectory, 530.
Watson, co. Meath, 521.
Welchetown, Diocese of Dublin, tithes, 543.
Weldon—Veldon:—
" Anne, 102.
" Thomas, pardon, 507.
" William, 77.
Werdon, see Verdon.
Wesby, see Westby.
Wessbexter, export of wool to, 87.
Wespalleston, co. Dub., rectory, 235.
Wesmley, Robert (Prior of Connall), pension, 147.
Westby—Wesby, Robert, 277, 259.
West Grange rectory, 513.
Wexford, 275, 342, 382.
" Castle, 409.
" Ferry, 75, 454.
" Lordship and county, Treasurer and Bailiff of, 63, 433.
" Hospital of S. John, 523.
" Monastery of Friars Minor, 400.
" S. Peter the less rectory, 342.
" see Salsker.
Whitchurche, co. Kilk., rectory, 342.
White—Whyte:—
" Alison (Prioress of Gracedieu), pension, 98.
" Christopher, licence to trade with Gascony, 8.
" Henry, 87.
" James, 152, 153, 154.
" John, Serjeant-at-Arms, 94.
" " knt., Constable of Castle of Dublin, 47, 44.

White—Whyte:—
" Laurence (Prior of S. John, Trym), pension, 74.
" Owen, Serjeant-at-Arms, 48.
" Patrick, appointed Second Baron of the Exchequer, 31; knt., lease of customs, 452.
" Patrick, presentation, 228.
" Richard, 101.
" Rowland, lease of customs, 482.
Whitechurch, co. Kildare, 80, 82, 120.
Whitchurche, co. Cork, rectory, 461.
Whitechurche—Whytchurche, co. Wex., 78, 484, 529.
Whitiston, parish of Palmerston by Grenoke (co. Dub.), 374.
Whitrell, John, 94.
Whitley. See Whytley.
Whyte. See White.
Whytechurche, co. Tip., rectory, 556.
Whytston, 440.
Whytley—Whitley:—
" Patrick, 522.
" Robert, 522.
" Walter, livery, 522.
" See Keting, David; Roche, Patrick.
Wicklowe—Wiclowe—Wykle—Wykeloo, 5, 374.
" constable of castle of, 46, 286.
" manor, 46.
Willie, John (Prior of Louth), pension, 86.
Windmyllmote in Drogheda, 26.
Wise—Wyse:—
" Andrew, 417.
" William, grant of land, 72.
" " knt., licence to alien, 483.
Wodstoke (co. Kild.), manor, 125.
Wodion, co. Meath, 318.
Wogan, Nicholas, 256.
Wolerston, co. Dub., 270.
Wolga vicarage, diocese of Clonfert, 263.
Wolfgrange—Woldgrang, co. Kilk., 135, 241.
Wonfeston, co. Kilkenny, 369.
Wothonia (Owney—Abington, co. Lim.), Cistercian Abbey, 149.
Washer (Usher), Christopher, 474.
" John, livery, 474.
Wstace. See Eustace.
Wycombe—Vicombe:—
" John, 280.
" Nicholas, 40, 280.
" Thomas, livery, 280.
Wykeloo. See Wicklowe.
Wykle—Wykeloo. See Wicklowe.
Wynomyll folde, co. Louth, 532.
Wyse. See Wise.

Yans, alias Delman, Robert, 51.
Ymokall, co. Cork, 461.
Ynyrteoke. See Eneotioke.
Yoghull, co. Cork, monastery of preachers, 343.
Yonge, David, 75.
Yongeston, co. Kild., 446.
Yougeston, co. Wex., 484.
Ywe, John, 402.

DUBLIN: Printed by ALEXANDER THOM, 87 & 88, Abbey-street,
For Her Majesty's Stationery Office.

STATE OF BAYS

ON

EAST AND WEST SIDES OF RECORD TREASURY,

31st DECEMBER, 1874.

(Work since last Report shown in Red)

	A	B	C	D	E	F	G	H	I	K
6	Vacant	Vacant.	Vacant.	Vacant.	Custom House Collectors' Accounts. Debentures	Custom House Collectors' Accounts. Miscellaneous.	Custom House Collectors' Accounts. Audit Rolls, &c.	Vacant.	Vacant.	Eq. Exchequer Recognizances.
5	Do.	Do.	Do.	Do	Benchers' Building Revenue Exchequer [illegible]	Law Exchequer Rule Books, Rolls, Inquisitions Crown Bonds	Law Exchequer Cognovits, Judgment Pleadings	Law Exchequer Judgment Pleadings. Pleadings. Affidavits.	Law Exchequer Affidavits, Writs, Memorials, Rolls, Warrants, [illegible]	Vacant.
4	Do	Do	Do	Chancery Bills to 1[illegible]	Eq. Exchequer, Affidavits, [illegible]	Vacant	Benchers' Building Eq. Exchequer Bills & Answers, [illegible]-1777	Benchers' Building Eq. Exchequer Bills & Answers, 1777-1800	Benchers' Building Eq. Exchequer Bills & Answers, 18[illegible] Depositions	Benchers' Building Eq. Exchequer Decrees Depositions, &c. [illegible]
3	Chancery Bills, 1791-1800	Chancery Answers, 1660-1771 Bills, [illegible] Tipperary Pleadings	Chancery Answers, 1771-1790	Chancery Rolls, Consent Petitions, Bonds, [illegible], Plea Rolls, [illegible] Entry Books, &c.	Common Pleas. Rolls, Judgments (Case), Recovery, Memorials, &c	Common Pleas. Fines, Writs of Entry, Warrants, [illegible], Memorials, &c	Common Pleas. Pleadings	Common Pleas. Affidavits. Writs.	Common Pleas. Writs.	Common Pleas. Judges' Books.
2	Chancery Answers, [illegible]	Chancery Answers, [illegible]-1814	Chancery Answers, 1814-60	Chancery Fitted up for Decrees and Rolls.	Queen's Bench Affidavits, Cognovits, Satisfactions, &c.	Queen's Bench Crown Office. Rules Office	Queen's Bench Cases, Judgments Rolls, Memorials, &c	[illegible]	[illegible]	Eq. Exchequer Crown Papers. Chancery Crown Papers, [illegible]
1	Vacant	Vacant	Vacant	Fitted up for [illegible] Inventions Patents.	Custom House Collections of Auditor-General, Surveyor General, Clerk of [illegible]	Custom House Temporary Books Teller and Vice Treasurer	Custom House Teller and Vice-Treasurer First Fruits Relief Commission, &c.	Custom House Poll Subsidy Hearth Money Returns, [illegible]	Testamentary Collection. Will Books, Grant Books, Bonds, &c.	Benchers' Building. Eq. Exchequer Books Decrees enrolled Rev. Exchequer Books
Vaults	Chancery Books [illegible]	Chancery Crown Papers. Books	Vacant	Chancery [illegible] Collection Crown Papers, Letters	Vacant	Vacant	Christ Church Cathedral Muniments	Law Exchequer Chancery Files and Writs	Fitted up with Presses	Fitted up with Presses.

State of Bays on West Side of Record Treasury, 31st December, 1874.

(Work since last Report shown in Red.)

L	M	N	O	P	Q	R	S	T	U
5 L. Misc. MSS. Commission	6 M. Sacks from Rolls.	6 N. Vacant	5 O. Vacant.	6 P. Vacant.	6 Q. Vacant.	6 R. Vacant.	6 S. Vacant.	6 T. Vacant.	6 U. Vacant
6 L. Chancery, Depositions-in-Chief.	5 M. Do.	5 N. Do	5 O. Record Tower Parliamentary Collection	5 P. Chancery Ancient Pleadings to A.D. 1714	5 Q. Do	5 R. Do	5 S. Do	5 T. Do.	5 U. Do
4 L. Chancery [illegible]	4 M. Vacant	4 N. Vacant	4 O. Testamentary [illegible]	4 P. Vacant.	4 Q. Court of Prerogative Wills, Bonds, Cause Papers, &c.	4 R. Prerogative and Diocesan Testamentary Collections. Additional do	4 S. Fitted up for Testamentary Collection	4 T. Fitted up for Testamentary Collection	4 U. Record Tower, Dublin Castle. The State Papers.
3 L. Chancery Decree Rolls	3 M. Queen's Bench [illegible] Collection	3 N. Queen's Bench [illegible] Collection	3 O. Queen's Bench [illegible] Collection.	3 P. Queen's Bench [illegible] Collection	3 Q. Chancery Recognizances Additional do	3 R. Fitted up for Eq. Exchequer Pleadings.	3 S. Fitted up for Eq. Exchequer Pleadings	3 T. Fitted up for Eq. Exchequer Pleadings.	3 U. Fitted up for Eq. Exchequer Pleadings.
2 L. Eq. Exchequer From Offices of Receivers Master in Chancery	2 M. Testamentary and Ecclesiastical Additional do	2 N. Testamentary and Ecclesiastical.	2 O. Chancery, Offices of Master [illegible] [illegible]	2 P. Chancery, Offices of Master [illegible] [illegible]	2 Q. Chancery Inquisitions Long Pleadings Cause Papers [illegible] Record Tower Fine Rolls. Pipe Rolls	2 R. Eq. Exchequer Pleadings. [illegible]	2 S. Eq. Exchequer Pleadings [illegible]	2 T. Do	2 U. Do
1 L. Chancery Fiants for Letters Patent	1 M. Chancery Registrars' Office.	1 N. Chancery Registrars' Office. Affidavit Office	1 O. Chancery Affidavit Office Notice	1 P. Chancery [illegible] Petitions [illegible] Special and Writ Office	1 Q. Chancery Commissioners. Bankrupts Office Collection Record Tower Record Commission Collection [illegible]	1 R. [illegible]	1 S. Fitted up for New Rolls.	1 T. In progress for New Rolls.	1 U. Fitted up for New Rolls
L. Crown and Hanaper Sacks Custom House Census, 1851	M. Custom House Imprest Accounts. Census, 1851	N. Custom House Imprest Accounts Census, 1851 Agricultural Returns, 1847	O. Custom House Imprest Accounts. Agricultural Returns. 1847–1854	P. Custom House Imprest Accounts, Agricultural Returns, 1854–1855.	Q. Custom House. Imprest Accounts Agricultural Returns, 1850 Exchequer Vouchers. 1688–1748.	R. Custom House Imprest Accounts Exchequer Vouchers. 1748–1818.	S. Custom House Imprest Accounts. Exch. Vouchers, 1818–1827 Agricultural Returns, 1854–1857	T. Custom House Imprest Accounts. Agricultural Returns, 1858–1860	U. Agricultural Returns, 18[illegible] Eq. Exchequer [illegible] Orders [illegible]

www.ingramcontent.com/pod-product-compliance
Lightning Source LLC
Chambersburg PA
CBHW020141170426
43199CB00010B/837